Myth Theorized

Myth Theorized

Robert A. Segal

eQuinox

SHEFFIELD UK   BRISTOL CT

Published by Equinox Publishing Ltd.

UK: Office 415, The Workstation, 15 Paternoster Row, Sheffield,
      South Yorkshire S1 2BX

USA: ISD, 70 Enterprise Drive, Bristol, CT 06010

www.equinoxpub.com

First published 2023

© Robert A. Segal 2023

British Library Cataloguing-in-Publication Data
A catalogue record for this book is available from the British Library.

ISBN-13   978 1 78179 863 8   (hardback)
          978 1 78179 864 5   (paperback)
          978 1 78179 865 2   (ePDF)
          978 1 80050 314 4   (ePub)

Library of Congress Cataloging-in-Publication Data
Names: Segal, Robert Alan author.
Title: Myth theorized / Robert A Segal.
Description: Sheffield, South Yorkshire ; Bristol, CT : Equinox Publishing
    Ltd, [2023] | Includes bibliographical references and index. | Summary:
    "Myth Theorized provides a survey of some key figures and topics in the
    modern study of myth"-- Provided by publisher.
Identifiers: LCCN 2022026163 (print) | LCCN 2022026164 (ebook) | ISBN
    9781781798638 (hardback) | ISBN 9781781798645 (paperback) | ISBN
    9781781798652 (epdf) | ISBN 9781800503144 (epub)
Subjects: LCSH: Myth. | Mythology.
Classification: LCC BL312 .S44 2023 (print) | LCC BL312 (ebook) | DDC
    398.2--dc23/eng20221026
LC record available at https://lccn.loc.gov/2022026163
LC ebook record available at https://lccn.loc.gov/2022026164

Typeset by S.J.I. Services, New Delhi, India

DEDICATION

To Golda, a beloved cat

Contents

Acknowledgments   ix

Introduction   1

1 From Nineteenth- to Twentieth-Century Theorizing about
  Myth in Britain and Germany: Tylor versus Blumenberg   10

2 Max Müller on Religion and Myth   33

3 Frazer on Adonis   45

4 Frazer on Osiris   55

5 Frazer and Campbell on Myth: Nineteenth- and Twentieth-
  Century Approaches   63

6 Campbell's Non-Jungian Approach to Myth   70

7 Are There Modern Myths for Eliade?   78

8 Eliade on Myth and Science   86

9 Dubuisson on Twentieth-Century Theorists of Myth:
  Foreword to Daniel Dubuisson, *Twentieth Century Mythologies:
  Dumézil, Lévi-Strauss, Eliade*   97

10 Myth and Literature   103

11 Hell and Paradise for Milton and Others   117

12 Must Mythic Heroes Be Male?   126

13 Does Synchronicity Bring Myth Back to the World?   138

14 The Bible as Myth, Science, Religion, and Philosophy   146

     Notes   171

     Bibliography   176

     Index   185

Acknowledgments

Seven of the chapters have been previously published. I would like to thank the following publishers for granting permission to use these materials in a revised form:

- Chapter 1 originally appeared as "Tylor versus Blumenberg." In *Edward Burnett Tylor, Religion and Culture*, edited by Paul-Francois Tremlett, Liam T. Sutherland, and Graham Harvey (London: Bloomsbury, 2017), 63–86.
  Published by permission by Bloomsbury Academic.
- Chapter 2 originally appeared as "From Nineteenth- to Twentieth-Century Theorizing about Myth in Britain and Germany." In *In the Embrace of the Swan: Anglo-German Mythologies in Literature, the Visual Arts and Cultural Theory*, edited by Rüdiger Görner and Angus Nicholls (Berlin and New York: De Gruyter, 2010), 41–64.
  Published by permission by Walter de Gruyter and Company.
- Chapter 4 originally appeared as "Frazer as Euhemerist: The Case of Osiris." In *Euhemerism and Its Uses: The Mortal Gods*, edited by Syrithe Pugh (London and New York: Routledge, 2021), 241–48.
  Published by permission by Taylor & Francis.
- Chapter 5 originally appeared as "Frazer and Campbell on Myth: Nineteenth- and Twentieth-Century Approaches." *Southern Review* 28 (Spring 1990), 470–76.
  Published by permission by The Editors, *The Southern Review*.
- Chapter 9 originally appeared as "Foreword to Daniel Dubuisson, *Twentieth Century Mythologies: Dumézil, Lévi-Strauss, Eliade*" (London: Equinox, 2006), ix–xiii.
  Published by permission by Equinox Publishing Ltd.
- Chapter 10 originally appeared as "Myth and Literature." In *Zwischen Präsenz und Repräsentation: Formen und Funktionen des*

Mythos in theoretischen und literarischen Diskursen, edited by Bent Gebert and Uwe Mayer (Berlin: De Gruyter, 2014), 258–73.
Published by permission by Walter de Gruyter and Company.

- Chapter 11 originally appeared as "Hell and Paradise for Milton: Physical Places and States of Mind." In *Fall Narratives*, edited by Zohar Hadromi-Allouche and Aine Larkin (London and New York: Routledge, 2017), 28–36.
Published by permission by Taylor & Francis.

Introduction

This collection of essays on myth is my third. The prior two are entitled *Theorizing about Myth* (1999) and *Myth Analyzed* (2021). All three collections are about theories of myth rather than about myths themselves. By theories I mean generalizations, either about myth per se or about a category of myth, such as hero myths. Some of the essays are about theories in their own right. Others are applications of theories to specific myths. Yet even applications serve to illuminate theories. The aim of a theory is to account for one or more of three things: the origin, the function, or the subject matter of myth.

Origin and function are two sides of the same coin. Both attribute myth to a need, which myth arises to fulfill and serves by fulfilling. Myth does not simply arise spontaneously and last on its own. It arises and lasts in response to a need. No need, no myth. No longer the need, no longer myth. The need may be eternal, such as the need for food. Or it may be more recent, such as a need for nationhood. But even if the need is eternal, myth may not be the sole or even the best way of fulfilling it and so may not itself be eternal. To take a classic example, myth for J. G. Frazer is not the first way of securing food—magic is—and is eventually succeeded by science.

A theory explains the *why* of myth—the need. But often, though not always, it also explains the *how*, or the means by which myth emerges and works—for example, in a group rather than individually.

Subject matter means what myth is really about. The subject can be either the apparent, literal subject or a symbolic one. A myth about a rain god can be taken as really about the god or about rain itself, or about a human father, or about a father archetype. Some theories deal with just the origin and function of myth. Others deal also with the subject matter. A few deal with just the subject matter.

Theories of the nineteenth century typically saw myth as an outdated, indeed "primitive," explanation of the physical world, an explanation taken literally. That explanation was succeeded by a scientific one. In this book this view is represented by F. Max Müller, E. B. Tylor, J. G. Frazer, Andrew Lang, Lucien Lévy-Bruhl, and Adalbert Kuhn.

By contrast, theories of the twentieth century have seen myth as almost anything else—that is, as anything other than a literal account of the origin or operation of the natural world. The subject of myth has become now not the physical world but instead the human world, whether taken as individuals or as a group. Or the need that myth originates and functions to fulfill has become other than explanatory. Or both. The need can be for anything save food. It can still be about the world, but to justify or simply to express the experience of the world. Or the need might have nothing to do with the physical world. It might be to explain or to justify the human world, such as ethics or rituals or laws. Myth might still be read literally, but at least as often it is read symbolically.

The twentieth-century view of myth is represented in this book by many figures: Bronislaw Malinowski, A. R. Radcliffe-Brown, Sigmund Freud, Otto Rank, Jacob Arlow, Géza Róheim, C. G. Jung, Johann Georg von Hahn, Jane Harrison, Gilbert Murray, F. M. Cornford, S. H. Hooke, Hans Blumenberg, Rudolf Bultmann, Hans Jonas, Albert Camus, Jessie Weston, Francis Fergusson, René Girard, Kenneth Burke, Northrop Frye, Georges Dumézil, Claude Lévi-Strauss, Joseph Campbell, and Mircea Eliade. At the same time some theorists in the twentieth century retain a nineteenth-century view—for example, David Bidney, Robin Horton, Samuel Noah Kramer, and Giorgio de Santillana.

Because the subject matter, origin, or function of myth in the twentieth century is usually different from that of science, myth and science are now compatible. One can have both. Myth and science are now like horses and cars, though with different origins, functions, or subject matters. For a few theorists, above all Campbell and Eliade, myth is not merely possible for all humans, modern as well as "primitive," but necessary. Without myth humans might not die, but they are less than complete humans.

Nineteenth-century theories saw myth as the "primitive" counterpart to natural science, which was considered modern, at least as the common explanation of events in the physical world. Ancient expressions of science were recognized—for example, among Sumerians, Babylonians, and Greeks and Romans. But these were the beliefs of intellectual elites, not of ordinary folk. In the nineteenth century myth and science were taken to be outright incompatible. One could not attribute the falling of rain to both the action of a god and meteorological processes. For God, it was assumed, did not let natural laws operate on their own, even if God had set them up. In this view, called Deism, God operates behind the scenes. In the nineteenth century God operated directly in the world, in place of natural laws. For example, God might have collected buckets of water and then each time dumped the water on a chosen spot below. True, a myth would be assuming the existence of mechanical laws or principles that explained why the buckets actually fell on the selected spot. But the emphasis was on the decision of the god and not on the course of the water.

Twentieth-century theories do not seek to reconcile myth with science. They seek to make myth merely compatible with science. The two are assumed to go their separate ways—in origin and function, in subject matter, or in both. The view that changes in the twentieth century is not that of science but that of myth.

Theories are attempts to make sense of the whole category of myths, even if some then focus on a variety of myths such as hero myths. Campbell at one point in his *Hero with a Thousand Faces* seems to be asserting that all myths are identical: "As we are told in the Vedas, 'Truth is one, the sages speak of it by many names'" (Segal 1997: 33). But he really means that myths are merely akin. They have the same origin, function, and subject matter. They are cases of the same "monomyth," to use the term that he takes from James Joyce. Campbell is in fact no different from other theorists. For all of them, myths are similar enough to share a common origin, function, and subject matter. The differences among myths are sheer details.

Specialists in one myth or mythology would demur. For them, the differences count more than the similarities, which are considered vague and superficial. Odysseus is a different kind of hero from Aeneas. The response from theorists: yes, there are differences, but they are secondary. They make sense only *in light of* the similarities. Interested in only the French Revolution? One will decipher it only vis-à-vis the Russian or the American Revolution. One will grasp the French Revolution only by first establishing what is meant by revolution per se. To explain the French Revolution is first to explain the origin, function, and subject matter of all revolutions. One can certainly be concerned with what makes the French Revolution distinctive, but one must first ask what makes it a revolution. One cannot say that one cares only about the French Revolution, for it is distinctively French only when matched up against any other revolution.

The essays in this book, as in my prior two books and also in my *Myth: A Very Short Introduction* (2004, revised 2015) are comparative. What they compare are not myths but theories, which come from at once the social sciences and the humanities.

In Chapter 1 I contrast Tylor's quintessentially nineteenth-century theory of myth—that myth serves to explain events in the physical world—to Blumenberg's equally quintessentially twentieth-century one—that myth serves to do anything but explain events in the physical world. Blumenberg attacks two kinds of theories: the rationalist one, as represented by Tylor, and the romantic one, as represented by Campbell, who himself is unnamed. Blumenberg takes an extreme view: that myth not merely no longer serves to explain the world but never did. Rather, myth has always served to alleviate anxiety about the arbitrariness of the world. Where science is about the world itself, myth, as also for Bultmann and Jonas and Camus, is about the human experience of the world. In this chapter the theories of both Tylor and Blumenberg are strongly criticized.

In Chapter 2 I contrast Müller's theory of myth to the theory of Tylor and also the theories of Jung and Lang. Where Tylor sees myth as an aspect of religion, at least of primitive religion, Müller pits myth against religion. For him, earliest religion has no myths, which arise only from a confusion in the use of seeming names for natural forces, such as the sun. The sun becomes not a mere name but a personality, the characteristics of whom need to be explained—by myth. Where Tylor insistently reads myth and religion literally, Müller reads religion symbolically—till the confusion. The original object of worship is not a physical phenomenon, such as the sun. Rather, it is an immaterial and impersonal Infinite. Where for Tylor myth and religion originate and function to explain physical events like the rising and setting of the sun, for Müller religion originates and functions to express the experience of the Infinite.

In Chapter 3 I present Frazer's theory of Adonis, who for Frazer is not a human being but either the god of vegetation or vegetation itself. Frazer sees Adonis as one of the key Mediterranean gods of vegetation. The others are Attis, Osiris, and Dionysus. Frazer applies his theory to all three of his pre-scientific stages of culture: magic, religion, and above all magic and religion combined. In the first stage, that of magic, there are no gods, only impersonal laws of nature. In the second stage, that of religion, gods are hypothesized to explain all physical events, not just the growth of crops. Through sacrifice and obedience gods are beseeched to provide necessities, above all food. There is no magic, which has been abandoned as an erroneous explanation of events. But eventually religion, while easily explained away as simply the refusal of the gods to grant requests for food, is itself abandoned, at least as the whole of a stage. It is replaced by a third stage, which brings back magic and combines it with religion to constitute "myth ritualism." In one version of myth ritualism the king, who is merely human, plays the role of the god of vegetation in a formal ritual. In the other version the king is himself divine and likewise participates in a formal ritual. In this chapter I apply Frazer's theory of all three pre-scientific stages of culture to the case of Adonis. In an endnote I refer to an essay of mine in which I compare Frazer on Adonis with Marcel Detienne and Jung on Adonis.

In Chapter 4 I present Frazer's interpretation of just one of his four main Mediterranean gods: Osiris. On the one hand Frazer treats all four examples as gods from the start, even if in their myths they by no means are. Frazer does not treat them as cases of euhemerism, or the transformation of an exceptional king into a god, either at death or even during life. On the other hand Frazer treats the case of Osiris as that of euhemerism. He offers scant evidence for euhemerism in Osiris. Yet Osiris does fit euhemerism more closely than do Frazer's other three Mediterranean gods of vegetation. For Frazer, Osiris parallels Jesus, who is prototypically euhemeristic.

In Chapter 5 I compare the theories of two of the most popular writers on myth: Frazer and Campbell. Frazer epitomizes the nineteenth-century view of myth: that myth is a primitive, pre-scientific account of the physical world, the function of which is not merely to explain the world but, even more, to control it, above all by providing food. Myth is succeeded by science and is incompatible with it. Myth and science are not akin to horses and cars: once science arises, one cannot still have myth. Myth is false, and science is true. By contrast to Frazer, Campbell epitomizes the twentieth-century view of myth: that myth is panhuman rather than merely primitive; that myth is not merely possible for moderns but even indispensable; that myth functions not to explain but to express; and that myth functions to express the mystical oneness between the immaterial and the material, between the soul and the body, and between the divine and the human. Where for Frazer myth is part of religion, for Campbell myth is separable from religion and survives the demise of religion by science. Myth as well as science is true. There can be secular myths. Where Frazer reads myth literally, at least usually, Campbell reads myth symbolically. Where for Frazer myth is about the physical world, for Campbell myth is about humans—specifically, about the human mind. At the same time Campbell parallels the human mind to the cosmos itself.

In Chapter 6 I argue that Campbell, despite the commonly applied characterization, is almost anything but a Jungian—even in his *Hero with a Thousand Faces*, his most Jungian book. Where Jung attributes myth to the unconscious, Campbell sometimes does so but other times attributes it to consciousness. Where for Jung the goal is the development of consciousness beyond the unconscious, for Campbell, at least in *Hero*, the goal is the return to primordial unconsciousness. Where Jung opposes diffusionism, Campbell sometimes adopts it. Later, Campbell attributes myth to ethological mechanisms. Where for Jung myth is not indispensable for psychological success, for Campbell it is. Where for Jung myth is not sufficient for psychological health, for Campbell it is. Where Jung usually confines himself to psychology, Campbell, at least in *Hero*, interprets myth not only psychologically but also metaphysically. Jung interprets myths variedly from myth to myth. In, most of all, *Hero* Campbell interprets myths almost identically. Yet above all in *The Masks of God* he interprets myths differently, culture by culture.

In Chapter 7 I ask whether Eliade's theory actually allows for modern myths, even in light of Eliade's fundamental claim that moderns, just like all other humans, have and must have myth. I maintain that by his own criteria modern myths fail to qualify as myths. They take place in the present or the future as often as in the past. If myths do take place in the past, reading or enacting them does not quite carry one back to the time of the myth. The characters in modern myths are humans rather than gods. To be present at the time and place of a modern myth is not to experience divinity. The characters are not usually models to be emulated. They do not always or even often establish a custom, a law, or an institution that continues to exist. Antithetically to Eliade stand Tylor and Frazer, for whom there are no modern myths. For them, "modern myths" would be a contradiction in terms. Also contrary to Eliade stand Jung and Campbell, both of whom allow for wholly secular myths and so who do not, like Eliade, seek religiosity in modern myths.

In Chapter 8 I consider Eliade on myth and science. In contrast to nineteenth-century theorists like Tylor and Frazer, Eliade, together with Malinowski, maintains that myth and science are compatible—not because their subject matter is other than the physical world, as for Bultmann, Jonas, Camus, Freud, and Jung, but even when their subject is the physical world, as it often is. For Malinowski, myth covers physical woes, such as flooding and illness, that science, at least for primitive peoples, is too rudimentary to cope with. Myth explains those woes by tracing them back to events from long ago, but it cannot remedy them.

It espouses resigned acceptance. Eliade, by contrast, does not seek to reconcile myth with science. For him, the fact that, especially, moderns have both means that they must be compatible. But how so? He does not even try to explain. He is left with two, purportedly compatible kinds of explanations of the origin of physical phenomena, one mythic and one scientific. He is similarly left with two, purportedly compatible kinds of explanations of social phenomena, such as race. One is mythic, the other social scientific. At the same time Eliade proposes functions that go far beyond that of science. Most important, myth, when read or heard or acted out, magically returns one to the time of the myth and thereby enables one to experience the gods in the myth.

In Chapter 9 I sum up the book *Twentieth Century Mythologies: Dumézil, Lévi-Strauss, Eliade* (2006) by Daniel Dubuisson. It was originally published in French in 1993. Dubuisson might have considered other theorists as well, but two of them, Freud and Jung, he does not even deem worthy of the term. Strikingly, he pits Dumézil and Lévi-Strauss against Eliade. He praises Dumézil and Lévi-Strauss as rigorous thinkers. He disparages Eliade as a fascist rather than a scholar. Where, for Dubuisson, Dumézil and Lévi-Strauss were open enough to change their minds, Eliade never was. He simply put his ideology in seemingly ethereal, apolitical terms. I consider whether, chronology aside, his three qualify as, in my terms, twentieth-century thinkers.

In Chapter 10 I present the array of views on the relationship between myth and literature. One relationship is the tracing of mythic themes in literature. The themes come above all from pagan, not biblical, mythology. Another relationship is the origin of literature from myth. The key theorist of myth here is Frazer. He himself does not apply his theory to literature, but many others do. They apply to specific myths his linkage of myth to ritual, or of story to action. Frazer, as noted, offers two distinct versions of what is called "myth ritualism." It is his second version which is applied more often. Among the myth ritualists discussed here are Jane Harrison, Gilbert Murray, F. M. Cornford, Jessie Weston, Francis Fergusson, Stanley Edgar Hyman, Northrop Frye, and René Girard. Girard himself, to be sure, sets myth against literature. Among theorists of myth, Tylor and Frazer downplay myth as story. For them, myth is a scientific-like explanation of external events that merely takes the form of a story. By contrast, Hans Blumenberg sees myth as a story and not as an explanation. The theorists who have offered plots, or patterns, for myth as story have focused on hero myths: Johann Georg von Hahn, Vladimir Propp, Otto Rank, Joseph

Campbell, and Lord Raglan. Rank, Campbell, and Raglan present their patterns as applications of theories: Freud's, Jung's, and Frazer's.

In Chapter 11 I compare various theorists on the nature of hell and heaven. In the myth of the Garden of Eden (Genesis 3) paradise means the garden. There is no hell. There is only life outside the garden, to which Adam and Eve are forever condemned. If one uses the favorite terms of Durkheim and Eliade, the sacred is both spatial and temporal. Sacred space is the garden. Profane space is the rest of earth. Sacred time is the time of life in the garden. Profane time is time after eviction from the garden. For Durkheim, the sacred is the group. The profane is the individual. The sacred is both spatial—the group, whenever it gathers—and temporal—the times when the group gathers. For Eliade as well, the sacred is both spatial—the location of altars, churches, and other sacred spaces—and temporal—the times, always in the past, when the gods resided on earth. For William Robertson Smith, the sacred means space above all. For primitive and ancient peoples, it was a physical location. Later it became, and remains, spiritualized and so can exist anywhere. For John Milton, uniquely, the sacred is at once physical and mental. For him, the garden, the world outside it, and hell are to be seen as at once physical and psychological: a place both "out there" and in one's head. For Freud and Jung alike, the outer world is psychologized: it refers to states of mind, which are wrongly projected onto the outer world. For D. W. Winnicott, the world of myth, which I compare with the world of play for him, is neither inner nor outer but in between.

In Chapter 12 I ask whether heroes of myth must be male. I go through each of the main theories of hero myths. Certainly the theories that deem heroes kings—for example, Frazer's—are obliged to make heroes male. Frazer's four chief gods of vegetation are male, though he does note the generic Mother Goddess of vegetation. But so, seemingly, does Campbell, whose heroes can come from any class. Whether he is in fact committed to male heroes, especially when his first example is of the Princess and the Frog, is debatable. On the one hand he gives many examples of female heroes, beginning with his first example in his *Hero with a Thousand Faces*. On the other hand heroism in the second of his three stages in *Hero* seems to require a male hero, and this despite the female cases he names! In his early, Freudian *Myth of the Birth of the Hero* Rank's hero, who can be an aristocrat and not necessarily a king, is always male. But once Rank breaks with Freud, the subject ceases to be the relationship between son and father and becomes that between either son or daughter and the mother. Heroes can therefore be of either gender. Raglan, who equates the hero with the king, clearly limits himself to male heroes. Some scholars have tried to allow for full-fledged female heroes for Campbell. Others have done the same with even Raglan's heroes.

In Chapter 13 I consider the concept, developed by Jung and the physicist Wolfgang Pauli, of a noncausal relationship between humans and the external world. According to this notion of synchronicity, what is going on in our unconscious matches but not causes what is going on in the outer world. Synchronicity is not the projection of dreams or fantasies or archetypes onto the world. Synchronicity is, rather, the sheer parallel between our unconscious beliefs and the world. It is coincidence, but it is more than coincidence. The question I ask is whether synchronicity thereby brings myth back to the outer world. I review the differing relationships between humans and the world espoused by theorists of the last two centuries. Where all prior theories assume that myth means the causing of events in the world by a personal god, in synchronicity there is no god and no causality. What part myth thereby plays is discussed.

In the fourteenth and final chapter I present the varying positions of theorists on the relationship among four categories: myth, science, religion, and philosophy. I first list the three main positions on myth and science: myth as true science, myth as modern science, and myth as primitive science. I then go theorist by theorist on myth and religion, myth and philosophy, and myth and science. I discuss Tylor, Frazer, Lévy-Bruhl, Malinowski, Lévi-Strauss, Karl Popper, Paul Radin, Ernst Cassirer, the Frankforts, Cornford, Bultmann, and Jonas. I apply each theory to the myth of Noah (Genesis 6–9).

Chapter 1

From Nineteenth- to Twentieth-Century Theorizing about Myth in Britain and Germany: Tylor versus Blumenberg

It is commonly said that theories of myth of the nineteenth century focused on the question of origin and that theories of the twentieth century have focused on the questions of function and subject matter. But this characterization confuses *historical* origin with *recurrent* one. Theories that profess to provide the origin of myth do not claim to know where and when myth first arose. Rather, they claim to know why and how myth arises wherever and whenever it does. The issue of recurrent origin has been as popular with twentieth-century theories as with nineteenth-century ones, and interest in function and subject matter was as common to nineteenth-century theories as to twentieth-century ones.

But there is one genuine difference between nineteenth- and twentieth-century theories. Nineteenth-century theories tended to see the subject matter of myth as the natural world and to see the origin and function of myth as the provision of a literal explanation of that world. Myth was typically taken to be the "primitive" counterpart to science, which was assumed to be wholly or overwhelmingly modern. It was recognized that the beginnings of science went back to ancient times, but science as the commonplace, everyday explanation of the world was considered to be only a few centuries old. Nineteenth-century theories assumed that science rendered myth not merely superfluous but impossible. Moderns, who by definition were scientific, therefore had to reject myth. By contrast, twentieth-century theories have tended to see myth as almost anything but an outdated counterpart to modern science, either in subject matter or in origin and function. Consequently, moderns can retain myth alongside science. For some twentieth-century theories, myth is not merely still possible for moderns but outright indispensable.

Twentieth-century theories have spurned nineteenth-century ones on many specific grounds: for pitting myth against science and thereby precluding modern myths, for subsuming myth under religion and thereby precluding secular myths, for deeming the function of myth intellectual, for deeming myth false, and for reading myth literally. Above all, twentieth-century theories have rejected nineteenth-century ones on the grounds that myths, far from dying out, are still "around." If myth is incompatible with science, how has myth survived—and survived not merely as a relic, which is what a "survival" meant in the nineteenth century, but as a living phenomenon? How has myth survived not *in place of* science—the way the Bible is for creationists—but *alongside* science? Surely the survival of living myth meant that whatever myth is, it is other than a literal explanation of the physical world.

Nineteenth-century theorists were not without a defense. They maintained that those who retained myth in the wake of science either did not recognize or, more, did not accept the incompatibility of myth with science. But their arguments scarcely persuaded twentieth-century theorists. Who, it is asked, does not recognize the incompatibility of attributing lightning to Zeus' thrusting a bolt and attributing lightning to meteorological processes? If moderns still do not accept the incompatibility of myth with science, why not consider the possibility that for them myth is doing something different from what science does? In that event nineteenth-century theories plainly got myth wrong.

The divide between nineteenth- and twentieth-century theories is not over whether primitive peoples have myth. That they do is taken for granted by both sides. The divide is over whether moderns, who for both sides have science, can also have myth. Twentieth-century theorists have argued that they can and do and even must. At the same time the divide between nineteenth- and twentieth-century theories is not over whether myth must be compatible with science. The authority of science is taken for granted by both sides. The twentieth-century approach is not to challenge science but to recharacterize myth. Only with the emergence of postmodernism has the deference to science assumed by both sides been questioned.

There have been three main twentieth-century responses to the nineteenth-century position. One response has been to take the origin and function of myth as other than explanatory, in which case myth diverges from science and can therefore coexist with it. Another response has been to read myth other than literally, in which case myth does not even refer to the physical world and can therefore likewise coexist with science. The most radical response has been to alter both the explanatory origin and function and the literal reading of myth.

This difference among theories of myth cuts across national boundaries. It is therefore to be found in both Britain and Germany as well as elsewhere in Europe and in North America. To illustrate the difference between the nineteenth-century view of myth and the twentieth-century one, I could, then, choose one Brit and one German from each period. There are many theorists I could choose. In the case of Britain I could choose the Scot J. G. (James George) Frazer, the first edition of whose opus, *The Golden Bough*, appeared in 1890. But as my exemplar I will choose the Englishman E. B. (Edward Burnett) Tylor, the first edition of whose key work, *Primitive Culture*, appeared in 1871. In the case of Germany I could choose from the group known as the nature mythologists, who, while not confined to Germany, were especially prominent there. The most eminent were Adalbert Kuhn and F. Max Müller, who, to be sure, spent most of his career at Oxford.

The list of possible twentieth-century theorists from both countries is longer. For example, I could choose any of the following Brits: Jane Harrison, F. M. Cornford, or S. H. Hooke. I could also choose non-British theorists who wrote in English: the Australian Gilbert Murray, the Americans Kenneth Burke and Joseph Campbell, or the Polish Bronislaw Malinowski. Similarly, I could choose any of the following Germans: Ernst Cassirer, Rudolf Bultmann, Hans Jonas, Walter Burkert, or Hans Blumenberg. And of course I could choose non-German theorists who wrote in German—above all the Austrian Sigmund Freud or the Swiss C. G. Jung.

Admittedly, the chronological divide between these camps is not rigid. Nineteenth-century views are to be found in the twentieth century—for example, in the English anthropologist Robin Horton (1967), who is even labelled a "neo-Tylorian," or in the American anthropologist David Bidney (1955, 1967: ch. 10), who could likewise be called a neo-Tylorian. The view that primitive myth is not the parallel to modern science but is itself scientific is to be found most grandly in the French structuralist Claude Lévi-Strauss (1966, 1970 [1969]). And the classic expression of the view that ancient myths record sophisticated scientific observations is the 1969 *Hamlet's Mill*, jointly written by the Italian historian of science Giorgio de Santillana and the Dutch historian of science Hertha von Dechend. Conversely, the nineteenth-century Friedrich Nietzsche psychologizes myth as fully as do Freud and Jung. Still, the chronological division, even if of degree only, remains.

Because the deepest divide among modern theorists is for me chronological rather than geographical, I will choose only one theorist each to evince it: Tylor for the nineteenth century and Blumenberg for the twentieth century.

Tylor

Tylor subsumes myth under religion and in turn subsumes both religion and science under philosophy. He divides philosophy into "primitive" and "modern." Primitive philosophy is identical with primitive religion. There is no primitive science. Modern philosophy, by contrast, has two divisions: religion and science. Of the two, science is by far the more important and is the modern counterpart to primitive religion. Modern religion is composed of two elements—metaphysics and ethics—neither of which is present in primitive religion. Metaphysics deals with nonphysical entities, of which primitive peoples have no conception. Ethics is not absent from primitive culture, but it falls outside primitive religion: "the conjunction of ethics and Animistic philosophy, so intimate and powerful in the higher culture, seems scarcely yet to have begun in the lower" (Tylor 1871, vol. 2: 11). Tylor uses the term "animism" for religion per se, modern and primitive alike, because he derives the belief in gods from the belief in souls (*anima* in Latin means soul). In primitive religion souls occupy all physical entities, beginning with the bodies of humans. Gods become the souls in all physical entities *except* humans, who are not themselves gods.

Primitive religion is the primitive counterpart to science because both are explanations of the physical world. Tylor thus characterizes primitive religion as "savage biology" (Tylor 1871, vol. 2: 20) and maintains that "mechanical astronomy gradually superseded the animistic astronomy of the lower races" and that today "biological pathology gradually supersedes animistic pathology" (Tylor 1871, vol. 2: 229). The religious explanation is personalistic: the decisions of gods explain events. The scientific explanation is impersonal: mechanical laws explain events. The natural sciences as a whole have replaced religion as the explanation of the physical world, so that "animistic astronomy" and "animistic pathology" refer only to primitive, not modern, animism. Modern religion has surrendered the physical world to science and has retreated to the immaterial world, especially to the realm of life after death—that is, of the life of the soul after the death of the body. Where in primitive religion souls are deemed material, in modern religion they are deemed immaterial and are limited to human beings:

In our own day and country, the notion of souls of beasts is to be seen dying out. Animism, indeed, seems to be drawing in its outposts, and concentrating itself on its first and main position, the doctrine of the human soul.... The soul has given up its ethereal substance, and become an immaterial entity, "the shadow of a shade." Its theory is becoming separated from the investigations of biology and mental science, which now discuss the phenomena of life and thought, the senses and the intellect, the emotions and the will, on a ground-work of pure experience. There has arisen an intellectual product whose very existence is of the deepest significance, a "psychology" which has no longer anything to do with "soul." The soul's place in modern thought is in the metaphysics of religion, and its especial office there is that of furnishing an intellectual side to the religious doctrine of the future. (Tylor 1871, vol. 2: 85)

Similarly, where in primitive religion gods are deemed material, in modern religion they are deemed immaterial. Gods thereby cease to be agents in the physical world—Tylor assumes that physical effects must have physical causes—and religion ceases to be an explanation of the physical world. Gods are relocated from the physical world to the social world. They become models for humans, just as they should be for Plato. One now reads the Bible not for the story of creation but for the Ten Commandments, just as for Plato a bowdlerized Homer would enable one to do. Jesus is to be emulated as the ideal human, not as a miracle worker.

This irenic position is also like that of the evolutionary biologist Stephen Jay Gould, for whom science, above all evolution, is compatible with religion because the two never intersect. Science explains the physical world; religion prescribes ethics and gives meaning to life: "Science tries to document the factual character of the natural world, and to develop theories that coordinate and explain these facts. Religion, on the other hand, operates in the equally important, but utterly different, realm of human purposes, meanings, and values" (Gould 2002 [1999]: 4). But where for Gould religion has *always* served a function different from that of science, for Tylor religion has been forced to retrain upon having been made compulsorily redundant by science. And its present function is a demotion. Tylor is closer to biologist Richard Dawkins, though Dawkins, unlike Tylor, is unprepared to grant religion even a lesser function in the wake of science.

For Tylor, the demise of religion as an explanation of the physical world has meant the demise of myth altogether, which for Tylor is thus confined to primitive religion. Even though myth is an elaboration on the belief in gods, the belief itself can survive the rise of science where somehow myth cannot. Apparently, myths are too closely tied to gods as agents in the world to permit any comparable transformation from physics to metaphysics. Where, then, there is "modern religion," albeit religion shorn of its key role as explanation, there are no modern myths. The term "modern myth" is an oxymoron.

For Tylor, science makes myth not merely superfluous but incompatible. Why? Because the explanations that science and myth give are. It is not simply that the mythic explanation is personalistic and the scientific one impersonal. It is that both are *direct* explanations. Gods operate not behind or through impersonal forces but in place of them. According to myth, the rain god, let us say, collects rain in buckets and then chooses to empty the buckets on some spot below. According to science, meteorological processes cause rain. One cannot stack the mythic account atop the scientific one, for the rain god, rather than utilizing meteorological processes, acts in place of them. Tylor thus notes the gradual displacement of the direct causes of religion, or "animism," by the equally direct ones of science: "But just as mechanical astronomy gradually superseded the animistic astronomy of the lower races, so biological pathology gradually supersedes animistic pathology, the *immediate* operation of personal spiritual beings in both cases giving place to the operation of natural processes" (Tylor 1871, vol. 2: 229; italics added).

Strictly, causation in myth is never entirely personalistic. The decision of the rain god to dump rain on a chosen spot below presupposes physical laws that account for the accumulation of rain in heaven, the capacity of the buckets to retain the rain, and the direction of the dumped rain. But to maintain his rigid hiatus between myth and science, Tylor would doubtless note that myths themselves ignore physical processes and focus instead on divine decisions.

Yet even if myth and science are incompatible, why for Tylor is myth unscientific? The answer must be that personal causes are unscientific. But why? Tylor never says. Among the possible reasons: that personal causes are mental—the decisions of divine agents—whereas impersonal causes are material; that personal causes are neither predictable nor testable, whereas impersonal ones are both predictable and testable; that personal causes are particularistic, whereas impersonal ones are generalized; and that personal causes are final, or teleological, whereas impersonal ones are efficient. But none of these reasons in fact differentiates personal from impersonal causes, so that it is not easy to see how Tylor could defend his conviction that myth is unscientific.

Because Tylor never questions this assumption, he takes for granted not merely that primitive peoples have only myth but, even more, that moderns have only science. Not coincidentally, he refers to the "myth-making stage" of culture. Rather than an eternal phenomenon, as such twentieth-century theorists as Mircea Eliade, Jung, and Campbell grandly proclaim, myth for Tylor is merely a passing, if slowly passing, one. Myth has admirably served its function, but its time is over. While Tylor does not date the beginning of the scientific stage, it is doubtless identical with the beginning of modernity and is therefore only a few centuries old. Dying in 1917, Tylor never quite envisioned a stage post the modern one.

One reason Tylor pits myth against science is that he subsumes myth under religion. For him, there is no myth outside religion, even though modern religion is without myth. Because primitive religion is the counterpart to science, myth must be as well. Because religion is to be taken literally, so must myth be.

Another reason Tylor pits myth against science is that he opposes those who read myth symbolically, poetically, or metaphorically—for him interchangeable terms. He opposes the "moral allegorizers," for whom the myth of Helius' daily driving his chariot across the sky is a way of instilling self-discipline. Likewise he opposes the "euhemerists," for whom the myth is simply a colorful way of describing the exploits of some local or national hero.[1] For Tylor, the myth is an explanation of why the sun rises and sets, and the explanatory function *requires* a literal reading. To read myth nonliterally is automatically to cede any explanatory function, and to cede the explanatory function is automatically to trivialize myth. Tylor thus writes that "the basis on which such [mythic] ideas as these are built is not to be narrowed down to poetic fancy and transformed metaphor. They rest upon a broad philosophy of nature, early and crude indeed, but thoughtful, consistent, and quite really and seriously meant" (Tylor 1871, vol. 1: 285). Myth makers are like modern scientists, not poets, and myth should be read as prose, not poetry (see Tylor 1871, vol. 1: 292).

For both the allegorizers and the euhemerists, myth is not the primitive counterpart to science because, read symbolically, it is about human beings rather than gods or the world. For the allegorizers, myth is also unlike science because, read symbolically, it functions to prescribe how humans ought to behave rather than to explain how they do behave. For the euhemerists, too, myth is also unlike science because it functions to describe rather than to explain heroic deeds. As interpretations of myth, moral allegory and euhemerism alike go back to antiquity, but Tylor sees contemporaneous exponents of both as motivated by a desire to preserve myth in the face of the distinctively modern challenge of science. In taking the subject matter of myth to be other than the world, and in taking the function of myth to be other than explanatory, both moral allegory and euhemerism are akin to twentieth-century theories.

Opposite to Tylor stands Müller (1856). Where for Tylor moderns misread myth by taking it symbolically, for Müller ancients themselves eventually came to misread their own myths, or mythical data, by gradually taking them literally. Originally symbolic descriptions of natural processes came to be read as literal descriptions of the attributes of gods. For example, the sea described poetically as "raging" was eventually taken as the characteristic of the personality responsible for the behavior of the sea, and a myth was then invented to account for this characteristic. Mythology for Müller arises from the absence in some ancient languages of a neuter gender. Speakers therefore had to refer to impersonal entities in the male or female gender, misleading later generations into taking the referent to be a person rather than a thing. But Müller is still the German counterpart to Tylor because for Müller as much as for Tylor myth is about the external world.

Since Tylor denies the reality of the gods, he himself might seem to be taking them as mere personifications of natural phenomena and thereby be taking myth nonliterally. But he is not. Unlike both the euhemerists and the moral allegorizers, he assumes that primitive peoples themselves take the gods literally. He breaks with primitive peoples in taking the gods as real only in intent, not also in fact.

Gods for Tylor are the purported causes of events in the physical world. Myths do not merely describe events but explain them. The ultimate subject matter of myth for Tylor is not events themselves, as it is for most nature mythologists and as it is at times for Frazer, but the causes of those events. As mere descriptions of events, myths would be unnecessary. Ever observant, primitive peoples for Tylor notice events on their own. They invent myths to account for their observations, not to record them. For Tylor, gods originate out of the personification of nature. But once conjured up, gods are more than mere personifications. They are the causes—the professed literal causes—of the origin and operation of the world.

Tylor's most telling argument for a literal reading of myth is the otherwise inexplicable beliefs of primitive peoples. Only persons who took myth literally would think the way they do:

> When the Aleutians thought that if anyone gave offence to the moon, he [i.e., moon] would fling down stones on the offender and kill him, or when the moon came down to an Indian squaw, appearing in the form of a beautiful woman with a child in her arms, and demanding an offering of tobacco and fur robes, what conceptions of personal life could be more distinct [i.e., real] than these? (Tylor 1871, vol. 1: 289–90)

While for Tylor taking the gods literally does not entail taking them as real, taking them as real does presuppose taking them literally.

For Tylor, myth stems from innate intellectual curiosity, which is as strong in primitive peoples as in moderns: "Man's craving to know the causes at work in each event he witnesses, the reasons why each state of things he surveys is such as it is and no other, is no product of high civilization, but a characteristic of his race down to its lowest stages" (Tylor 1871, vol. 1: 368–69). More than idle curiosity, the quest for knowledge among even primitive peoples "is already an intellectual appetite whose satisfaction claims many of the moments not engrossed by war or sport, food or sleep" (Tylor 1871, vol. 1: 369).

For Tylor, the postulation of first souls and then gods is a rational inference from the data: "the primitive animistic doctrine is thoroughly at home among savages, who appear to hold it on the very evidence of their senses, interpreted on the biological principle which seems to them most reasonable" (Tylor 1871, vol. 2: 83–84; see also, for example, vol. 2: 29–31, 62, 194). We moderns consider even more madcap the postulation of souls and gods in inanimate objects like "stocks and stones, weapons, boats, food, clothes, ornaments, and other objects," for to us these objects "are not merely soulless but [underlying it] lifeless" (Tylor 1871, vol. 2: 61). But "if we place ourselves by an effort in the intellectual position of an uncultured tribe, and examine the theory of object-souls from their point of view, we shall hardly pronounce it irrational" (Tylor 1871, vol. 2: 61). A stone over which one trips can seem to have placed itself there. Plants as well as animals do seem to be exercising their wills in their varying responses to human effort.

Once primitive peoples hypothesize souls and gods as the causes of natural events, they *experience*, not just *explain*, the world as filled with souls and gods:

> They [primitives] could see the flame licking its yet undevoured prey with tongues of fire, or the serpent gliding along the waving sword from hilt to point; they could feel a live creature gnawing within their bodies in the pangs of hunger; they heard the voices of the hill-dwarfs answering in the echo, and the chariot of the Heaven-god rattling in thunder over the solid firmament. (Tylor 1871, vol. 1: 297)

But unlike such theorists as Lucien Lévy-Bruhl, Cassirer, and Henri Frankfort, for all of whom primitive religion shapes experience from the outset, Tylor maintains that primitive peoples initially experience the world no differently from moderns. Primitive peoples see and hear what moderns do. They merely trust their eyes and ears and on the basis of them reason out, not assume or project, the existence of souls and gods. Primitive peoples may be uncritical, but they are not illogical. Like moderns, they work scrupulously inductively—from observations to inferences to generalizations. Tylor thus preserves the parallel between primitive religion and modern science, or his conception of modern science.

As much as Tylor stresses the role of reason in myth and religion, he accords a place to imagination, at least in myth. Like the rest of religion, myth functions to explain the world. But unlike the rest of religion, myth does so in the form of stories, which are in part the product of imagination.

It is imagination that transforms the rational belief in Helius as the sun god into the fantastic story of Helius' daily driving a chariot across the sky. Undeniably, Tylor vigorously decries the view that myth stems from *unrestrained* imagination:

> Among those opinions which are produced by a little knowledge, to be dispelled by a little more, is the belief in an almost boundless creative power of the human imagination. The superficial student, mazed in a crowd of seemingly wild and lawless fancies, which he thinks to have no reason in nature nor pattern in this material world, at first concludes them to be new births from the imagination of the poet, the tale-teller, and the seer. (Tylor 1871, vol. 1: 273)

Tylor even maintains that both the euhemerists and the moral allegorizers fail to take myth seriously *because* they attribute it to unbridled imagination, which he equates with "poetic fancy" (see, for example, Tylor 1871, vol. 1: 285, 289–90). For Tylor, to attribute myth to imagination is invariably to make its subject other than the physical world and is thereby to make its function other than explanatory.

Still, Tylor accords a commodious place to *restrained* imagination: imagination restrained by reason. The comparative approach, which he takes for granted neither the euhemerists nor the moral allegorizers employ (see Tylor 1871, vol. 1: 280–82), "makes it possible to trace in mythology the operation of imaginative processes recurring with the evident regularity of mental law" (Tylor 1871, vol. 1: 282; see also vol. 1: 274–75). Tylor assumes that untethered imagination would never yield the patterns he finds in myths, so that regularities constitute *ipso facto* evidence of the subordination of imagination to reason. The stories may be fantastic, but they are fantastic in uniform ways. Tylor asks rhetorically, "What would be popularly thought more indefinite and uncontrolled than the products of the imagination in myths and fables?" (Tylor 1871, vol. 1: 18). Here he anticipates Lévi-Strauss. For both, the demonstration of uniformity in myth, the seemingly least orderly of artifacts, proves that not only it but also its primitive creators are rational (see Lévi-Strauss 1955: 430; 1970 [1969]: 10). For both Tylor and Lévi-Strauss as well, the rational function of myth must be scientific-like.

Tylor's subordination of imagination to reason is symptomatic of the central limitation of his overall theory of myth: his overemphasis on myth as akin to science and his underemphasis on it as akin to literature. Myth for him is a scientific-like hypothesis that merely happens to take the form of a story. Like Lévi-Strauss, he downplays the format in order to uphold the content. He assumes that myth, like the rest of religion, is an explanation of the physical world, is taken seriously only when it is taken as an explanation of the physical world, and is taken as an explanation of the physical world only when the form is taken as merely a colorful way of presenting the content. Form and content are separable, and content alone counts. To treat the form as anything more is to reduce a set of truth-claims about the world to fiction.

Tylor's attempt at minimizing both narrative and imagination fails. First, he simply cannot confine the subject of myth to the physical world or even the human one. He cannot disregard the divine world. Even if gods are postulated in order to explain the physical world, surely they become of interest in their own right, if only for their power over the physical world. Surely the intellectual inquisitiveness that Tylor is so zealous to credit to primitive peoples does not abate with the postulation of gods as the causes of events in the world. Exactly insofar as myths for Tylor are stories about gods, surely there is interest in gods in themselves. The Hebrew Bible may present God only in relation to humans and the world, but Homer and Hesiod, for example, also depict the gods amongst themselves. Certainly in science the microscopic world, even if initially postulated to account for the macroscopic world, becomes of interest in itself.

Second, descriptions of the divine world are surely the work of imagination. Gods may be postulated on analogy to human beings, but they are more than human beings. Whatever qualities make gods gods and make heaven heaven are surely the product of imagination. Far from constricting the exercise of imagination, the belief in gods spurs it.

Third, the content of myth does not readily evince "the operation of imaginative processes recurring with the evident regularity of mental law" (Tylor 1871, vol. 1: 282). Strikingly, Tylor barely discusses the content of myth—beyond stipulating that myth presents a divine explanation of natural phenomena. What form that explanation takes, he never says. Unlike some other theorists such as Frazer, he provides no common pattern for myths. The sole myths for which he provides any regularity are hero myths, in which, according to him, the subjects are exposed at birth, are saved, and grow up to become national heroes (see Tylor 1871, vol. 1: 281–82). But his pattern is neither universal nor detailed. And hero myths for Tylor are an anomaly within his characterization of myths as explanations of physical events. He offers no comparable pattern for creation myths, flood myths, or myths of recurrent natural processes.

In the light of postmodernism, Tylor's approach doubtless seems not simply one-sided but hopelessly out of date. Where postmodernists would view myth as a mere story and not an explanation, Tylor views myth as an explanation and only incidentally a story. What is needed is not the replacement of myth as explanation by myth as story but instead the integration of the two: the working out of how form and content, story and explanation, operate together.

Blumenberg

In *Work on Myth* (1985) Hans Blumenberg attacks two leading modern views of myth: that of the Enlightenment and that of Romanticism. Tylor, though cited only once (see Blumenberg 1985: 151), and Campbell, though never cited, are standard exemplars of each view.

Blumenberg sums up the Enlightenment view, which he by no means limits to the eighteenth century, in the familiar phrase "from *mythos* to *logos*" (see, for example, Blumenberg 1985: 49).[2] Tylor, epitomizing that view, assumes an evolution from myth, which he subsumes under religion, to science. For him, primitive peoples alone have myth and moderns alone science. Myth and science not only are incompatible in content but also duplicate each other in function.

Blumenberg assumes that the contrast between *mythos* and *logos* necessarily makes myth irrational: "What [to the Enlightenment] was meant by the antithesis of reason and myth was in fact that of science and myth" (Blumenberg 1985: 49). He thus berates the Enlightenment for failing to see myth "as itself [serving] a rational function" (Blumenberg 1985: 48). But his criticism does not hold for all "Enlightened" theorists and certainly not for Tylor. Far from either blind superstition or frivolous storytelling, myth for Tylor is a scrupulously logical and reflective enterprise. As quoted: "The basis on which such [mythic] ideas as these are built is not to be narrowed down to poetic fancy and transformed metaphor. They rest upon a broad philosophy of nature, early and crude indeed, but thoughtful, consistent, and quite really and seriously meant" (Tylor 1871, vol. 1: 285). Tylor does judge myth false, but not irrational. Otherwise it could not be the primitive counterpart to science—a point about the Enlightenment missed by Blumenberg. As the primitive counterpart to science, myth for Tylor and others offers a rigorous and systematic account of the world.

Having been displaced by science as the explanation of the world, myth, according to Blumenberg, is left by Enlightened theorists with a merely aesthetic role:

> In his discussion of myth Fontenelle expressed the Enlightenment's amazement at the fact that the myths of the Greeks had still not disappeared from the world. Religion [i.e., Christianity] and reason had, it is true, weaned people from them, but poetry and painting had given them the means by which to survive. They had known how to make themselves indispensable to these arts. (Blumenberg 1985: 263)

Ironically, Tylor here goes even further than Blumenberg assumes that Enlightened theorists go. In the wake of science myth, unlike the rest of religion, is for Tylor left with no role at all and will eventually die out.

Blumenberg rejects the Enlightenment view of myth on two grounds: that myth continues to exist in modernity (see Blumenberg 1985: 263–64, 274) and that myth was never an explanation of the world. Combining these arguments, Blumenberg states:

> That does not yet mean that the *explanation* of phenomena has always had priority and that myths are something like early ways of dealing with the difficulty of lacking theory. If they were an expression of the lack of science or of prescientific explanation, they would have been disposed of automatically at the latest when science ... made its entrance. The opposite was the case. (Blumenberg 1985: 274)

For Blumenberg, the survival of living myth in the wake of science proves that its function was never scientific.

Of course, what Tylor claims of religion *minus* myth someone else might claim of myth itself: that not serving to explain the world now hardly proves that it never served to explain the world. For Bultmann (1953), for example, myth prior to the rise of science served both to explain the world and to depict the state of human beings in the world, which remains its sole (and proper) function. Blumenberg needs an additional argument for his claim that myth never served a scientific-like function. He offers multiple arguments.

By a scientific explanation Blumenberg means a genetic, or etiological, one. As he writes in criticism of the Enlightenment view, "That the relationship between the 'prejudice' called myth and the new science should [for the Enlightenment] be one of competition necessarily presupposes the interpretation of individual myths as etiological" (Blumenberg 1985: 265).

On four grounds, asserts Blumenberg, myth is nonetiological. First, even standard creation myths like Hesiod's *Theogony* and Genesis 1–2 give no ultimate origin of the world. Rather, they presuppose the existence of something and explain the creation of the world either by or from it:

> Flaubert noted in his Egyptian diary on June 12, 1850, that during the day his group had climbed a mountain on the summit of which there was a great number of large round stones that almost resembled cannonballs. He was told that these had originally been melons, which God had turned into stones. The story is over, the narrator is evidently satisfied; but not the traveler, who has to ask for the reason why. Because it pleased God, is the answer, and the story simply goes no further. (Blumenberg 1985: 257; see also 126–27, 128, 161, 257–59)

Second, myths tell stories rather than give reasons: "In the [erroneous] etiological explanation of myth ... the recognition of myth as an archaic accomplishment of reason has to be justified by its having initially and especially given answers to questions, rather than having [in actuality] been the implied rejection of those questions by means of storytelling" (Blumenberg 1985: 166; see also 184–85, 257–59).

Third, within a myth anything can derive from anything else, in which case there must be scant interest in accurate derivation and therefore in derivation itself: "When anything can be derived from anything, then there just is no explaining, and no demand for explanation. One just tells stories" (Blumenberg 1985: 127). Indeed, myth presents mere "sequences" rather than "chronology," by which he means causality (Blumenberg 1985: 126; see also 128).

Fourth and most important, myth describes more the significance than the origin of phenomena. Thus the Bible tells not how but why God created the rainbow:

> He [God] gives those who have just escaped the Flood a first specimen of the sequence of agreements and covenants that were to characterize his dealings with his people: "This is the token of the covenant which I make between me and you and every living creature that is with you, for perpetual generations ...." One will not want to say that this is an "explanation" of the rainbow, which would have had to be replaced as quickly as possible, with arrival at a higher level of knowledge, by a physical [i.e., scientific] theory. (Blumenberg 1985: 265)

Blumenberg asserts not only that myth fails to give the origin of phenomena but also that the origin of myth itself is unknowable: "But theories about the origin of myths are idle. Here the rule is: *Ignorabimus* [We will not know]" (Blumenberg 1985: 45; see also 59). If so, then Blumenberg's consequent turning from the origin of myth to the function makes sense. What does not is his seeming additional justification for so doing: that myth itself is not concerned with the origin of things! Surely even if Blumenberg's claim that myth itself scorns the question of the origin of phenomena is correct, a *theory* of myth need not therefore scorn the question of the origin of *myth*. Yet Blumenberg repeatedly implies that the issues that myth itself considers somehow determine the issues that theories of myth should consider.

Blumenberg argues that the function, or "work," of myth is not, as for the Enlightenment, to explain the world but to allay anxiety over the world, to fulfill the need "to be at home in the world" (Blumenberg 1985: 113). Like Freud in *The Future of an Illusion* (1961), Blumenberg asserts that humans wish the world were nicer than it is. For Freud, humans fulfill their wish by transforming an indifferent, impersonal world into one ruled by a caring, human-like god.

For Blumenberg, there are many stages in between. First, the still impersonal world gets named—as Fate, for example. Anxiety, which has no object, thereby gets reduced to fear, which does. The impersonal force then gets transformed into animal gods, who in turn become human-like gods. Initially nameless and vague gods acquire names and attributes, both of which make them easier to control. Initially capricious gods become predictable. Initially indifferent gods become just and then merciful. Initially implacable gods become appeasable through rituals and ethics. The originally single cosmic force, which is omnipotent, becomes multiple gods, who neutralize one another's power. Many gods in turn ultimately become a single god, but one whose omnipotence is tempered by justice and mercy (see Blumenberg 1985, esp. 5–6, 13–14, 18, 22–23, 35–36, 42–43, 117, 124–25).[3]

For the Enlightenment, according to Blumenberg, myth creates anxiety by turning the natural world into a world filled with terrifying supernatural figures. For Blumenberg himself, by contrast, myth *alleviates* anxiety by turning a terrifying *natural* world into one filled with supernatural figures who can be placated. Myth "is a way of expressing the fact that the world and the powers that hold sway in it are not abandoned to pure arbitrariness" (Blumenberg 1985: 42).[4]

For Freud, the transformation of the world under myth serves less to control than to justify the world. For Blumenberg, the transformation serves less to control or even to justify the world than, in a nonetiological sense to be spelled out, to "explain" it. Freud assumes that humans seek above all to justify the world and that a world ruled by personal agents offers the possibility of a rationale and therefore of a justification. Blumenberg assumes that a world ruled, like society, by personalities is more familiar and therefore less alien than an impersonal one.[5]

Unlike Freud, Blumenberg attributes human helplessness to biology, not to the environment. He is here like the early psychoanalyst Géza Róheim (1943) and the sociologist Peter Berger (1967), among others. Róheim argues that humans are born much too soon and are thus more dependent on their mothers than are other animals. Culture, including myth, arises to provide a substitute for the mother and thereby to restore some control over the world. Berger maintains that humans are born less premature than, in existentialist fashion, "unfixed." Culture, again including myth, arises not, as for Róheim, to tame the world but to make sense of it—above all by justifying the experiences that cannot be ameliorated: suffering, especially death. The justification provided gives humans a settled place in the world. While Blumenberg singles out myth, he, too, sees all of culture as serving to compensate for the limits of human biology—but, again, primarily by "explaining" rather than by either controlling or justifying the world.

When Blumenberg writes that myth "explains," that it provides "explanations for the inexplicable" (Blumenberg 1985: 5), he likely means that myth explains the *operation* rather than the *origin* of the world and in that sense is nonetiological. But myth for Tylor explains the operation more than the origin of the world, though Tylor is not, like Blumenberg, preoccupied with the distinction. How much Blumenberg's view of myth really differs from that of his Enlightened nemeses will be considered after presenting the view of his other nemeses: the Romantics.

Where the Enlightenment sees myth as superseded by science, Romanticism, itself no more restricted to the nineteenth century than the Enlightenment is to the eighteenth, sees myth as eternal. Where the Enlightenment believes that myth gets superseded by something that better serves the same *function*, Romanticism believes that myth can never be superseded because nothing else bears the same *content*. As representative Romantic, Campbell thus applauds the view of fellow Romantic Jung that myths "are telling us in picture language of powers of the psyche to be recognized and integrated in our lives, powers that have been common to the human spirit forever, and which represent that wisdom of the species by which man has weathered the milleniums. Thus they have not been, and can never be, displaced by the findings of science" (Campbell 1973 [1972]: 13).

Romanticism argues that myth not only offers eternal wisdom but also has always offered it. Moderns thus lack not only a superior successor to myth but also superior myths: ancient myths contain all the wisdom to be had. Still, moderns are not bereft of myths of their own. For Campbell, all humans are continually spinning them. He himself cites the distinctively modern myths of space travel, as typified by the *Star Wars* saga. Moderns harbor no superior myths because there are none: all myths are the same because all say the same. "Romanticism," writes Blumenberg, "set up the more or less distinct idea of a substance of tradition that changes only in form" (Blumenberg 1985: 49; see also 130–31). Not coincidentally, Campbell is an arch-comparativist, seeking only similarities and dismissing differences as trivial.

For Romantics, moderns no more possess superior interpretations of traditional myths than possess superior myths: ancients already intuited the deepest meanings of their own myths. Only obtuse moderns need sophisticated theories to extricate those meanings. Romanticism, writes Blumenberg, "attaches the seriousness of the conjecture that in it [myth] there is hidden [to moderns] the unrecognized, smuggled contents of an earliest revelation to mankind, perhaps of the recollection of Paradise, which was so nicely interchangeable with Platonic anamnesis" (Blumenberg 1985: 48; see also 273–74).

To be sure, Blumenberg may not be claiming that for Romantics ancients themselves were conscious of this revelation, only that it was present in their myths. But at least for Campbell they were fully conscious of it. Hence Campbell employs Freud and Jung alike to raise to modern consciousness the meaning of which our forebears were fully aware:

> The old teachers knew what they were saying. Once we have learned to read again their symbolic language, it requires no more than the talent of an anthologist [i.e., Campbell] to let their teaching be heard. But first we must learn the grammar of the symbols, and as a key to this mystery I know of no better tool than psychoanalysis. (Campbell 1949: vii)

Freud and Jung themselves never credit early humanity with superior consciousness. Quite the opposite.

Against Romanticism, Blumenberg argues, first, that new myths are not constantly being created. Rather, old myths are continually getting reworked, and by a Darwinian competition only the most effective myths or versions of myths survive. Blumenberg argues, second, that the meaning of myths changes. If, then, on the one hand there are no new myths, on the other hand there are new meanings to old ones—a process of reinterpretation that he calls "work on" myth.[6]

Blumenberg is consequently a staunch particularist rather than a comparativist. Echoing the philosopher R. G. Collingwood, he goes as far as to claim that even though the myths remain the same, the reinterpretations change the questions and not merely give new answers to perennial ones (see Blumenberg 1985: 182–84; Collingwood 1939: ch. 5). At the same time new interpreters feel obliged to answer old questions in order to prove their worth—a process that Blumenberg calls "reoccupation" (see Blumenberg 1985: 27–28).[7] The effort of new interpreters to meet their predecessors on their predecessors' home grounds bolsters the false, Romantic view that there is nothing new under the sun.[8]

Blumenberg's arguments against both Romanticism and the Enlightenment are moot. Even though he traces brilliantly the sharply shifting meanings of the Prometheus myth, to which three of the five parts of his book are devoted, his Romantic adversaries would surely emphasize the persistence of the myth itself. The debate between comparativists and particularists seems unresolvable. Just as particularists can always point to differences between one myth and another or to differences between one interpretation of a myth and another, so comparativists can always point to similarities. More accurately, each side need deny only the importance, not the existence, of the other. Particularists maintain that the similarities deciphered by comparativists are vague and superficial. Comparativists contend that the differences etched by particularists are trivial and incidental.

So what, say Campbell's critics, if all heroes undertake a dangerous trek to a distant world and return to spread the word? The differences between one heroic quest and another count more. Where, for example, Odysseus is seeking to return home, Aeneas is seeking a new home. Where Odysseus is at least eventually eager to reach Ithaca, Aeneas must relentlessly be prodded to proceed to Italy. Where Odysseus encounters largely supernatural entities along the way, Aeneas encounters largely human ones. Where Odysseus' triumph is entirely personal, Aeneas' is that of a whole people. Campbell would retort that, as different as Odysseus and Aeneas are, both are heroes. Blumenberg's appeal to the differences thus convinces only confirmed particularists.

As for Blumenberg's arguments against the Enlightenment, first, the undeniable survival of myth in modernity scarcely proves that its function must be nonscientific. Surely myth and science can simultaneously serve the same function, whether or not compatibly. Like Bultmann, Blumenberg wrongly assumes that myth actually does yield explanation to science. Fundamentalists are not the only ones who seemingly manage to espouse both mythic and scientific explanations.

Second, even if science does preclude a mythic explanation of the world, *prior to* science myth might have functioned as an explanation. So maintains Tylor. Or myth might have functioned concurrently as both explanation and something else—the nonexplanatory function alone now remaining. So maintains Bultmann. To make his case, Blumenberg must rebut these alternatives.

It would be one thing for Blumenberg, like numerous other theorists, to deny that myth is the primitive counterpart to modern science on the grounds that the real subject of myth is human nature (Freud, Jung), society (Emile Durkheim, A. R. Radcliffe-Brown, Malinowski), or ultimate reality (Bultmann, Campbell) *rather than* the physical world (Tylor, Frazer). It is another thing for him to deny that myth is the primitive counterpart to modern science *even though* its subject matter is the physical world. Here Blumenberg and Tylor are akin. For both, myth is about gods, not humans, but it is about the actions of gods in the human world.

That Blumenberg deems the subject matter of myth the physical world is clear from his criticism of Freud for rooting myth in pleasure—the "absolutism of images and wishes"—rather than in "reality" (Blumenberg 1985: 8). It is even clearer from his castigation of the Enlightenment for contrasting *logos*, which deals with physical reality, to myth, which supposedly does not: "The boundary line between myth and logos is imaginary and does not obviate the need to inquire about the logos of myth in the process of working free of the absolutism of reality" (Blumenberg 1985: 12). Myth helps humans master the physical world and is itself "a piece of high-carat 'work of logos'" (Blumenberg 1985: 12; see also 3ff., 26, 27, 48). For Blumenberg, the shift from *mythos* to *logos* begins within *mythos* itself.

Certainly, myth can refer to the physical world and still not be the primitive counterpart to modern science. For Samuel Noah Kramer, for example, Sumerian myth is merely a metaphorical description of the physical world: stripped of the metaphor, myth is not primitive but *modern* science—observationally, even if not theoretically (see Kramer 1961: 73). For Lévy-Bruhl, myth functions to unite primitive peoples mystically with the physical world rather than to explain the world (see Lévy-Bruhl 1926: 368–71). For Lévi-Strauss, whom Blumenberg berates on other grounds, myth is outright primitive science, but it is not, as for the Enlightenment, inferior science (see Lévi-Strauss 1966, especially ch. 1). Certainly for Malinowski (1954b) and Eliade (1959b: ch. 2), myths about the physical world are more than scientific in function. Whether or not these strategies succeed in reconciling myth with science without sacrificing a common subject matter, they at least confront the problem. Blumenberg evades it. He says *that*, never *how*, myth and science manage to deal compatibly with the same subject.

Blumenberg himself waxes ambivalent about the relationship between myth and science. In faulting the Enlightenment for failing to give myth credit for beginning the process of mastering the physical world—of overcoming the "absolutism of reality" (see Blumenberg 1985: 3ff.)—he surely implies that science continues the process. In that case myth must be serving the same function as science:

> Theory [i.e., science] is the better adapted mode of mastering the episodic *tremenda* [terrors] of recurring world events. But leisure and dispassion in viewing the world, which theory presupposes, are already results of that millenniums-long work of myth itself .... [T]he antithesis between myth and reason [i.e., science] is a late and a poor invention, because it forgoes seeing the function of myth, in the overcoming of that archaic unfamiliarity of the world, as itself a rational function, however due for expiration its means may seem after the event. (Blumenberg 1985: 26, 48)

Even in asserting that science can never fully master the world, so that a place for myth always remains, Blumenberg must still mean that the two serve the same function: science cannot be merely "reoccupying" the position of myth.

Blumenberg's other arguments for myth as nonetiological are even more tenuous. First, if creation myths provide no etiology because they presuppose the existence of something, then science provides no etiology either, as Blumenberg himself concedes. Explaining the origin of anything means explaining out of what it came (see Blumenberg 1985: 126–27). Ironically, science often gets faulted for failing to do what religion, including myth, purportedly does: explaining "where it all began" (see Hempel 1973, section 6).

Second, myths undeniably tell stories rather than give arguments. But this difference in form need scarcely mean a difference in function. Tylor, for his part, disregards the form for the content and sees myth as presenting arguments in the form of stories. Plato, Plotinus, and other ancient critics of myth *as* story take for granted that the function of myth is the same as that of philosophy, which Blumenberg rightly associates with science. Insofar as Thales and other Presocratics succeed Homer and Hesiod, Homer and especially Hesiod must be providing etiologies of their own. Again, philosophy cannot be merely reoccupying the place vacated by myth.

Third, undeniably in myth anything can derive from anything else. Indeed, nearly anything at all can happen. But even the most fantastic etiologies are not therefore less etiological. Even if anything can happen in myth, myth is still reporting how it did happen.

Fourth, myth provides above all the significance, not the origin, of the world. But the significance still depends on the origin. The Bible may not explain how God created the rainbow, but only the divine origin of the rainbow gives it its clout. As a merely natural occurrence, the rainbow would not quite represent God's covenant with future humanity. The significance of woman in the *Theogony* and in Genesis 2 stems considerably from the circumstances of her origin. All of the world in Genesis 1 is good because God created it. For theorists of myth like Malinowski (1926) and Eliade (1959b: ch. 2), the significance of the phenomena considered by myth stems entirely, not just partly, from their primordial lineage.

Blumenberg declares that myths, as stories, block, not merely ignore, etiological questions: "The stories that it is our purpose to discuss here simply weren't told in order to answer questions, but rather in order to dispel uneasiness and discontent, which have to be present in the beginning for questions to be able to form themselves" (Blumenberg 1985: 184; see also 166). Augustine, he writes, asks why God created the world, not "in order to give an answer, but rather in order simply to discredit inquiry"

(Blumenberg 1985: 258). Hence Augustine's sole answer: "Because he wanted to" (Blumenberg 1985: 258)—an answer as satisfying as Bartley the Scrivener's "I would prefer not to." Myth takes events back to what Eliade calls "primordial time" to make its account of events sacrosanct: "Myths do not answer questions; they make things unquestionable. Anything that could give rise to demands for explanation is shifted into the position of something that legitimates the rejection of such claims" (Blumenberg 1985: 126; see also 127).

If, however, myth gives either arbitrary answers to etiological questions or none at all, how is it managing to quell anxiety? How is it "a way of expressing the fact that the world and the powers that hold sway in it are not abandoned to pure arbitrariness, ... a system of the elimination of arbirariness" (Blumenberg 1985: 42–43)? Blumenberg never says. Perhaps he would reply that myth eliminates arbitrariness by cogently explaining the operation rather than the origin of the world. But myth typically explains how things *are* by explaining how they *came to be*. Hesiod provides no cosmology in *addition* to his cosmogony. From his cosmogony *comes* the cosmology. The same is true of the Bible. Even if, contrary to Aristotle, Thales is offering a cosmology *rather than* a cosmogony, Hesiod and the Bible are not.

Blumenberg boasts that the meaning myth provides rests on no scientific grounds: "No one will want to maintain that myth has better arguments than science .... Nevertheless it has something to offer that— even with reduced claims to reliability, certainty, faith, realism, and intersubjectivity—still constitutes satisfaction of intelligent expectations. The quality on which this depends can be designated by the term *significance [Bedeutsamkeit]*, taken from Dilthey" (Blumenberg 1985: 67). But if neither evidence nor etiology supports mythic pronouncements of significance, what does? Blumenberg never says.

Blumenberg notes that classical, not biblical, myths are the ones that survive (see Blumenberg 1985: 215–18, 238–40). The use of biblical myths by modern writers like Thomas Mann is presumably an exception. Blumenberg's justification for nevertheless claiming that mythology generally did not die out with science must be his argument that the Bible remained tied to a fixed text and to adherents controlling its interpretation: "What prevents the [modern] poet from making use of the figures in the Bible ... is the way they are fixed in a written book, and the incomparable presence of this book in people's memories" (Blumenberg 1985: 216). In proceeding to assert that classical mythology was free of not only a single text and disciples but also a priesthood and dogma, Blumenberg is really asserting that it was free of religion (see Blumenberg 1985: 237–40). But is classical mythology thereby typical of mythology worldwide? Does, then, mythology generally survive science? If only because of the presence in myths of gods and other supernatural elements, many theorists subsume myth under religion. The Enlightenment shift from myth to science is thus, as for Tylor, also a shift from religion, or religion as it had traditionally operated.

Even suppose that Enlightened theorists wrongly assume that myth survives only as literature or art. By contrasting the survival of classical mythology to the demise of its biblical counterpart, Blumenberg himself appears to be agreeing with them that the survival of myth in any form requires its severance from religion. Whether a state exists for myth between religion and aesthetics is the question. Truncated from Greek religion, Prometheus ceases to be an actual entity and becomes only a symbol of something else, presumably human. Is he not thus reduced to a literary or artistic figure?

Yet Blumenberg, despite his peremptory dismissal of the quest for origin, does not himself forsake the quest. He may refuse to speculate on *how* myth arose, but he certainly hypothesizes *why* and even *when*.[9] He denies both the Enlightenment view that myth arose to satisfy intellectual curiosity and the Romantic view that myth simply arose spontaneously. Rather, he says, myth arose to cope with the anxiety felt by those who had ventured from the shelter and security of the forest to the expanse and uncertainty of the savanna:

> It was a situational leap, which made the unoccupied distant horizon into the ongoing expectation of hitherto unknown things. What came about through the combination of leaving the shrinking forest for the savanna and settling in caves was a combination of the meeting of new requirements for performance in obtaining food outside the living places and the old advantage of undisturbed reproduction and rearing of the next generation .... (Blumenberg 1985: 4)

Surely this is speculation at its grandest.

Chapter 2

Max Müller on Religion and Myth

Friedrich Max Müller was the founder of the "science of religion," which became identical with the field of religious studies. He also sought to establish a science of mythology and of language. He used "scientific" as synonymous with "comparative." The comparative study of anything seeks similarities among the members of the category. Müller does not deny differences. In fact, he groups religions into categories, each with its own distinctive origin: "As all the Semitic languages had one unmistakable type, and all Aryan languages another, every Semitic religion turned out to possess one physiognomy, every Aryan religion another. Hence, to derive any Aryan religion from a Semitic source was, in ancient times, at least as impossible and unscientific as to derive Greek from Hebrew" (Müller 2002: 354). At the same time the ultimate origin of religion per se was the same: the need to express the universal experience of what Müller calls the Infinite.

What for Müller made religious studies scientific was threefold: a distinctive subject matter, the comparative approach to that subject matter, and the attribution of religion to other than revelation. Religion is created by human beings, not disclosed by a god. Yet religion is a reaction by humans to their actual experience of god—or the Infinite—in the physical world. That experience is taken by Müller to be the actual experience of the Infinite. In these ways Müller is like present-day defenders of the autonomy of the discipline such as Mircea Eliade. But there is one big difference. Eliade takes scientific to mean reductive and anti-religious and so would never characterize the field as scientific (see Segal 1989).

Müller's theory of religion and theory of myth are two sides of the same proverbial coin, and this despite Müller's oddly pitting myth against religion. Not all theorists of myth are also theorists of religion, and not all theorists of religion are also theorists of myth. Eliade, for one, is both. Some theorists of myth, especially twentieth-century ones, allow for nonreligious myths. For example, the scores of myths that Freud's original disciple Otto Rank amasses in *The Myth of the Birth of the Hero* (1914) are as often nonreligious as religious. There are plenty of theorists of religion who simply do not focus on myth. Few of the theorists in E. E. Evans-Pritchard's classic *Theories of Primitive Religion* (1965) are also theorists of myth. In his *Lectures on the Religion of the Semites* (1889) William Robertson Smith asserts that ritual rather than myth was central to ancient or "primitive" religion. Still, Müller is unique among theorists of myth and theorists of religion alike not because he tends equally to both but because he sets myth against religion.

Müller's Theory of Religion

Let us start with Müller as a theorist of religion. The key divide in theories of religion is between those theories that hail from the social sciences and those that hail from religious studies itself. Social scientific theories deem the origin and function of religion nonreligious. The need that religion arises to fulfill can be for almost anything. It can be physical—for example, for food, health, or prosperity. Or it can be nonphysical—for example, for a scientific-like explanation of events in the physical world, as for E. B. Tylor (1871), or for justification for suffering, as in the highest stage of religion for Max Weber (1963: ch. 9). The need can be on the part of individuals (Weber) or on the part of society (Emile Durkheim). For all social scientific theories, the need that religion fulfills, whatever it is, is secular. Religion can be an excellent means to the end or even be the best means, but the end is not itself religious.

By contrast, theories from religious studies deem the origin and function of religion distinctively religious: religion arises and serves to provide an experience of god. This is really the sole theory of religion from religious studies. Adherents to it I call "religionists." They include, besides Müller and Eliade, Gerardus van der Leeuw (1933), Raffaele Pettazzoni (1954), and Joachim Wach (1962). *Like* rather than *unlike* many social scientists, religionists typically confine themselves to the issues of origin and function—the need to encounter (not to become) god—and shy away from the issue of truth: whether god exists. Where social scientists entrust the issue of truth to philosophers, religionists entrust it to theologians.

For religionists, human beings need contact with god as an end in itself. They need contact with god because they need contact with god. To ask why humans need that contact is to miss the point. An encounter with god may yield peace of mind and other benefits, but the need is still for the encounter itself. The need is considered as fundamental as the need for food or water. Without that contact humans may not die, but they will languish. Because the need is for god, nothing secular can substitute for religion. There may be secular, or seemingly secular, *expressions* of religion, but there are in fact no secular *substitutes* for religion. For the social scientist Durkheim, for example, nationalism is not an alternative to religion but an "updated" form of it. He cites the emergence of nationalism during the French Revolution as an alternative to French Catholicism (see Durkheim 1915: 240). For religionists, by contrast, nationalism would be a false substitute for religion.

Religionists consider the need for god not only distinctive but also universal: "Wherever there is human life, there is religion" (Müller 1878: 7). "We may safely say that, in spite of all researches, no human beings have been found anywhere who do not possess something which is to them religion" (Müller 1878: 76). By contrast to Müller, Tylor notes that we simply do not have evidence of the situation of the earliest humans.

By religion Müller means, as we shall see, "a belief in something beyond what they can see with their eyes" (Müller 1878: 76). To demonstrate the universality of religion, religionists point to its presence both among early humanity (Müller and also the nonreligionist Tylor) and among professedly atheistic moderns (Eliade).

Strictly speaking, there are two versions of the religionist theory. One is the form just described: religion originates within human beings, who seek contact with god. The exemplar of this form is Eliade, who stresses the yearning for god or, so he prefers, the sacred: "But since religious man cannot live except in an atmosphere impregnated with the sacred, we must expect to find a large number of techniques for consecrating space" (Eliade 1959a: 28). Sacred places, or spaces, are one venue for encountering god. Religious sites, such as churches and mosques, are built on those spots where god is believed to have appeared. The assumption is that wherever god has once appeared, god, even if formally present everywhere, is more likely to appear anew. Sacred times, or time, is the other venue for encountering god. Myths, which describe the creation by god of physical and social phenomena, carry one back to the time of creation, when, it is believed, god was closer at hand than god has been ever since: "Now, what took place 'in the beginning' was this: the divine or semidivine beings were active on earth.... Man desires to recover the active presence of the gods .... [T]he mythical time whose reactualization is periodically attempted is a time sanctified by the divine presence" (Eliade 1959a: 92).

This version of the religionist theory bypasses the issue of the existence of god. The theory is committed to the existence of only the *need* for god. The catch is that if religionists claim that religion actually fulfills the need—and why else would they advocate religion?—then god must exist. Religionists thus prove to be theologians despite themselves. Still, the emphasis is on the need.

The other version of the religionist theory, epitomized by Müller, roots religion not in the need for god but in the *experience* of god. However indispensable the experience of god may be for human fulfillment, religion originates not in the quest for god but in an unexpected encounter with god. Müller himself singles out the sun and other celestial phenomena as the occasion where god or, for Müller, the Infinite is most fully encountered: "Thus sunrise was the revelation of nature, awakening in the human mind that feeling of dependence, of helplessness, of hope, of joy and faith in higher powers, which is the source of all wisdom, the spring of all religion" (Müller 1867: 96).

The two versions of the religionist theory are compatible. The quest for an encounter with god may be fulfilled by an uninitiated encounter, and an uninitiated encounter can lead to a quest for further encounters. Still, the approaches differ. One starts with a need; the other, with an experience. Deriving religion from a need for god makes the religionist theory more easily comparable with social scientific theories, nearly all of which do the same.

Friedrich Schleiermacher (1996) is a religionist because, going beyond Kant, he roots religion in an irreducibly religious faculty. By contrast, Müller attributes, or comes to attribute, religion not to any uniquely religious consciousness but instead to the senses: "Let it not be supposed, however, that there is a separate consciousness for religion. There is but one self and one consciousness ..." (Müller 1878: 20).

Müller claims that the senses can decipher not only what they can actually see or hear or smell or taste but also what they cannot—that is, what lies beyond them:

> When our eye has apprehended the farthest distance which it can reach, with or without instruments, the limit to which it clings is always fixed on one side by the finite, but on the other side by what to the eye is not finite, or Infinite.... In fact, our very idea of limit implies the idea of a beyond, and thus forces the idea of the Infinite upon us, whether we like it or not. (Müller 1878: 34)

It is not just "civilized man" who senses the Infinite. The "primitive" does so as well: "We have accepted the primitive savage with nothing but his five senses.... [I]t is his senses which give him the first impression of the infinite things, and supply him in the end with an intimation of the infinite" (Müller 1878: 35). Where "most philosophers ... derive the idea of the infinite from a necessity of our human reason" (Müller 1878: 34), Müller assumes that "primitives" lack reason and instead derive the idea from the senses: "The infinite, therefore, instead of being merely a late abstraction [i.e., of reason], is really implied in the earliest manifestations of our sensuous knowledge" (Müller 1878: 36).

What in the physical world arouses the sense of the Infinite? Seemingly, it can be anything majestic:

> After we have seen how it is possible for man to gain a presentiment of something beyond the finite, we shall watch him looking for the infinite in mountains, trees, and rivers, in the storm and lightning, in the moon and the sun, in the sky and what is beyond the sky, trying name upon name to comprehend it, calling it thunderer, bringer of light, wielder of the thunder-bolt, giver of rain, bestower of food and life; and, after a time, speaking of it as maker, ruler, and preserver, king and father, lord of lords, god of gods, cause of causes, the Eternal, the Unknown, the Unknowable. (Müller 1878: 46)

Yet some sources of the Infinite are more equal than others, and the most imposing are celestial—not just the sun, as many incorrectly take Müller to be asserting, but the world above us as a whole. Müller distinguishes "three classes of things which we can perceive with our senses, but which leave in us three very distinct kinds of impression of reality" (Müller 1878: 174).

The lowest are tangible objects, "such as stones, shells, bones, and the rest" (Müller 1878: 174). They become *fetishes*. But even though the then-reigning theory rooted religion in these objects, for Müller the objects are too mundane to stir any sense of the Infinite. The next highest are semi-tangible objects, "such as trees, mountains, rivers, the sea, the earth" (Müller 1878: 174). These objects, much grander, "supply the material for what I should propose to call *semi-deities*" (Müller 1878: 174). But only the highest class, that of intangible objects, "such as the sky, the stars, the sun, the dawn, the moon" (Müller 1878: 174), is sublime enough to produce outright *deities*. So it turns out that Müller is a celestial, just not an exclusively solar, mythologist. Still, on the one hand he is prepared to stress that the Vedas contain hymns addressed to semi-deities as well as to deities, and on the other hand he singles out the sun for the highest praise: "People wonder why so much of the old mythology, the daily talk, of the Aryans, was solar: what else could it have been?" (Müller 1878: 200). While Müller is offering a theory of religion per se, he limits himself to Indo-European, or Aryan, religion (see Müller 1878: 48). (On Semitic religion, see Müller 1860.)

Religion for Müller is not the worship of intangibles themselves. It is the worship of the Infinite aroused by the experience of tangibles. Müller is therefore not just one more nature mythologist (contrary to, for example, van den Bosch 2002: 274–75, 519–20), and not just because he declines to rest religion on any specific celestial phenomenon. And he is not like Tylor, for whom religion arises not, as for Müller, to *express* the experience of the Infinite but to *explain* the experience of the finite—of why the sun rises and sets and why rain falls and ceases. And for Tylor, primitive gods are material rather than immaterial.

Müller maintains that deities get named by worshipers. They get named on the basis of the behavior, or actions, of the deity:

> Primitive men, no doubt, had their own ideas very different from our own; but do not let us suppose for one moment that they were idiots, and that, because they saw some similarity between their own acts and the acts of rivers, mountains, the moon, the sun, and the sky, and because they called them by names expressive of those acts, they therefore saw no difference between a man, called a measurer, and the moon, called a measurer, between a real mother and a river called the mother. (Müller 1878: 181)

Natural phenomena were, then, assumed to be living beings—deities or semi-deities. But they were not anthropomorphized—a distinction never drawn by Tylor. Man, Müller tells us, "never dreams at first that, because the river is called a defender, that therefore the river has legs, and arms, and weapons of defence; or that the moon, because he divides and measures the sky, is a carpenter" (Müller 1878: 183–84). In other words, the words naming natural phenomena are meant metaphorically. When, eventually, the names wrongly come to be taken literally, mythology arises to explain the names, which means the names of what are now personalities. Prior to this process of degeneration—or the "disease of language"—the river, according to Müller, is a god but not a personality. By contrast, for Tylor, a god *is* a personality.

This distinction between god and personality is not very clear. But let me quote Müller's clearest statement: "Thus the sun and the moon were spoken of, no doubt, as moving about, but *not* as animals; the rivers were roaring and fighting, but they were *not* men; the mountains were not to be thrown down, but they were *not* warriors; the fire was eating up the forest, yet it was *not* a lion" (Müller 1878: 188). More important, the river is a metaphor for the Infinite. But the relationship between a god and the Infinite is not clear either.

Müller versus Tylor

Antithetically to Müller stands Tylor, his chief rival theorist of religion and of myth. Tylor emphatically reads religion and myth literally. He opposes those who read the two poetically, metaphorically, or symbolically—for him interchangeable terms. Tylor assumes that the explanatory function of religion and myth *requires* a literal reading. To read religion and myth nonliterally is automatically to cede any explanatory function, and to cede the explanatory function is automatically to trivialize the two. He thus writes that "the basis on which such [primitive] ideas ... are built is not to be narrowed down to poetic fancy and transformed metaphor. They rest upon a broad philosophy of nature, early and crude indeed, but thoughtful, consistent, and quite really and seriously meant" (Tylor 1871, vol. 1: 285). Tylor even assumes that modern theorists who take religion and myth nonliterally do so because they project their own incredulity onto primitives. Never taking religion and myth seriously themselves, these moderns cannot conceive that anyone else has ever done so.

According to Tylor, moderns who interpret religion and myth nonliterally for primitives are anachronistically interpreting it as poetry:

> Poetry has so far kept alive in our minds the old animative [i.e., mythic] theory of nature, that it is no great effort to us to fancy the [inanimate] waterspout a huge giant or sea-monster, and to depict in what we call appropriate metaphor its march across the fields of ocean. But where such forms of speech are current among less educated races, they are underlaid by a distinct prosaic [i.e., literal] meaning of [actual] fact. (Tylor 1871, vol. 1: 292)

Modern nature poets like Wordsworth intend images like that of a "raging sea" to be taken symbolically. For Tylor, "primitives" always took myth literally. For Müller, "primitives" originally took the image symbolically and only eventually came to misread it literally. For Müller, "primitives" are like poets. For Tylor, they are like scientists.

Gods for Tylor are the purported causes of events in the physical world. Myths do not merely describe events but explain them. The ultimate subject matter of myth for Tylor is not events themselves, as it sometimes is for J. G. Frazer, but the causes of those events. As mere descriptions of events, myths would be unnecessary. Ever observant, "primitives" for Tylor notice events on their own. They invent myths to account for their observations, not merely to record them. For Tylor, gods originate out of the personification of nature. But they are not a merely metaphorical way of talking about nature—for example, the "raging sea" as a poetic description of a storm at sea. On the contrary, gods are an actual explanation of the storm, which is caused by a decision by the god of the sea. Myth explains how gods cause events.

Where for Tylor religion and myth are really about the physical world, for Müller religion is really about the immaterial Infinite, simply symbolized by the grandeur of celestial bodies and events. Yet in nineteenth-century fashion religion is still thereby rooted in the physical world. Where for Tylor religion and myth seek to explain the physical world, for Müller religion seeks to transcend it.

For Müller, religion is anything but the projection of something human or social onto the physical world (though see Müller 1878: 180). Religion is not the confusion of something outside the physical world with something in it, as C. G. Jung above all would maintain:

> This latter analogy [between god and natural phenomenon] explains the well-attested connection between the renewal of the god and seasonal and vegetational phenomena. One is naturally inclined to assume that seasonal, vegetational, lunar, and solar myths underlie these analogies. But that is to forget that a myth, like everything psychic, cannot be solely conditioned by external events. Anything psychic brings its own internal conditions with it, so that one might assert with equal right that the myth is purely psychological and uses meteorological or astronomical events merely as a means of expression. The whimsicality and absurdity of many primitive myths often makes the latter explanation seem far more appropriate than any other. (Jung 1971: 193–94, cited in Segal 1998a: 5)

For Müller, antithetically to Jung, religion is about a quality of the physical world, even if that quality symbolizes something beyond itself. Myth may be a corruption of religion, but myth, in nineteenth-century fashion, is part of religion. In the twentieth century, by contrast, myth was often severed from at once religion and the physical world.

While Müller was a Christian, his theory of religion is more typical of pagan or pantheistic nature mythology, according to which religion, which goes hand in hand with mythology, is the worship of one natural phenomenon or another. Yet Müller was not really a nature mythologist because, again, for him the object of worship is not the physical world but the immaterial Infinite. He was the founder of religious studies precisely because he did not reduce god to the sun or to any other natural entity.

Müller was a leading Indo-Europeanist and espoused Sanskrit as the original Indo-European language. For him, as for many others, language was the key to culture. Conventionally, he pitted Indo-European, or Aryan, language and culture against Semitic language and culture. But to his credit he did not, like so many others, extend culture to race, and he was appalled at the extension. More accurately, he defended Indian culture in its pristine form and contrasted that form to a subsequent, degenerate form. He sought to show the kinship among Indo-European peoples. Yet he remained a staunch Christian, specifically a Lutheran, and somehow managed to reconcile the superiority of Christianity with a common source for all Indo-European religions.

For Tylor, myth arises within religion. Without myth there would still be the belief in Zeus as the god of thunder and lightning. But there would be no account of the life of Zeus, of the acquisition of his powers, or of his use of those powers. Myth provides all three. For Tylor, both myth and the rest of religion were meant to be read literally. Symbolic readings of myth seek to preserve myth for moderns, who cannot accept a literal reading because of the conflict with science.

Where, then, for Tylor moderns misread myth by taking it symbolically, for Müller ancients themselves mistakenly came to take literally their originally symbolic personifications of natural phenomena, for which myths then had to be created. Originally, religion flourished without myth. There were no gods. There was only the Infinite. For Tylor, "primitives" were incapable of symbolism. Frazer assumes the same. Take the earliest stage of culture for Frazer: that of magic. Piercing a voodoo doll, for example, works only because the doll is taken to be identical with the person of whom it is a doll rather than being taken to be a mere symbol of the person. For Müller, by contrast to both Tylor and Frazer, "primitives" were supremely capable of symbolism.

Yet gradually, mere metaphors for the physical manifestations of the Infinite came to be taken literally. The sea initially described poetically as "raging" was taken to be the characteristic of the personality responsible for the sea, and a myth was then invented to account for this characteristic. The metaphors properly recognized as metaphors by earliest humanity came to be misunderstood by later, if still early, humanity. Myth itself was taken literally from the outset. Mythology for Müller stems from the absence in at least some ancient languages, such as Hebrew, of a neuter gender. Speakers therefore had to refer to impersonal entities in the male or female gender, forever after misleading their descendants into taking the referent to be a person rather than a thing.

As opposed to Müller's view of myth as Tylor is, he grants Müller's disease of language a secondary place in the "formation of myth." Contrary to Müller, Tylor insists that myth arises primarily from reality—from the actual experience of the physical world, not from a metaphor for it. The primitive, and also modern, experience of the world is above all of motion, such as that of the falling of rain or the growing of a plant. Myth is a scientific-like inference to account for the motion, and the inference comes from an analogy to the purposeful behavior of human beings. For Tylor, "the difference in nature between myth founded on fact [Tylor] and myth founded on word [Müller] is sufficiently manifest" (Tylor 1871, vol. 1: 199). Tylor is prepared to concede that more advanced peoples would have been capable of thinking symbolically, so that the mistaking of initial metaphor for literal personification could have emerged among them. But primitive peoples are for him at once too materialist and too literalist ever to have turned mere language into reality, which is to say into gods.

Müller versus Lang

In his time Müller engaged in many famous debates with the Scottish man of letters Andrew Lang. In Lang's earlier writings—*Custom and Myth* (1884), the first edition of *Myth, Ritual and Religion* (1887), and *Modern Mythology* (1897)—he seeks to refute Müller's theory of myth. Lang is here a faithful follower of Tylor, to whom he dedicates *Custom and Myth*. Accordingly, myth presupposes "animism," which is Tylor's term for religion, or the belief in gods, in all natural phenomena. The decisions of gods account for events in the natural world. For earlier Lang, as for Tylor, myth and the rest of religion arise and operate in tandem. Religion does not degenerate into myth. Where Tylor accepts Müller's linguistic explanation of myth as a secondary origin of myth, Lang rejects it altogether, and does so in the name of Tylor:

> The general problem is this: Has language—especially language in a
> state of "disease," been the great source of the mythology of the world?
> Or does mythology, on the whole, represent the survival of an old
> stage of thought—not caused by language—from which civilised men

have slowly emancipated themselves? Mr. Max Müller is of the former,
anthropologists are of the latter, opinion. Both, of course, agree that
myths are a product of thought, of a kind of thought almost extinct in
civilised races; but Mr. Max Müller holds that language caused that kind
of thought. We, on the other hand, think that language only gave it one
means of expressing itself. (Lang 1897: x)

By anthropologists Lang means Tylor. By primitive thought he means
the personification of the physical world. One might say that, for Lang,
Müller anticipates what one hundred years later Richard Rorty called
"the linguistic turn."

In Lang's later writings—*The Making of Religion* (1898), the second edition of *Myth, Ritual and Religion* (1901), and *Magic and Religion* (1901)—he
seeks to *refute* Tylor's theory, not of myth but of religion. There is no
mythology in this first stage of religion both because there is only one
god, who therefore cannot interact with other gods, and because that god
is nonanthropomorphic and so does not act in human-like ways. So ethereal and sublime is this pristine conception of god, known as the High
God view of religion, that it simply cannot last and eventually degenerates into Tylor's polytheism, which now becomes the second stage of
religion rather than, as for Tylor, the first. Only now does mythology
arise—to account for the nature of these gods. While mythology still
serves to account for events in the natural world, as part of degenerate
religion, it is now itself considered degenerate. Lang's view of the course
of religion as degenerative is the opposite of Tylor's evolutionary view of
the course of religion:

> The conception of a powerful spirit of a dead father, worshipped by his
> children, is supposed to have been gradually raised to [i.e., evolved into]
> the power of a god. Against this theory I have elsewhere urged that
> superior beings are [already] found among races who do not worship
> ancestral spirits; and again that these superior beings are not envisaged
> as spirits, but rather as supernormal magnified men, of unbounded
> power (an idea often contradicted in savage as in Greek mythology) and
> of limitless duration. (Lang 1901b: 16–17)

Most ironically, Lang's position thus becomes almost identical with
Müller's: the pristine worship of an impersonal god degenerates into the
worship of many anthropomorphic gods, the nature of whom mythology arises to explain. Where for earlier Lang, as for Tylor, myth is part
of religion and completes the explanatory function of religion, for later
Lang, as for Müller, myth is pitted against religion, which is to say against
original, prelapsarian, true religion. Yet Lang never enlists Müller against

Tylor. Why would he? He had been Müller's nemesis for decades, and by now Müller had lost his luster.

Müller's theory of religion and of myth seems at best quaint. Present-day theorizing is a throwback to Tylor in its focus on personification, or anthropomorphism, as the heart of religion rather than any degeneration from it. A work like Stewart Guthrie's cognitivist *Faces in the Clouds* (1993) seeks to explain the naturalness of personification, just as Tylor does. But rather than a fall from a pre-personified stage, religion for Guthrie is deemed personification from the start, and even religions apparently without gods are assumed to have them. Müller's equation of personification with a fall in the course of religion is nowhere accepted today.

Chapter 3

Frazer on Adonis

Of all the interpretations of the myth of Adonis, J. G. Frazer's remains the most popular. Frazer wrote about Adonis in all three editions of *The Golden Bough* (1890, 1900, 1911–15) and also in his abridged edition (1922), which virtually repeats the chapters on Adonis from the second and third editions and from which the quotations here are taken.

Frazer's Stages

From the second edition on, Frazer works out three pre-scientific stages of culture, and he places Adonis in all three stages: those of magic, religion, and magic and religion combined. Though to differing degrees, in all three stages Adonis for Frazer is a mere personification of vegetation rather than a personality. Frazer assumes that the myth of Adonis is not about gods or even about human beings but about the physical world, which the gods personify. Adonis is only a symbol of vegetation. Vegetation does not symbolize Adonis. Adonis symbolizes vegetation. The heart of vegetation is that it dies and is reborn.

While Frazer is best known for his tripartite division of all culture into the stages of magic, religion, and science, the bulk of *The Golden Bough* is devoted to an intermediate stage between religion and science—a stage of magic and religion combined. This in-between stage combines not only magic with religion but also ritual with myth. In the stage of sheer magic there are rituals—the routines involved in carrying out the directions—but no myths. For there are no gods. In the stage of religion there are both myths and rituals, but they are barely connected. Myths describe the character and behavior of gods. Rituals seek to curry divine favor. Rituals may presuppose myths, which would suggest what activities would most please the gods, but they are otherwise independent of myths.

By contrast, in the following stage of magic and religion combined, myths and rituals work together in what is called "myth ritualism."

Frazer, rarely consistent, actually presents two distinct versions of myth ritualism. In the first version the myth provides the biography of the god of vegetation, and the ritual enacts the myth—better, that portion of the myth describing the death and rebirth of the god. The myth constitutes the script of the ritual. The ritual operates on the basis of the Law of Similarity, according to which the imitation of an action causes it to happen. The ritual does not manipulate vegetation directly. Rather, it manipulates the god of vegetation. But as the god goes, so goes vegetation. The assumption that vegetation is under the control of a god is the legacy of religion. The assumption that vegetation can be controlled, even if only through the god, is the legacy of magic. The combination of myth and ritual is the combination of religion and magic:

> Thus the old magical theory of the seasons was displaced, or rather supplemented, by a religious theory. For although men now attributed the annual cycle of change primarily to corresponding changes in their deities, they still thought that by performing certain magical rites they could aid the god[,] who was the principle of life, in his struggle with the opposing principle of death. They imagined that they could recruit his failing energies and even raise him from the dead. (Frazer 1922: 377)

In the ritual a human being plays the role of the god and acts out what he magically causes the god to do. While the actor may be the king, Frazer does not strongly tie this version of myth ritualism to kingship.

Whoever plays the role of the god of vegetation is not himself killed. At the outset of the ritual the god is already dead—the reason that the crops have died. The ritual imitates the death of the god only as the necessary starting point of his resurrection. Certainly, the ritual is not responsible for the death of the god in the first place.

Violence is still central to this first version of myth ritualism. For the god has been killed rather than has died a natural death. Frazer's main examples of gods of vegetation are Adonis (Babylonian and Syrian–Greek), also known as Tammuz (Babylonian); Attis (Syrian); Osiris (Egyptian); and Dionysus (Greek). Adonis is gored to death by a wild boar while hunting. Or worse, he is murdered by either a spurned lover, Artemis, or a jealous rival, Ares, "who turned himself into the likeness of a boar in order to compass the death of his rival" (Frazer 1922: 380). Attis, too, is the victim of a spurned lover, Cybele, who in her jealousy drives him to madness and to self-castration and death. Frazer, ever attentive to variants of myths, writes of "two different accounts of the death of Attis." According to one variant, "he was killed by a boar, like Adonis." According to the other, "he unmanned himself under a pine-tree, and bled to death on the spot" (Frazer 1922: 404).

Osiris is killed by his brother Set, who nails him into a coffer that is flung into the Nile. Isis, Osiris' wife (and sister), eventually finds the coffer, but Set discovers it and cuts up the body into fourteen pieces, which he then scatters. Isis manages to find all the pieces but one, which has been eaten by fish. Eventually, the body is pieced together, and Osiris is reborn as god of the underworld. In Frazer's summary line, "Thus according to what seems to have been the general native tradition Osiris was a good and beloved king of Egypt, who suffered a violent death but rose from the dead and was henceforth worshipped as a deity" (Frazer 1922: 426).

Of Dionysus, Frazer writes, "Like other gods of vegetation Dionysus was believed to have died a violent death, but to have been brought to life again" (Frazer 1922: 450). According to one version of the myth, "[T]he treacherous Titans," who were enemies of Dionysus' father, Zeus, "attacked him with knives while he was looking at himself in the mirror. For a time he evaded their assaults by turning himself into various shapes .... Finally, in the form of a bull, he was cut to pieces by the murderous knives of his enemies" (Frazer 1922: 450–51). The Cretan version is even more bestial, for it was Jupiter's wife, Juno, who set the Titans against Dionysus, and they "cut him limb from limb, boiled his body with various herbs, and ate it" (Frazer 1922: 451).

In Frazer's second version of myth ritualism the king is central. In the first version the king may not even participate in the ritual. In the second he must. In the first version the king, even when he is the actor in the ritual, is merely human. In the second version he is divine, by which Frazer means that the god resides in him. Just as the health of vegetation depends on the health of its god, so now the health of the god depends on the health of the king: as the king goes, so goes the god of vegetation, and so in turn goes vegetation itself. Where in the first version the king at most merely plays the role of the god, in the second version the king is the god. Above all, where in the first version the king is not killed, in the second version he is. For to ensure a steady supply of food, the community kills its king while he is still in his prime and thereby safely transfers the soul of the god to his successor:

> For [primitives] believe ... that the king's life or spirit is so sympathetically bound up with the prosperity of the whole country, that if he fell ill or grew senile the cattle would sicken and cease to multiply, the crops would rot in the fields, and men would perish of widespread disease. Hence, in their opinion, the only way of averting these calamities is to

put the king to death while he is still hale and hearty, in order that the divine spirit which he has inherited from his predecessors may be transmitted in turn by him to his successor while it is still in full vigour and has not yet been impaired by the weakness of disease and old age. (Frazer 1922: 312–13)

The king is killed either at the end of a fixed term or at the first sign of infirmity. Doubtless the sudden death of a king can never be precluded, but the killing of the king before his likely passing guarantees as nearly as possible the continuous health of the god and so of vegetation. The aim is to fend off winter. The withering of vegetation during the winter of even a year-long reign is ascribed to the weakening of the king.

While Frazer presents two distinct and seemingly incompatible versions of myth ritualism, he somehow manages to combine them in his description of the myths and rituals of his key gods. He combines the imitation of the death and rebirth of the god with the actual killing of a human being, who sometimes is the king. Presumably, the actual killing of a human is, to paraphrase the line, the sincerest form of imitation, but the effect of it is unclear. After all, the god is already dead, so that the killing of a human does not cause it. Unless the human victim is himself resurrected, his killing cannot magically resurrect the god. Oblivious to the different versions of myth ritualism that he is trying to combine, Frazer is likely oblivious to the difficulty of combining them.

Of Adonis, he writes,

> There is some reason to think that in early times Adonis was sometimes personated by a living man who died a violent death in the character of the god. Further, there is evidence which goes to show that among the agricultural peoples of the Eastern Mediterranean, the corn-spirit, by whatever name he was known, was often represented, year by year, by human victims slain on the harvest-field. (Frazer 1922: 394)

Here the human victim is not the king.

Frazer goes as far as to link the cult of Adonis to an outright cult of death:

> In the summer after the battle of Landen, the most sanguinary battle of the seventeenth century in Europe, the earth, saturated with the blood of twenty thousand slain, broke forth into millions of poppies, and the traveller who passed that vast sheet of scarlet might well fancy that the earth had indeed given up her death. At Athens the great Commemoration of the Dead fell in early spring about the middle of March, when the early flowers are in bloom. Then the dead were believed to rise from their graves and go about the streets, vainly

endeavouring to enter the temples and dwellings, which were barred against these perturbed spirits with ropes, buckthorn, and pitch.... There may therefore be a measure of truth in the theory of Renan, who saw in the Adonis worship a dreamy voluptuous cult of death .... (Frazer 1922: 395)

The imitation here is of Adonis' final death, not of his annual death and then rebirth, and it is imitation in the sense of emulation, not of magical efficacy. Adonis himself is not affected. Still, the ritual is no less violent. And if death does not lead to rebirth, the violence cannot be taken as merely an ineluctable means to an irenic end.

Frazer likewise links the myth of Attis to ritualistic violence and death but not to the death of the king: "The story of the self-mutilation of Attis is clearly an attempt to account for the self-mutilation of his priests, who regularly castrated themselves on entering the service of the goddess [Cybele]" (Frazer 1922: 404). Frazer also notes an annual festival of Cybele and Attis in Rome and elsewhere:

On the second day of the festival, ... the chief ceremony seems to have been a blowing of trumpets. The third day ... was known as the Day of Blood: the Archigallus or high-priest drew blood from his arms and presented it as an offering. Nor was he alone in making this bloody sacrifice. Stirred by the wild barbaric music of clashing cymbals, rumbling drums, droning horns, and screaming lutes, the inferior clergy whirled about in the dance with waggling heads and streaming hair, until, rapt into a frenzy of excitement and insensible to pain, they gashed their bodies with potsherds or slashed them with knives in order to bespatter the altar and the sacred tree with their flowing blood. (Frazer 1922: 405)

Again, the imitation here is sheer emulation, but again not thereby any less violent.

The Life of Adonis

The myth of Adonis, the main sources for which are Apollodorus and Ovid, describes the miraculous birth of a preternaturally beautiful human out of a tree, the fighting over him by Aphrodite and Persephone, his annual division of the year into a third with Persephone in Hades and two thirds on earth with Aphrodite, and his eventual death while hunting.

Frazer locates the potted gardens of Adonis in his first, magical stage. Since in this stage humans believe that impersonal forces rather than personalities cause events in the physical world, Adonis here cannot be a personality. Without personality there is no myth, so that this first stage is pre-mythic as well as pre-religious. Greeks would be planting seeds in earth-filled pots not to persuade a divine personality to grant growth but, by the magical Law of Imitation, to force the impersonal earth itself to grow: "For ignorant people suppose that by mimicking the effect which they desire to produce they actually help to produce it" (Frazer 1922: 396). Mimicking the growth of crops would ensure their actual growth. Magic, like religion and in turn like magic and religion combined, originates and functions to secure food. If our forebears had had science, they would have used it instead of magic or religion.

In Frazer's second, religious stage Adonis is an outright personality. He is the god of vegetation. In fact, Frazer distinguishes religion from magic on precisely the grounds that divine personalities rather than impersonal forces now cause events in the physical world. As the god of vegetation, Adonis could, most straightforwardly, be asked for crops. Or the request could be reinforced by ritualistic and ethical obedience. Just as there is now religion, so there is now myth: the biography of Adonis. Information from that biography would help worshipers figure out how best to get Adonis to grant crops. Frazer himself says that rites of mourning were performed for Adonis—not, as in the next stage, to undo his death but to seek his forgiveness for it (see Frazer 1922: 393–94). For Adonis has died not, as in the next stage, because he has descended to the underworld but because in cutting, stamping, and grinding the corn—the specific part of vegetation he symbolizes—humans have killed him. Yet Adonis is somehow still sufficiently alive to be capable of punishing humans, something that the rituals of forgiveness are intended to avert. Since, however, Adonis dies because vegetation itself does, the god is here really only a metaphor for the element that he supposedly controls. As vegetation goes, so goes Adonis.

In Frazer's third pre-scientific stage, which combines the first with the second, Adonis' death means his descent to the underworld for his stay with Persephone. If in stage two as vegetation goes, so goes Adonis, in stage three as Adonis goes, so seemingly goes vegetation. Frazer assumes that whether or not Adonis wills his descent, he is too weak to ascend by himself. By acting out his rebirth, humans facilitate it. On the one hand the enactment employs the magical Law of Imitation. On the other hand it does not, as in the first stage, compel but only bolsters Adonis, who, despite his present state of death, is somehow still hearty enough to revive himself, just not fully. He needs a catalyst, which the enactment provides. In this stage gods still control the physical world, but their effect on it is automatic rather than deliberate. To enact the rebirth of Adonis is to spur his rebirth and thereby the rebirth of vegetation (see Frazer 1922: 377).

Yet even if Adonis chooses to descend to the underworld, he is not choosing infertility, which is just the automatic consequence of his sojourn below. Similarly, even if he chooses to return, he is not thereby choosing fertility, which likewise simply follows automatically from his resurfacing. Adonis proves to be not the cause of the fate of vegetation but only a metaphor for that fate, so that in fact in stage three as well as in stage two as vegetation goes, so goes Adonis. For Frazer, the myth that Adonis spent a portion of the year in the underworld "is explained most simply and naturally by supposing that he represented vegetation, especially the corn," which lies buried half the year and re-emerges the other half (Frazer 1922: 392).

In a much larger sense Frazer, in all three of his pre-scientific stages, reduces Adonis to the mere personification of vegetation. For even where Frazer does deem Adonis an independent personality, the only aspect of his life he considers is that which parallels the natural course of vegetation: Adonis' death and rebirth. Yet Adonis' life, from his birth to his "permanent" death, is anything but natural. For both Apollodorus and Ovid, his birth results from his mother's incestuous yearning for her father. Adonis' split schedule may become routine, but it is not therefore natural. For Apollodorus, it stems from love and jealousy on the part of Aphrodite and Persephone. Nor is Adonis' eventual death natural. His final death terminates, not perpetuates, the change of seasons. He is killed and in some versions is even murdered. This final death Frazer ignores. It is not hard to see why. Only if Adonis is reborn forever can his life symbolize the course of vegetation.

Not only Ovid's version, which does not involve a trek to the underworld and therefore a cycle of death and rebirth, but even Apollodorus', which does, ends in Adonis' permanent demise. By whatever means Adonis has overcome death annually, he cannot do so now. He is gone forever, which is why, in Ovid's version, Aphrodite is so disconsolate. How, then, can his mortal life symbolize eternal rebirth? How, then, can he be a god, who may die but does not stay dead, rather than a human being, who does?

Other Key Gods

Frazer speculates that at Attis' festival he "was also represented at these ceremonies by an effigy" (Frazer 1922: 411). For Frazer, the killing of an effigy is always a watered-down survival of the previous killing of a living being. Hence he writes of instances in which "the divine being is first represented by a living person and afterwards by an effigy, which is then burned or otherwise destroyed." He "conjectures" that "this mimic killing of the priest, accompanied by a real effusion of his blood, was ... a substitute for a human sacrifice which in earlier times was actually offered" (Frazer 1922: 411). The chronology would thus have been as follows: first Attis' self-castration, then the castration of human victims, then priests' self-castration, and finally the castration of an effigy.

Frazer links the violent rituals of Osiris to the king:

> With regard to the ancient Egyptians we have it on the authority of Manetho that they used to burn red-haired men and scatter their ashes with winnowing fans, and it is highly significant that this barbarous sacrifice was offered by the kings at the grave of Osiris. We may conjecture that the victims represented Osiris himself, who was annually slain, dismembered, and buried in their persons that he might quicken the seed in the earth. Possibly in prehistoric times the kings themselves played the part of the god and were slain and dismembered in that character. (Frazer 1922: 439)

Frazer notes a story in which "Romulus, the first king of Rome, was cut in pieces by the senators, who buried the fragments of him in the ground" (Frazer 1922: 439). Osiris himself is king of Egypt when killed. In contrast to the cults of Adonis and Attis, death here is a means to rebirth: "that he might quicken the seed in the earth" (Frazer 1922: 439). But the rejuvenation of the crops comes from the death, not the resurrection, of the king.

The Cretan followers of Dionysus celebrated a biennial festival, in which "all that he had done or suffered in his last moments was enacted before the eyes of his worshippers, who tore a live bull to pieces with their teeth and roamed the woods with frantic shouts" (Frazer 1922: 452). More significant are the cases of the killings of Pentheus and Lycurgus, "two kings who are said to have been torn to pieces, the one by Bachanals, the other by horses, for their opposition to the rites of Dionysus" (Frazer 1922: 455). Frazer suggests that their deaths might in fact have been "distorted reminiscences of a custom of sacrificing divine kings in the character of Dionysus and of dispersing the fragments of their broken bodies over the fields for the purpose of fertilising them" (Frazer 1922: 455).

As with Osiris, so here with Dionysus: the rejuvenation of the crops comes from the death, not the resurrection, of the king. Furthermore, "It is probably no mere coincidence that Dionysus himself is said to have been torn in pieces at Thebes, the very place where according to legend the same fate befell king Pentheus at the hands of the frenzied votaries of the vine-god" (Frazer 1922: 455). Unlike most kings, Pentheus was an unwitting substitute for the god. Tying yet further god to king, Frazer notes "the legend ... that in his infancy Dionysus occupied for a short time the throne of his father Zeus" (Frazer 1922: 451)—a role which to Frazer suggests that in primeval times sons were substitute sacrifices for their reigning fathers (see Frazer 1922: 451).

When Frazer analyzes the myths of gods other than Adonis, he does not have the convenience of a dual death to portion out between his varieties of myth ritualism. Attis, Osiris, and Dionysus each die only once. Because all three die violently, their deaths parallel the death of the king in Frazer's second version of myth ritualism. But in order to make these three gods fit the first version as well, Frazer must argue that the three were believed to be resurrected annually, so that their seemingly one-time deaths become annual affairs. The myth of at least Osiris does include his resurrection, but he becomes king of the underworld and never returns to the world of the living. Some variants of the myth of Dionysus include his resurrection, but others do not. No variant of the myth of Attis offers any resurrection. Still, insofar as Frazer fuses a god's one-time death, which always comes through violence, with a god's annual death, he is tying both versions of myth ritualism to violence.

Violence

Frazer's theory of myth connects religion to violence. Religion is literally about life and death. Humans need food to survive. Crops would continue to grow if they did not die. Their death is not natural, even if recurrent. They die because the god of vegetation dies, and in Frazer's first scenario that god dies because he has been killed. Religion—better, religion and magic combined—arises for the sheer purpose of restoring to life a god who would have lived forever had he not been killed. Had the god not been murdered, the combined stage would never have arisen. Religion plus magic thus arises to undo a murder. That religion and magic restore to life the god and thereby the crops make this combined stage ultimately life-giving, but again only by reversing a murder.

In Frazer's second scenario the king, or a substitute, is killed. His death is anything but natural since he is killed prior to succumbing to natural causes. Because he is killed as a sacrifice for the community, he cannot be said to be murdered. But killed he still is. He is barred from serving out an otherwise lifetime post. "The king must die" is the familiar line. The king is killed so that the god of vegetation residing within him can be brought back to full health. True, the king and therefore the god are not initially dead but at most only weak, so that the king is really being brought back from weakness to strength. But the king is then outright killed to ensure that he does not die naturally while still reigning. Abdication is not an option. Again, had the king not been weak, even if from wholly natural causes, the crops would never have wilted, and the combined stage would never have arisen.

Conclusion

Like all other theories of myth, Frazer's is a theory of a far bigger domain than myth, which is merely a case in point. Frazer's theory is a theory of culture, of which religion is a part and myth in turn a part of religion. Other parts include magic and science. Frazer's theory is, even more basically, a theory of human nature. All of culture is for him a series of elaborate ways of getting food on the table. Frazer's theory—of myth, religion, culture, and human nature—has been forever debated. But Frazer brings to the fore more than a classicist's mastery of a specific myth. He brings a twelve- and really thirteen-volume tome, *The Golden Bough* in its third edition. He enlists information from almost the whole world. Of course, his theory can still be wholly wrong, as many critics have asserted. But his analysis of the myth of Adonis rests on more than the ability to interpret a story.[1]

Chapter 4

Frazer on Osiris

In all four editions of *The Golden Bough* (1890, 1900, 1911–15, 1922) J. G. Frazer treats his four key Mediterranean gods of vegetation—Adonis, Attis, Osiris, and Dionysus—as gods from the start. Frazer places them all within the second of his three (really four) stages of culture. Magic, which is without gods, is the first stage. Impersonal laws of nature cause events in the physical world. Like scientists, who come later, magicians discover and enlist those laws to manipulate the world. The epitome of magic is voodoo.

The second stage is that of religion, in which gods rather than impersonal forces are believed to cause events in the physical world. Here it rains because a god decides to send rain, and does so by, say, dropping buckets of water on a chosen spot rather than by using any meteorological processes.

The last stage is that of science, which marks a return to impersonal causes. Science means natural, not social, science. It means biology, chemistry, and physics above all.

But in between the stage of religion and the stage of science Frazer introduces a stage which combines magic with religion. Here gods rather than impersonal forces still cause physical events, but humans can magically control the gods and thereby the events. This stage, barely announced, proves to be the central one in the whole of *The Golden Bough*. Frazer introduces this stage in his first chapter on Adonis (see Frazer 1911–15, part 4, vol. 1: 4; 1922: 377).

Frazer's theory of religion and of myth and ritual is confusing in many ways, especially for euhemerism. In the first version of Frazer's stage of myth ritualism the king plays the part of the god of vegetation but himself never becomes divine. So no euhemerism, or the transformation of a human into a god.[1] Only in the second version is the king divine. But the king here is divine from the outset. The soul of the god resides in the body of the king. Therefore the ritualistic death and rebirth of the king does not make the king divine. So again, no euhemerism.

In combining magic with religion, this in-between stage also combines ritual with myth. In the stage of sheer magic there are rituals—the routines involved in carrying out the directions—but no myths, for there are no gods. There are, instead, impersonal, mechanical laws. These laws of sympathetic magic are the pre-scientific counterpart to all the laws of natural science. In the stage of sheer religion there are both myths and rituals, but they are barely connected. Myths describe the character and behavior of gods. Rituals, such as sacrifices, seek to curry divine favor. Rituals may presuppose myths, which would suggest what activities would most please the gods, but rituals are otherwise independent of myths.

By contrast, in the following stage, that of magic and religion combined, rituals and myths work together in what is called "myth ritualism." In a further confusion Frazer actually presents two versions of myth ritualism and fails to disentangle them.[2]

In the first version the myth provides the biography of the god of vegetation, and the ritual enacts it. More precisely, the ritual enacts that portion of the myth which describes the death and rebirth of the god. The myth constitutes the script of the ritual. The ritual operates on the basis of the magical Law of Similarity, according to which the imitation of an action causes it to happen. The ritual does not manipulate vegetation directly. Rather, it manipulates the god of vegetation. But as the god goes, so goes vegetation. The assumption that vegetation is under the control of a god is the legacy of religion. The assumption that vegetation can be controlled, even if only through the god, is the legacy of magic. The combination of myth with ritual is the combination of religion with magic.

In this first version of myth ritualism the actor need not be the king. And whoever plays the role of the god of vegetation is not himself killed. The ritual does not cause the death of the god, which, on the contrary, is presupposed as the necessary starting point of the rebirth of the god and thereby of the crops. The ritual causes—magically—the rebirth of the god.

In Frazer's second version of myth ritualism the king is central. In the first version the king may not even participate in the ritual. In the second he must. In the first version the king, even when the actor in the ritual, is merely human: he imitates, not becomes, the god. In the second version the king is divine, by which Frazer means that the god resides in him. Just as the health of vegetation depends on the health of its god, so now the health of the god depends on the health of the king: as the king goes, so goes the god of vegetation, and so in turn goes vegetation itself. Above all, where in the first version the king does not even die, let alone get killed, in the second version he is killed.

The king is killed either at the end of a fixed term or at the first sign of illness. Doubtless the sudden death of a king can never be precluded, but the killing of the king before his likely passing most nearly guarantees the continuous health of the god and so of vegetation. The aim is to fend off winter. The withering of vegetation during the winter of even a year-long reign is attributed to the weakening of the king.

This second version of myth ritualism has proved the more influential by far, but ironically it in fact provides only a tenuous link between myth and ritual and in turn between religion and magic. Instead of enacting the myth of the god of vegetation, the ritual merely changes the residence of the god. The king dies not in imitation of the death of the god but as a sacrifice to preserve the health of the god. Myth, hence religion, plays a scant part here. Nor does magic play any part. Instead of reviving the god by magical imitation, the ritual revives the god by substitution. By contrast, in Frazer's first myth-ritualist scenario one would not ritualistically enact the rebirth of the god of vegetation without the myth of the death and rebirth of that god.

Frazer's Main Gods

When Frazer discusses Adonis, Attis, Osiris, and Dionysus, he considers them as gods—gods of vegetation. He does not consider them as human beings, even though, most confusingly, their myths sometimes do. Of Osiris, he writes that "there are good grounds for classing him in one of his aspects with Adonis and Attis as a personification of the great yearly vicissitudes of nature, especially of the corn" (Frazer 1922: 420). "Under the names of Osiris, Tammuz [i.e., Adonis], Adonis, and Attis, the peoples of Egypt and Western Asia represented the yearly decay and revival of life, especially of vegetable life, which they personified as a god who annually died and rose again from the dead" (Frazer 1922: 378).

Yet Osiris, and only Osiris, is considered by Frazer to have been a king as well as a god:

> Reigning as a king on earth, Osiris reclaimed the Egyptians from savagery, gave them laws, and taught them to worship the gods. Before his time the Egyptians had been cannibals. But Isis, the sister and wife of Osiris, discovered wheat and barley growing wild, and Osiris introduced the cultivation of these grains amongst his people, who forthwith

abandoned cannibalism and took kindly to a corn diet. Moreover, Osiris is said to have been the first to gather fruit from trees, to train the vine to poles, and to tread the grapes. Eager to communicate these beneficent discoveries to all mankind, he committed the whole government of Egypt to his wife Isis, and travelled all over the world, diffusing the blessings of civilisation and agriculture wherever he went .... Loaded with the wealth that had been showered upon him by grateful nations, he returned to Egypt, and on account of the benefits he had conferred on mankind he was unanimously hailed and worshipped as a deity. (Frazer 1922: 421–22)

But Osiris is then killed by his evil brother Set (or Typhon), who eventually cuts up his body into fourteen pieces and scatters them abroad. Osiris' wife, Isis, manages to find thirteen of the "body parts," to construct the missing part (his genitals), and to revive him. But he never returns to the world of the living. Instead, he reigns over the dead. He is called Lord of the Underworld, Lord of Eternity, and Ruler of the Dead. He judges the dead and rewards and punishes them accordingly.

Osiris is the son of gods. But he is obviously not thereby immortal. (It is wrong to assume that gods are always immortal, though perhaps all immortals are gods.) Osiris becomes immortal when he is resurrected. And with his resurrection comes the worship of him as a god. Here, and here alone in Frazer's corpus, do we have euhemerism, or the transformation of a human into a god.

While Frazer presents two distinct and incompatible versions of myth ritualism, he combines, or tries to combine, them in his description of the myths and rituals of his key gods. Of Adonis, he writes,

There is some reason to think that in early times Adonis was sometimes personated by a living man who died a violent death in the character of the god. Further, there is evidence which goes to show that among the agricultural peoples of the Eastern Mediterranean, the corn-spirit, by whatever name he was known, was often represented, year by year, by human victims slain on the harvest-field. (Frazer 1922: 394)

Here Frazer tries to combine the imitation of the death and rebirth of the god—"Adonis was sometimes personated by a living man ... in the character of the god"—with the killing of a human being—"a living man who died a violent death." But unless the human victim harbors the god within him, the victim's death duplicates, not imitates, Adonis'. There is no magical efficacy, only emulation. Adonis himself is unaffected. Kingship is not even mentioned.

Furthermore, the emulation here is of Adonis' final death, not of his annual descent to the land of the dead. Therefore the death here does not lead to rebirth and so cannot be considered merely a violent means to renewal. In fact, Frazer splits the myth in two to serve his dual goals. He focuses on Adonis' annual trip to and from Hades because that trip parallels, and can thereby be said to cause, the annual death and rebirth of the crops, as Frazer's first version of myth ritualism dictates. Adonis' death here is wholly irenic: he dies only because he enters—while alive—the land of the dead. Here Adonis' final, violent death is ignored. Alternatively, Frazer focuses on that violent death, from which there is no return, because it parallels, though not causes, the death of the king, as Frazer's second version of myth ritualism requires. Adonis' annual, peaceful sojourn is ignored.

When Frazer turns to the myths of his other main gods of vegetation, he does not have the convenience of an annual event to tout. Attis, Osiris, and Dionysus each die only once. The deaths of those who die violently parallel the death of the king in Frazer's second version of myth ritualism. But in order to make these three gods fit the first version as well, Frazer must argue that the three were believed to be resurrected annually, so that their seemingly one-time deaths become annual affairs. The myth of at least Osiris does include his resurrection, but he becomes king of the underworld and never returns to the world of the living. Some variants of the myth of Dionysus include his resurrection, but others do not. And in some versions he does not even die but instead goes directly to Olympus. No variant of the myth of Attis offers any resurrection. Attis, driven mad, kills himself—by castration.

Frazer does not link the violent rituals of either Adonis or Attis to kingship. But he does tie the violent rituals of both Osiris and Dionysus to kingship. To take the case of Osiris: while Osiris was king of Egypt when killed, subsequent Egyptian kings, while "playing the part" of Osiris, die in emulation, not magical imitation, of Osiris. Moreover, Osiris as king is not said to harbor the god within himself, so that the link between king and god is even more distant. Nevertheless, the death of the king is now a means to rebirth: "that he might quicken the seed in the earth." Yet the rejuvenation of the crops comes from the death and replacement, not the resurrection, of the king.

Where, then, is the possible euhemerism? The evidence for Osiris' ever having been a human being is absent. He is a god—the son of the earth god and the sky goddess. True, he is said to have reigned as a king on earth, but there is no tying of him to Egypt. The benefits that he bestowed on humanity are the kinds that are typically credited to culture heroes, such as Prometheus. There is no place in Egypt connected to him. Osiris has no personality. No writings or sayings are attributed to him. He has no disciples or cult. He has no genealogy. Nevertheless, Frazer deems Osiris a case of euhemerism.

Jesus

For Frazer, Christianity is just another vegetation cult, simply the most successful of the lot. Christianity takes over from Judaism the primitive practice of putting a human being to death not for the ethereal purpose of atoning for sin but for the mundane purpose of putting food on the table. Jesus was a human king in whom, it was believed, resided the soul of the god of vegetation. The annual spring celebration of Jesus' death and resurrection was a ritual intended to revive the crops, with Jesus the King of the Jews. At work here is Frazer's second myth-ritualist scenario exclusively, not any combination with the first one. Jesus was not an actor imitating the death and rebirth of a god but a divine king who was himself killed and replaced, though Frazer never discloses who his successor was.

Frazer takes the section on Jesus from the second edition of *The Golden Bough* (1900) and puts it as an appendix to volume 9 of the third edition (1911–15)—this on the grounds that "the hypothesis which it sets forth has not been confirmed by subsequent research, and is admittedly in a high degree speculative and uncertain" (Frazer 1911–15, vol. 11: 412 n. 1). But instead of yanking the section altogether, Frazer retains it "as an appendix on the chance that, under a pile of conjectures, it contains some grain of truth" (Frazer 1911–15, vol. 11: 412 n. 1).

Trying to account for the "remarkably rapid diffusion of Christianity in Asia Minor," Frazer argues that "the new faith had elements in it which appealed powerfully to the Asiatic mind"—namely, an annual spring ritual of regicide (Frazer 1900, vol. 3: 195–96):

> All over Western Asia from time immemorial the mournful death and happy resurrection of a divine being appear to have been annually celebrated with alternative rites of bitter lamentation and exultant joy; and through the veil which mythic fancy has woven round this tragic figure we can still detect the features of those great yearly changes in earth and sky which, under all distinctions of race and religion, must always touch the natural human heart with alternative emotions of gladness and regret, because they exhibit on the vastest scale open to

our observation the mysterious struggle between life and death. But man has not always been willing to watch passively this momentous conflict; he has felt that he has too great a stake in its issue to stand by with folded hands while it is being fought out .... Nowhere do these efforts, vain and pitiful yet pathetic, appear to have been made more persistently and systematically than in Western Asia. In name they varied from place to place, but in substance they were all alike. A man, whom the fond imagination of his worshippers invested with the attributes of a god, gave his life for the life of the world; after infusing from his own body a fresh current of vital energy into the stagnant veins of nature, he was cut off from among the living before his failing strength should initiate a universal decay, and his place was taken by another who played, like all his predecessors, the ever-recurring drama of the divine resurrection and death. Such a drama, if our interpretation of it is right, was the original story of Esther and Mordecai or, to give them their older names, of Ishtar and Marduk.... A chain of causes ... determined that the part of the dying god in this annual play should be thrust upon Jesus of Nazareth, whom the enemies he had made in high places by his outspoken strictures were resolved to put out of the way. (Frazer 1911–15, vol. 3: 196–97)

Frazer does not explicitly compare Jesus with Osiris. He ties Jesus to the annual killing at Purim of Haman but then ties this Jewish ritual to the pagan and indeed worldwide killing and resurrecting not of a human but of a god—the god of vegetation. The god, while residing in the body of the incumbent king, dies insofar as the king dies and is resurrected insofar as the king is replaced. The soul of the god is transferred from one body to another. The king himself is not revived but replaced.

Of Frazer's main gods of vegetation—Adonis, Attis, Dionysus, and Osiris—Osiris comes closest to Jesus (a) because he is king, (b) because he is killed, (c) because he is killed by his enemies, and (d) because he is resurrected—though now as King of Hades rather than as King of Egypt. By contrast, Adonis' death falls outside his annual descent to Hades. Attis kills himself. In some versions Dionysus simply ascends to Olympus.

Many others have tied Jesus to Osiris.[3] Frazer is struck by the similarities. For Frazer, Osiris, like Jesus, somehow despite a divine lineage, was born a human being and became a god only after he had been killed and resurrected. So here we definitely have euhemerism. Frazer, a nonbeliever, objects strongly and almost bitterly to the denial of the historicity of Jesus: "The historical reality both of Buddha and of Christ has sometimes been doubted or denied. It would be just as reasonable to question the historical existence of Alexander the Great and of Charlemagne on account of the legends which have gathered round them" (Frazer

1911–15, vol. 5: 311 n. 2).[4] At the same time he sees Jesus as the son of sheer humans, Mary and Joseph, and not at all of God. Jesus becomes divine not with his baptism but with his resurrection. Osiris is the god of vegetation in general and of corn in particular. Jesus is the god of vegetation generally. Just like Jesus, Osiris is put to death by his enemies but is then brought back to life.[5]

Chapter 5

Frazer and Campbell on Myth: Nineteenth- and Twentieth-Century Approaches

No two writers on myth have been more popular than J. G. Frazer, author of *The Golden Bough* (1st edition 1890), and Joseph Campbell, author of *The Hero with a Thousand Faces* (1st edition 1949). Yet few others have had more mixed professional receptions. Frazer sought acclaim among anthropologists but became outdated within his lifetime. Campbell cultivated a popular rather than an academic following and was never taken seriously in anthropological or folkloristic circles.

Both figures have nevertheless thrived as authorities elsewhere in the intellectual world, in literary circles above all. Frazer influenced not only leading modernist poets and novelists—notably, Yeats, Eliot, Lawrence, and Joyce—but also many leading scholars of literature—for example, Jessie Weston on the Grail legend, E. M. Butler on the Faust legend, C. L. Barber and Herbert Weisinger on Shakespeare, Jane Harrison on Greek religion and art, F. M. Cornford on Greek philosophy and comedy, Gilbert Murray on Greek epic and tragedy, Francis Fergusson on tragedy, Lord Raglan on hero myths, and Stanley Edgar Hyman and Northrop Frye on literature as a whole. The link to Frazer is the tracing back of literature to myths that were originally primitive vegetation rituals. To be sure, some of these literary myth ritualists connect myth and ritual differently from Frazer, reconstruct the ritual differently, make the king other than an outright god, ignore the king altogether, or make the aim of the ritual more than food. Still, the influence of Frazer, who himself does not apply his theory of myth to literature, has been inestimable.[1]

Campbell's impact on literary scholars has likewise been vast, though far more confined. Most of his followers apply to novels and movies the hero myth pattern of his *Hero with a Thousand Faces*. But they often adopt only the pattern itself and disregard Campbell's Jungian and mystical interpretation of it.

Frazer and Campbell share various fundamental convictions. Both despise religion—for Frazer, all religions; for Campbell, at first just Western ones but later Eastern ones, too. Where Frazer berates Christianity above all, Campbell more narrowly condemns Roman Catholicism. Robert Ackerman, author of the definitive biography, *J. G. Frazer* (1987), denies that his subject's lifelong animus toward Christianity was a reaction to an overbearing childhood religiosity. Rather, religion in Frazer just did not "take." By contrast, Campbell's hatred of Catholicism was conspicuously a reaction to his Catholic upbringing. But until a biographer uncovers a more visceral source of this hostility, the explanation must remain Campbell's own: that Catholicism, like other Western religions, misconstrues its own myths and thereby robs adherents of their benefits. Campbell writes as if personally betrayed by Catholicism.

Frazer damns religion by demoting it to a primitive phenomenon—more advanced than magic but still pre-scientific. He damns Christianity in particular by relegating it to just another vegetation cult—for Frazer, the core of all religion. Writes Ackerman: "Jesus was really (and therefore, in Frazer's reductionist analysis, only) a member of the group of dying and reviving gods that included ... Attis, Adonis, and Osiris" (Ackerman 1987: 169). Similarly, Campbell damns Western religion by demoting it to a pre-scientific enterprise and damns Catholicism in particular by transforming its would-be distinctive, historical claims into mere instances of universal archetypes.

The differences between Frazer and Campbell are, however, even keener than the similarities. Frazer damns myth as well as religion by subsuming myth under religion. Like the rest of religion, myth is a wholly primitive phenomenon. Frazer's assumptions that religion serves the same explanatory function as science, that the religious explanation is incompatible with the scientific one, and that the scientific explanation is true all render religion and so myth not only superfluous but also impossible for moderns, who by definition have science. For Frazer, modern believers are remnants of a fading religious age.

Campbell does the opposite: he saves myth by severing it from religion, which itself he views no differently than Frazer. Unlike religion, which at least in the West is for Campbell dying, myth for him is perennial. Deeming myth perennial is the extreme version of the twentieth-century view that myth is not at odds with science and is, at the least, still possible for moderns. Campbell's assumptions that myth does not serve to explain the world, that the functions myth does serve are indispensable, and that myth is indispensable to serving them all make myth not merely open to moderns but mandatory for them. Frazer's view of myth as not just unnecessary but also impossible for moderns constitutes the quintessentially nineteenth-century stance.

Frazer reads myths literally, as descriptions of the activities of gods of nature. While for him gods originate as metaphors for natural phenomena, myths about gods are meant literally, though at times he reads myths as symbols of the life not of the god of vegetation but of vegetation itself. Campbell, by contrast, always reads myths symbolically, as descriptions of the contents of at once the human mind and the cosmos. For him, only obtuse Westerners, brainwashed by religion, take myths literally.

Until 1987, there had been no scholarly biography of Frazer—perhaps because, as Ackerman acknowledges, Frazer's life largely was his work. There had been only the two hagiographical memoirs of Frazer's secretary, R. Angus Downie: *James George Frazer: The Portrait of a Scholar* (1940) and *Frazer and The Golden Bough* (1970). There had also been Bronislaw Malinowski's ambivalent sketch in his *A Scientific Theory of Culture and Other Essays* (1960 [1944]: 177–221). Ackerman brilliantly melds Frazer's life with his work.

Correcting caricatures of Frazer as unworldly, Ackerman shows that, contrary to Downie and Malinowski, Frazer, if never quite gregarious, became withdrawn only in middle age—the result of both the death of William Robertson Smith, his mentor and best friend, and the overprotectiveness of his wife, whom he married shortly afterwards at age forty-two. Ackerman also shows that Frazer, while incontestably bookish and diffident, was not beyond ambition and even controversy. Nor, contrary to Downie and Malinowski, was he unable to stomach criticism. Most surprisingly, Frazer, the prototypical armchair anthropologist, considered joining what became a celebrated anthropological expedition to New Guinea. Downie notes merely the invitation.

Ackerman corrects caricatures of not only Frazer's life but also his ideas. On the one hand he observes that many of the views for which Frazer has long been castigated—most of all his hopeless ethnocentrism and relentless rationalism—were commonplaces of his time. On the other hand Ackerman reveals how much more mixed Frazer's views really were. Frazer, it turns out, was at times skeptical of progress: the masses would always remain benighted, and only an elite was capable of enlightenment. In singling out individual geniuses as the carriers of civilization, Frazer was more romantic than rationalist. Frazer even stressed the similarities as well as the differences between primitives and moderns: the West arose *out of* its primitive foil (see Frazer 1909).

Perhaps the most egregious popular assumption is that Frazer never changed his mind. Ackerman meticulously traces the changes in Frazer's views, especially from the first edition of *The Golden Bough* (1890) to the third (1911–15). For example, the very distinction between magic and religion arises only in the second edition. In the third edition Frazer unexpectedly entertains diffusion as a source of cultural similarities. The explicitness with which he mockingly parallels Christianity and primitive religion varies from edition to edition. Even the importance of the case of the priest of Nemi, the formal spur to the whole opus, changes with the editions.

Ackerman never contests many standard criticisms of Frazer. For example, he grants that Frazer was an inconsistent theorist, that Frazer's theories are often derivative, that Frazer overintellectualizes both primitive peoples and religion, that Frazer over-literalizes both, that the rigid division into magic and religion does not hold, that primitive cultures include protoscience alongside magic and religion, and that Frazer's version of comparativism severs phenomena from their contexts. Nevertheless, Ackerman respects Frazer's achievements: not just Frazer's influence but his works themselves.

As exact as Ackerman's mastery of his subject is, he does, I think, confuse William Robertson Smith's form of myth ritualism with Frazer's. For Smith, myth is inferior to ritual: it arises as an explanation of ritual only once the magical meaning of a ritual has been forgotten. While Ackerman documents assiduously how far from a uniform myth ritualist Frazer is, insofar as Frazer is a myth ritualist, he makes myth the equal of ritual: it is the script for ritual. Assuming that the script provides only "a description of what the performers or dancers were doing as they imitated the gods" rather than "'stories of the gods' actions themselves—myths" (Ackerman 1987: 232), Ackerman thereby restricts myth ritualism to Smith's version. But for Frazer the script is the story, which is thus inextricably linked to ritual from the start. Because the heart of especially the second and third editions of *The Golden Bough* is, as Ackerman himself emphasizes, the ritualistic enactment of the myths of dying and rising gods, Frazer necessarily remains a full-fledged myth ritualist par excellence—even in the face of such contrary theoretical statements as his denunciation of myth-ritualism in his Loeb Library translation of Apollodorus (see Apollodorus 1921: xxviii, n. 1).[2]

An authorized biography of Campbell is still to be written. So far, the sole book on his theory is my own, *Joseph Campbell: An Introduction* (1987 and 1990), which has a brief introductory chapter on Campbell's life (see

Segal 1987 and 1990/1997: ch. 1). *The Power of Myth*, an edited transcript of the US Public Broadcasting Service interviews with Bill Moyers, sums up Campbell's lifelong views. While continuing to grant differences among myths, Campbell still stresses the similarities: "What does it say about what all of us have in common that so many of these stories contain similar elements—the forbidden fruit, the woman" (Campbell 1988b: 51). Though he divides the earlier *Masks of God* into primitive, Eastern, Western, and modern mythologies, even there he concludes that all mythologies are finally one—the firm view of his *Hero with a Thousand Faces*.

Campbell assumes that the moment one discovers that every people has its own myths of creation, paradise, the flood, and ancestral heroes, one can no longer take one's own myths literally. Yet instead of abandoning one's myths, as Frazer would urge, one should reread them symbolically: "Read other peoples' myths, not those of your own religion, because you tend to interpret your own religion in terms of [literal] facts—but if you read the other ones, you begin to get the [symbolic] message" (Campbell 1988b: 6).

A myth of paradise that literally describes a place on earth initially occupied by the first humans symbolically describes both the unconscious, out of which consciousness arose, and invisible, immaterial reality, out of which the created, material world emerged: "The Garden of Eden is a metaphor for that innocence that is innocent of time, innocent of opposites, and that is the prime center out of which consciousness then becomes aware of the changes" (Campbell 1988b: 50).

As the quotation evinces, the symbolic meaning of myths is mystical. Myths proclaim all oppositions and all distinctions illusory. Psychologically, myths say not only that there exists an unconscious as well as a conscious mind but also that those two minds are one. Metaphysically, myths say not only that there exists an immaterial world beyond the material one but also that those two worlds are one. For Frazer, by contrast, myths refer to the material world alone. Gods are material.

The mysticism that, according to Campbell, all myths espouse is the most radical variety of monism. Myths preach not that everything is immaterial rather than material but that everything is a single, indissoluble substance combining immateriality with matter. Myths preach not that there is heaven rather than earth, soul rather than body, or god rather than humanity but that heaven and earth are identical, soul and body identical, and god and humanity identical. Campbell's hero thus returns to the everyday world to find within it the strange new world seemingly left behind. All who heed the message of myth find the strange new world within, not beyond, the everyday one. As Campbell puts it, "Divinity informs the world." The Bible, taken literally, wrongly teaches that "God is separate from nature": "[O]ur [literal] story of the Fall in the Garden sees nature as corrupt; and that myth corrupts the whole world for us" (Campbell 1988b: 99). The brand of mysticism that Campbell deciphers everywhere is the world-affirming nature mysticism of Emerson and Thoreau.

Campbell's interpretation of myths worldwide scarcely tallies with conventional interpretations of the myths of Western religions. Mainstream Christianity, Judaism, Islam, and ancient Greek and Roman religions do not teach that heaven and earth or soul and body, let alone god and humans, are one. Indeed, the worst sin in the West is the attempted effacement of the divide between god and humanity. Mysticism is a minor strain in the West and typically takes the form of world rejection. Campbell's unruffled response is that Western religions misconstrue their own myths, which get reduced from pristine expressions of universal, symbolic, mystical truths to degenerate pronouncements of local, literal, nonmystical pseudofacts: "Mythology is very fluid.... You may even find four or five myths in a given culture, all giving different [symbolic] versions of the same mystery. Then theology comes along and says it has got to be just this [literal] way. Mythology is poetry, and the poetic language is very flexible. Religion turns poetry into prose" (Campbell 1988b: 141–42).

For Campbell, as for Frazer, myth taken literally conflicts with science. But for Campbell, myth taken symbolically does not even directly refer to the material world and so does not conflict with science. In fact, science for Campbell is itself mythic—for Frazer an unimaginable possibility. Writes Campbell: "No, they [myth and science] don't conflict. Science is breaking through now into the mystery dimensions. It's pushed itself into the sphere that myth is talking about" (Campbell 1988b: 132).

Campbell assumes that the true, mystical meaning of myth is itself true: "No, mythology is not a lie, mythology is poetry, it is metaphorical. It has been well said that mythology is the penultimate truth—penultimate [only] because the ultimate cannot be put into words" (Campbell 1988b: 163). Endorsing the mysticism that he maintains all myths preach, Campbell is thus a mystic himself. Where for Frazer myth is congenitally false, for Campbell myth ineluctably harbors the deepest truths.

Campbell sometimes bemoans and sometimes denies the absence of modern myths. Like Frazer, he takes for granted that traditional Western myths, by which he means biblical rather than classical ones, no longer work because moderns take them literally. Often he declares that, in the wake of the demise of biblical mythology, "What we have today is a demythologized world" (Campbell 1988b: 9). He even ascribes social problems like crime to the paucity of myths.

Other times Campbell says that moderns are continually creating myths:

MOYERS: Where do the kids growing up in the city—on 125th and Broadway, for example—where do these kids get their myths today?

CAMPBELL: They make them up themselves. This is why we have graffiti all over the city. These kids have their own gangs and their own initiations and their own morality, and they're doing the best they can. (Campbell 1988b: 8)

Campbell predicts that new myths, typified by the *Star Wars* saga, will focus on outer space. Whatever their literal subject, not theologians but artists will be inventing those "secular myths"—for Frazer, a contradiction in terms.

Because I am comparing a book *by* Campbell with one *on* Frazer, my criticisms of the Campbell book are necessarily of Campbell's theory itself rather than of someone else's presentation of it. Like Frazer's theory, Campbell's is weak less because it is wrong than because it is inconsistent. While the interpretations both give of the meaning of myth are unwavering, their explanations of the origin and function of it fluctuate wildly. Just as Frazer, as Ackerman shows, is alternatively and even simultaneously a myth ritualist, an intellectualist, and a euhemerist, so Campbell is alternatively and even simultaneously a Freudian, a Jungian, an ethologist, and a diffusionist.

Where, however, Frazer, a consummate scholar, adduces inexhaustible evidence to bolster his claims, Campbell, a guru, appeals instead to some unshakable intuition. For example, Frazer painstakingly tries to justify his radical interpretation of Judaism and Christianity as primitive religions. Campbell blithely interprets them equally wildly as mystical religions.

Frazer will never cease to be of interest to poets and critics because he never turns away from the plot of myth. Campbell does. Only in *Hero with a Thousand Faces* does he, like Frazer, focus on the plot. Elsewhere he concentrates instead either on the themes underlying the plot or on specific archetypes within the plot. For all Campbell's deserved fame as a masterly storyteller, he is, as a theorist, surprisingly uninterested in myths as stories.

Chapter 6

Campbell's Non-Jungian Approach to Myth

Despite the commonly applied epithet, Joseph Campbell was never a straightforward "Jungian." He did edit both *The Portable Jung* and the six-volume selection from the *Eranos-Jahrbüch*, which, while not uniformly Jungian, is Jungian in spirit. Campbell himself twice gave lectures published in the *Jahrbüch*. Several volumes of his works appear in the Bollingen Series, which is likewise broadly Jungian. Two of Campbell's works even constitute the inaugural and final entries in the series. He also edited other Bollingen volumes. He was both a fellow and a trustee of the Bollingen Foundation.

Still, Campbell was not a Jungian analyst and underwent no analysis. Not only did he never call himself a Jungian, but he even denied that he was: "You know, for some people, 'Jungian' is a nasty word, and it has been flung at me by certain reviewers as though to say, 'Don't bother with Joe Campbell: he's a Jungian.' I'm not a Jungian!" (Campbell 1988b: 123). True, of all theorists of myth, Campbell does praise Jung the most: "As far as interpreting myths, Jung gives me the best clues I've got" (Campbell 1988b: 123). But Campbell, fancying himself a theorist in his own right, refuses to defer to Jung: "he [Jung]'s not the final word—I don't think there is a final word" (Campbell 1988b: 121).

Campbell differs most with Jung over the origin and function of myth. Where for Jung the contents of myth arise out of the unconscious, in only some works of Campbell's do they do so. Even then, sometimes the unconscious for Campbell is acquired rather than, as for Jung, inherited. Other times the contents of myth—contents that Campbell loosely calls "archetypal" simply because they are similar worldwide—emerge from the imprint of either recurrent or traumatic experiences. In all of these cases, as for Jung, each society creates its own myths—whatever the source of the material it uses. Other times, however, myths for Campbell, in contrast to Jung, originate in one society and spread elsewhere.

Where for Jung myth functions at once to reveal the existence of the archetypes of the unconscious, to enable humans to encounter those archetypes, and to guide humans in encountering them, for Campbell myth serves additional functions as well. Campbell comes to declare repeatedly that myth serves four distinct functions: to instill and maintain a sense of awe and mystery before the world; to provide a symbolic image for the world, such as that of the Great Chain of Being; to maintain the social order by giving divine justification to social practices like the Indian caste system; and above all to harmonize human beings with the cosmos, society, and the parts of themselves. Jung, ever seeking a balance between the internal and the external worlds, would doubtless applaud many of these functions for keeping humans anchored to the outer, everyday, conscious world. But he himself is more concerned with reconnecting humans to the inner, unconscious world, with which they have ordinarily lost contact. Since only the fourth of Campbell's litany of functions deals with the relationship of humans to themselves, and since even it deals with more than the unconscious, Jung would likely consider Campbell's quaternity of functions distinct from his own.

For all Jung's praise of myth, he does not regard it as indispensable. Religion, art, dream, and what he calls the "active imagination" can work as well, even if at times Jung uses the term "myth" so loosely as to encompass these alternatives to it. For Campbell, by contrast, myth is irreplaceable. Campbell attributes to myth so many disparate functions that it is hard to envision any possible substitute. Moreover, he, like Jung at times, defines myth so broadly that religion, art, and dreams become instances of myth rather than substitutes for it.

Jung considers myth neither necessary nor sufficient for human fulfillment. Campbell considers it both. Where for Jung therapy supplements myth, for Campbell myth precludes therapy, which is only for those bereft of myth. For Jung, one should reflect on a myth rather than heed it blindly. For Campbell, one should follow a myth—any myth—faithfully. Where for Jung a myth can lead one astray, for Campbell it never can.

Despite these conspicuous differences, Campbell stands close to Jung and stands closest in *The Hero with a Thousand Faces*, which remains the classic Jungian analysis of hero myths. Campbell himself, to be sure, states that he became ever more of a Jungian *after* writing *Hero*: "When I wrote *The Hero with a Thousand Faces* they [Freud and Jung] were equal in my thinking: Freud served in one context, Jung in another. But then, in the years following, Jung became more and more eloquent to me. I think the longer you live, the more Jung can say to you" (Campbell 1988b: 121). But Campbell is likely basing this characterization of *Hero* on his reliance on the Freudian Géza Róheim, who, however, strays from Freudian orthodoxy in a manner that Campbell adopts and carries still further to Jung.[1]

Where for Freud and his then-disciple Otto Rank heroism is limited to the first half of life, for C. G. Jung it involves the second half.[2] For Freud and Rank, heroism involves relations with parents and instincts. For Jung, heroism in even the first half involves, in addition, relations with the unconscious. Heroism here means separation not only from parents and anti-social instincts but even more from the unconscious: every child's managing to forge consciousness is for Jung a supremely heroic feat.

For Freud, the unconscious is the product of the repression of instincts. For Jung, it is inherited rather than created and includes far more than repressed instincts. Independence of the Jungian unconscious therefore means more than independence of instincts. It means the formation of consciousness, the object of which in the first half of life is the external world.

The goal of the uniquely Jungian second half of life is likewise consciousness, but now consciousness of the Jungian unconscious rather than of the external world. One must return to the unconscious, from which one has invariably become severed. But the aim is not thereby to sever one's ties to the external world. On the contrary, the aim is still to return to the external world. The ideal is a balance between consciousness of the external world and consciousness of the unconscious. The aim of the second half of life is to supplement, not abandon, the achievements of the first half.

Just as classic Freudian problems involve the failure to establish oneself externally, so distinctively Jungian problems involve the failure to re-establish oneself internally. Freudian problems stem from excessive attachment to the world of childhood. Jungian problems stem from excessive attachment to the world one enters upon breaking free of the childhood world: the external world. To be severed from the internal world is to feel empty and lost.

Jung himself allows for heroism in both halves of life, but Campbell does not (see Campbell 1972: 318–34). Just as Rank confines heroism to the first half of life, so Campbell restricts it to the second half. Rank's scheme begins with the hero's birth; Campbell's, with his adventure. Where Rank's scheme ends, Campbell's begins: with the adult hero ensconced at home. Rank's hero must be young enough for his father and in some cases even his grandfather still to be ruling. Campbell does not specify the age of his hero, but the hero must be no younger than the age at which Rank's hero myth therefore ends: young adulthood. He must, again, be in the second half of life. Campbell does acknowledge heroism in the first half of life and even cites Rank's monograph, but he demotes this youthful heroism to mere preparation for adult heroism. He calls it the "childhood of the human hero." Birth itself he dismisses as unheroic because it is not done consciously (see Campbell 1988b: 125).[3] At the same time Campbell is egregiously inconsistent: his first example of heroism is that of the young girl in "The Princess and the Frog."

Rank's hero must be the son of royal or at least distinguished parents. Campbell's need not be, though often he is. Campbell later allows for female heroes,[4] but in *Hero* he, like Rank, in effect limits himself to male ones. More accurately, his scheme necessitates male heroes, even though many of his examples, including that of the Princess, are female! For the middle stage of his three-stage hero's journey requires a male hero. Finally, Campbell's scheme, in which the hero ventures to a wholly different, unknown world, commits him to human heroes, even though many of his heroes are divine! Rank's pattern, by contrast, allows for divine as well as human heroes.

Where Rank's hero returns to his birthplace, Campbell's marches forth to a strange, new world, which he has never visited or even known existed: "destiny has summoned the hero and transferred his spiritual center of gravity from within the pale of his society to a zone unknown. This fateful region of both treasure and danger may be variously represented: as a distant land, a forest, a kingdom underground, beneath the waves, or above the sky, a secret island, lofty mountaintop, or profound dream state" (Campbell 1972: 58). This extraordinary world is the world of the gods, and the hero should hail from the human world precisely for the worlds to stand in contrast.

In this exotic, supernatural world the hero encounters above all a supreme female god and a supreme male god. The maternal goddess is loving and caring: "She is the paragon of all paragons of beauty, the reply to all desire, the bliss-bestowing goal of every hero's earthly and unearthly quest" (Campbell 1972: 110–11). By contrast, the male god is tyrannical and merciless—an "ogre" (Campbell 1972: 126). The hero has sex with the goddess and marries her. He then kills and eats the god. Yet with both, not just the goddess, he becomes mystically one and thereby becomes divine himself.

Where Rank's hero *returns* home to encounter his father and mother, Campbell's hero *leaves* home to encounter a male and a female god, who are neither his parents nor a couple. Yet the two heroes' encounters are remarkably akin: just as Rank's hero kills his father and, if usually only latently, marries his mother, so Campbell's hero, in reverse order, first marries the goddess and then kills the god.

The differences, however, are even more significant. Because the goddess is not the hero's mother, sex with her does not constitute incest. Moreover, the two not only marry but also become mystically one.

Despite appearances, the hero's relationship to the male god is for Campbell no less positive. Seemingly, the relationship is blatantly Oedipal. Campbell even cites Róheim's Freudian analysis of aboriginal myths and rituals of initiation, which evince the son's fear of castration by his father and the father's prior fear of death at the hands of his son:

> The native Australian mythologies teach that the first initiation rites were carried out in such a way that all the young men were killed. The ritual is thus ... a dramatized expression of the Oedipal [counter-] aggression [on the part] of the elder generation; and the circumcision, a mitigated castration. But the rites provide also for the cannibal, patricidal impulse of the younger, rising group of males. (Campbell 1972: 139)

Róheim, however, departs from a strictly Freudian interpretation. The sons seek not sex with their mothers but *reunion* with them. They seek to fulfill not their Oedipal desires but their even earlier, infantile ones—a booming echo of the post-Freudian Rank. Their fathers oppose those desires not because they want to keep their wives for themselves but because they want to break their sons' prenatal ties to their mothers. If the fathers try to break those ties by threatening their sons with castration, they also try to break the ties by offering themselves as substitutes for their wives. The fathers selflessly nourish their sons with their own blood, occasionally dying in the process.

Campbell adopts Róheim's more harmonious, non-Freudian interpretation of the clash between sons and fathers and carries it even further. Since Campbell's hero is in the second half of life, he is not, like Róheim's initiates, seeking separation from his mother—for Róheim, as for the renegade Rank, the central experience of life. He is seeking reintegration with her. Furthermore, he is seeking reintegration with his father as well. Indeed, he is not really fighting with his father over his mother. For again, the two gods are neither his parents nor a couple. The hero is seeking from the god the same love that he has just won from the goddess. To secure it he need not give up the goddess but need only trust in the god, who is symbolized by the father: "One must have a faith that the father is merciful, and then a reliance on that mercy" (Campbell 1972: 130). The father sacrifices himself to his son.

When Campbell writes that initiation rituals and myths "reveal the benign self-giving aspect of the *archetypal* father [italics added]," he is using the term in its Jungian sense (Campbell 1972: 139-40). For Freudians, gods symbolize parents. For Jungians, parents symbolize gods, who in turn symbolize father and mother archetypes, which are components of the hero's personality. The hero's relationship to these gods symbolizes not, as for Freud, Rank, and Róheim, a son's relationship to other persons—his parents—but the relationship of one side of a male's personality—his ego—to another side—his unconscious. The father and the mother are but two of the archetypes of which the Jungian, or collective, unconscious is composed. Archetypes are unconscious not because they have been repressed but because they have never been conscious. For Jung and Campbell, myth originates and functions not, as for Freud and Rank, to satisfy neurotic urges that cannot be manifested openly but to express normal sides of the personality that have just not had a chance at realization.

By identifying himself with the hero of a myth, Rank's myth maker or reader vicariously lives out in his mind an adventure that, if ever directly fulfilled, would be acted out on his parents themselves. While also identifying himself with the hero of a myth, Campbell's myth maker or reader vicariously lives out in his mind an adventure that even when directly fulfilled would still be taking place in his mind. For parts of the mind are what he is really encountering.

Having managed to break free of the secure, everyday world and go off to a dangerous new one, Campbell's hero, to complete his journey, must in turn break free of the new world, in which he has by now become ensconced, and return to the everyday one. So enticing is the new world that leaving it proves harder than leaving home was. Circe, Calypso, the Sirens, and the Lotus Eaters thus tempt Odysseus with not just a comfortable, long life but a carefree, immortal one.

Though often misconstrued, Jung no less than Freud opposes a state of sheer unconsciousness. Both strive to make the unconscious conscious. While they differ over the origin of the unconscious and over its capacity to become conscious, the ideal for both remains consciousness. Jung opposes the rejection of ordinary, or ego, consciousness for unconsciousness as vigorously as he opposes the rejection of unconsciousness for ego consciousness. He seeks a balance between ego consciousness and the unconscious, between consciousness of the external world and consciousness of the unconscious. For Jung, the hero's failure to return to the everyday world would spell his failure to resist the allure of the unconscious.

By contrast to Jung, Campbell seeks pure unconsciousness. Campbell's hero never returns to the everyday world. He surrenders to the unconscious. Yet Campbell himself demands the hero's return to the everyday world. How, then, can his hero really be spurning it? The answer is that the world to which Campbell's hero returns is not really the everyday world. It is the strange, new world, which turns out to pervade the everyday one. No separate everyday world exists. The everyday world and the new world are really one:

> The two worlds, the divine [i.e., new] and the human [i.e. everyday], can be pictured only as distinct from each other—different as life and death, as day and night.... Nevertheless ... the two kingdoms are actually one.... The values and distinctions that in normal life seem important disappear with the terrifying assimilation of [what is now] the self into what formerly was [to the ego] only otherness. (Campbell 1972: 217)

If only the hero had known, he need never have left home after all: "Hence separateness, withdrawal, is no longer necessary. Wherever the hero may wander, whatever he may do, he is ever in the presence of his own essence—for he has the perfected eye to see. There is no separateness" (Campbell 1972: 386). Still, the hero needed to undertake the journey to learn this.

To say that the everyday world and the new world are one is to say that no distinctive everyday world exists. Campbell thus dismisses as illusory the "values and distinctions" of the everyday world. But if no everyday world exists, then the hero's apparent return to it is a sham. And if no everyday world exists, then the ego, which provides consciousness of it, is itself a sham as well.

By contrast to Campbell, Jung never denies the existence of the everyday world and therefore of the ego. He rejects the everyday world, the object of ego consciousness, as the *sole* reality, not as *a* reality. While he seeks to integrate the everyday world with the new one, ego consciousness with the unconscious, he denies that it is possible to fuse them, at least without thereby dissolving both the everyday world and the ego itself.

Campbell's hero returns home not only because he finds the new world back home but also because he wants selflessly to save others: "The full round, the norm of the monomyth, requires that the hero shall now begin the labor of bringing the runes of wisdom, the Golden Fleece, or his sleeping princess, back into the kingdom of humanity, where the boon may redound to the renewing of the community, the nation, the planet, or the ten thousand worlds" (Campbell 1972: 193). But if the hero's return is selfless, then the everyday world to which he is returning is inferior to the new one, if not illusory. Indeed, the hero is returning only to apprise others of the fact: whatever the literal "boon," the symbolic one is knowledge, knowledge of the real status of the everyday world. Campbell's chief heroes consequently include the selfless Buddha, Moses, Aeneas, and Jesus.

Furthermore, the journey, once psychologized, is a personal one. It is from one part of the hero's mind to another. Others are not involved. Nobody else is being saved.

Campbell's characterization of the hero's return as triumphant reveals another fundamental departure from Jung: Campbell's hero ironically remains bound to the *first* half of life. Even though Campbell's hero has undeniably already accomplished the goals of the first half of life, truly reencounters the unconscious, must even guard against succumbing to it, and returns home transformed, he also returns *triumphant*. He thinks he has tamed the unconscious and can do the same for others.

Jung would say that Campbell's hero has in fact missed the power and depth of the unconscious. A Jungian hero would return home humbled rather than elevated, wary rather than brash, the saved rather than the savior. A Jungian hero would seek only a *modus vivendi* with the unconscious, not control over it. Campbell's hero is, in Jungian lingo, merely an "inflated" ego. Only Jung's is a full-fledged "self." If on the one hand Campbell ventures well beyond Jung in seeing heroism as the transcendence of the ego in mystical oneness with the unconscious, on the other hand he stops far short of Jung in simultaneously seeing heroism as the ego's mastery over the unconscious. Only because Campbell assumes that the ego stays in control can he, without trepidation, espouse the fusion of the ego with the unconscious. Jung would deny that in a deeper encounter with the unconscious the ego either could or should remain in control. To underscore the difference between Campbell's and Jung's notions of heroism, Jungian analyst Joseph Henderson goes as far as to restrict heroism per se to Campbell's variety and to relabel the Jungian ideal "initiation" (see Henderson 1967: 101–102, 134–35, 151–52, 159, 178–80).[5]

Chapter 7

Are There Modern Myths for Eliade?

In all his writings Mircea Eliade strives to show that religiosity is innate to human beings and, more, that it is as insatiable a drive as hunger. Rather than arguing the case philosophically, by analyzing the concept of human nature or of religion, Eliade argues it empirically, by amassing evidence of the universality of religion. For him, the two main expressions of religion are myths and rituals.

Eliade's greatest challenge is to demonstrate the presence of religion among modern Westerners, who for him are almost by definition professed nonbelievers.[1] To be able to show that even they, who spurn religion, still evince it would surely be a strong, whether or not clinching, argument for its ineluctability. How convincing is Eliade's argument that moderns harbor myths?

Traditional Myths

According to Eliade, in "primitive" and "archaic" societies myth is "the very foundation of social life and culture" (Eliade 1967: 23). Operating at its fullest, myth here fulfills several functions. First, it explains the origin of present-day phenomena, tracing them back to the primordial deeds of gods:

> Myth narrates a sacred history; it relates an event that took place in primordial Time, the fabled time of the "beginnings." In other words, myths tell how, through the deeds of Supernatural Beings, a reality came into existence, be it the whole of reality, the Cosmos, or only a fragment of reality—an island, a species of plant, a particular kind of human behavior, an institution. Myth, then, is always an account of a "creation": it relates how something was produced, began to *be*. (Eliade 1975: 5–6)

Second, myth provides models for behavior. The deeds of gods recounted in myth serve as norms to be imitated: "the myth becomes exemplary, and consequently repeatable, for it serves as a model, and by the same token as a justification, for all human actions" (Eliade 1967: 23).

Third, either the outright imitation of a primordial deed or the sheer recounting of it takes one out of present time and, as if on a magic carpet, takes one back to the time of the deed itself: "In imitating the exemplary acts of a god or of a mythic hero, or simply by recounting their adventures, the man of an archaic society detaches himself from profane time and magically re-enters the Great Time, the sacred time" (Eliade 1967: 23). The payoff is less escapism than rejuvenation: "What is involved is, in short, a return to the original time, the therapeutic purpose of which is to begin life once again, a symbolic rebirth" (Eliade 1959a: 82). That rejuvenation comes from returning to the time when, it is believed, the gods were close at hand. The rejuvenation comes not from becoming divine oneself—Eliade stresses the hiatus between the human and the divine, between the profane and the sacred—but from brushing up against divinity. Humans are rejuvenated by *encountering* the sacred, not by *becoming* sacred. What Eliade writes of creation myths, which for him are the fundamental myths, applies to other myths as well: "*In illo tempore* the gods had displayed their greatest powers. The cosmogony is the supreme divine manifestation, the paradigmatic act of strength, superabundance, and creativity. Religious man thirsts for the real. By every means at his disposal, he seeks to reside at the very source of primordial reality, when the world was *in statu nascendi*" (Eliade 1959a: 80).

Modern Myths

If moderns have myths, as Eliade contends, then surely those myths must fulfill the same three functions as traditional myths.[2] Indeed, Eliade virtually determines the existence of myths by their efficacy. By modern myths he means both new, distinctively modern myths and, even more, earlier myths that continue to exist in modernity. Most often, he means a combination of the two: distinctively modern *versions* of older, "archetypal" myths. To use one of his favorite examples, Marxism represents an updated version of the traditional mythic motifs of an original golden age, a fall, a battle between good and evil forces, the triumph of good, and the restoration of the golden age:

> For whatever we may think of the scientific claims of Marx, it is clear that the author of the *Communist Manifesto* takes up and carries on one of the great eschatological myths of the Middle Eastern and Mediterranean

world, namely: the redemptive part to be played by the Just (the "elect", the "anointed", the "innocent", the "missioners", in our own days by the proletariat), whose sufferings are invoked to change the ontological status of the world. In fact, Marx's classless society, and the consequent disappearance of all historical tensions, find their most exact precedent in the myth of the Golden Age which, according to a number of traditions, lies at the beginning and the end of History. Marx has enriched this venerable myth with a truly messianic Judaeo-Christian ideology; on the one hand, by the prophetic and soteriological function he ascribes to the proletariat; and, on the other, by the final struggle between Good and Evil, which may well be compared with the apocalyptic conflict between Christ and Antichrist, ending in the decisive victory of the former. (Eliade 1967: 25–26)

Similarly, modern literature evinces perennial mythic motifs in contemporary guise:

> The successive stages of myth, legend, epic and modern literature have often been pointed out and need not detain us here. Let us merely recall the fact that the mythical archetypes survive to some degree in the great modern novels. The difficulties and trials that the novelist's hero has to pass through are prefigured in the adventures of the mythic Heroes. It has been possible also to show how the mythic themes of the primordial waters, of the isles of Paradise, of the quest of the Holy Grail, of heroic and mystical initiation, etc., still dominate modern European literature. Quite recently we have seen, in surrealism, a prodigious outburst of mythical themes and primordial symbols. As for the literature of the bookstalls, its mythological character is obvious. Every popular novel has to present the exemplary struggle between Good and Evil, the hero and the villain (modern incarnation of the Demon), and repeat one of those universal motives [sic] of folklore, the persecuted young woman, salvation by love, the unknown protector, etc. Even detective novels, as Roger Caillois has so well demonstrated, are full of mythological themes. (Eliade 1967: 35)

Eliade finds mythic themes everywhere in modern culture, even if he sometimes takes rituals as myths (see Eliade 1967: 28). The question is whether the themes amount to myths: whether they constitute stories, and stories that fulfill Eliade's three mythic functions. Eliade tries to fend off the charge that would-be modern myths fall short by characterizing them as "private," "camouflaged," and "degenerated." But do these diminished cases still qualify as myths?

Private Myths

Eliade regularly compares psychoanalysis with religion. Both activities seek to reconnect human beings to a reality from which they have become severed:

> Two of Freud's ideas are relevant to our subject: (1) the bliss of the "origin" and "beginnings" of the human being, and (2) the idea that through memory, or by a "going back," one can relive certain traumatic incidents of early childhood. The bliss of the "origin" is, we have seen, a quite frequent theme in the archaic religions; it is attested in India, Iran, Greece, and in Judaeo-Christianity. (Eliade 1975: 78)

Psychoanalysis as well as religion employs myth as a vehicle for returning to the past. But psychoanalytic myths—"dreams, reveries, fantasies, and so forth"—are merely "private mythologies." They "never rise to the ontological status of myths, precisely because they are not experienced by the whole man and therefore do not transform a particular situation into a situation that is paradigmatic" (Eliade 1975: 211). Private myths help solve personal problems, but they do not link their creators or users to anything cosmic. They open up human beings to the unconscious but not, like traditional myths, to the sacred: "the nonreligious man of modern societies is still nourished and aided by the activity of his unconscious, yet without thereby attaining to a properly religious experience and vision of the world. The unconscious offers him solutions for the difficulties of his own life, and in this way plays the role of religion" (Eliade 1959a: 212).

By Eliade's three criteria, or functions, of myth, private myths fail altogether. First, they do not explain anything. Dreams and fantasies may *express* unconscious wishes, but they do not account for them. Psychoanalytic *theory* accounts for the wishes, but dreams and fantasies are not themselves the explanation. The wishes expressed by dreams and fantasies may explain adult feelings and actions, and explain them as the legacy of childhood, but again the explanation is not provided by dreams and fantasies themselves, which do not even take coherent form.

Second, dreams and fantasies, as the repositories for Freud of antisocial impulses, hardly provide models for behavior. Moreover, since private myths are autobiographical, the model offered would be of only oneself!

Third and most important, while private myths may well carry one back to the character-forming, precedent-setting time of childhood, no gods are to be found in this private primordial time. In childhood, parents do take on the role of gods, but parents are in fact mere human beings—one of the lessons to be learned in analysis. It might be argued that private myths do put subjects in touch with the psychological counterpart to the sacred—the unconscious—but the payoff is still merely psychological: one encounters not god but only another side of oneself.

Jungian psychology would here work better for Eliade than Freudian since Jung both characterizes the unconscious as god-like and makes the unconscious largely independent of consciousness. Even so, the payoff for Jung no less than for Freud is psychological and not religious: one encounters a god-like side of oneself, not a god independent of oneself. Eliade recognizes Jung's psychological reductionism and consequently distances himself from Jung. Only the later Jungian concept of synchronicity, which Eliade never mentions, reconnects humans to the world, and even that world remains profane. In fact, synchronicity, as the coincidence of inner reality with outer, presupposes the differentiation of the two, and that differentiation presupposes the withdrawal of the divinity projected onto outer reality.

Camouflaged Myths

Eliade by no means limits modern myths to private ones, which he recognizes barely qualify as myths. He gives more weight to public myths. He calls them "camouflaged" because they go unrecognized as myths by their adherents. They are to be found above all in plays, films, and books:

> A whole volume could well be written on the myths of modern man, on the mythologies camouflaged in the plays that he enjoys, in the books that he reads. The cinema, that "dream factory," takes over and employs countless mythical motifs—the fight between hero and monster, initiatory combats and ordeals, paradigmatic figures and images (the maiden, the hero, the paradisal landscape, hell, and so on). Even reading includes a mythological function ... because, through reading, the modern man succeeds in obtaining an escape through time comparable to the "emergence from time" effected by myths. Whether modern man "kills" time with a detective story or enters such a foreign temporal universe as is represented by any novel, reading projects him out of his personal duration and incorporates him into other rhythms, makes him live in another "history." (Eliade 1959a: 205)

Eliade is labeling "mythic" two elements in plays, movies, and books: superhuman figures, and escape to another time and place. Myths here are public because they are shared. They are camouflaged because theatergoers, movie fans, and readers, as moderns, miss the religious nature of the themes: "The majority of the irreligious still behave religiously, even though they are not aware of the fact. We refer not only to the modern man's many 'superstitions' and 'tabus,' all of them magico-religious in structure. But the modern man who feels and claims that he is nonreligious still retains a large stock of camouflaged myths and degenerated rituals" (Eliade 1959a: 204–205).

What, however, is religious about these camouflaged myths? Are the figures in them gods? The figures in, say, science fiction may be supernatural, but surely the characters in most modern plays, movies, and books are not. Most are merely human, even all too human. Even if some human heroes veer to the superhuman—for example, Rambo—most do not.

The divinity of the characters aside, do the stories in modern drama, film, and literature function as myths? First, do they trace the establishment long ago of a natural or social phenomenon of any kind that continues to exist today? Certainly, historical plays, movies, and books often describe the establishment of enduring social institutions such as nations, forms of government, ideologies, occupations, laws, and customs. But clearly many plays, movies, and books do not. Most take place in the present or even in the future. And even those that take place in the past by no means always involve the establishment of any phenomenon.

Second, do the characters in modern plays, movies, and books serve as models for others? Some may, but surely many modern protagonists are anti-heroes rather than heroes. Many live on the margins of society. Many reject society rather than seek to alter it.

Third and last, does the modern spectator or reader travel to the time and place of the story? It may be true that stories work only when one gets lost in them, forgetting where one is and getting caught up in the events described. Doubtless the emotions that stories elicit—fear, pity, admiration, love—require absorption in the lives of the characters, even identification with the characters. A horror movie works only when the audience as well as the victims on the screen is scared, only when the audience imagines itself to be part of the action. Still, the spectator or reader is scarcely carried away for more than the duration of the story. When it is over, the emotion stirred may linger, but only as a memory. Reality takes over. Few think that they have *really* been carried to the time and place of the plot. They only feel *as if* they have been.

Those who continue to consider the story real are considered crazy. They have confused fiction with reality. By no coincidence it is nowadays a commonplace to ask whether children who harm, even kill, others have taken their cues from movies. The contrast between impressionable children and detached adults reinforces the common assumption that movies are not the real world. The saddest lesson learned by the boy in *Cinema Paradiso* is that movies are no guide to the real world. Indeed, movies are often seen more as sheer escapism than as a perspective on reality. A committed fan may see the same movie again and again, but ordinarily the fan still distinguishes the movie from reality. The fan may *wish* reality were like the movie, but ordinarily the fan manages to differentiate the two.

Finally, what payoff would a fan derive from somehow managing to enter the world of the movie, play, or book? Eliade insists that immersion in the time of myths provides rejuvenation and not mere escapism. But how many filmgoers, theatergoers, or readers feel permanently rejuvenated after their experiences? Are their lives transformed?

Far closer to gods are not the characters in movies but the actors. Movie stars are not merely revered but worshiped. Even more than celebrities from other walks of life, movie stars are associated with the traditional characteristics of gods: they are bigger, handsomer, and richer than ordinary folk. After all, they are seen writ large on the screen, and with physical flaws and limitations erased. Thus it comes as a shock to fans to learn that "in reality" Mel Gibson and Tom Cruise are relatively short. Movie stars are free of the constraints that bind the rest of us, so that we are disconcerted to discover that even they cannot always get away with, for example, drug or spousal abuse. At the same time everyone wants to be a movie star, and the behavior of stars influences others. Like gods, movie stars are inaccessible, off screen as well as on, and if one ever does get near them, the thrill is simply to touch them, to brush up against them. Above all, movie stars, like gods and unlike other kinds of celebrities, are immortal: they live on in their movies.

Unfortunately, movie stars are not usually linked to myths—one reason perhaps that Eliade ignores them. Stars are not usually credited with establishing phenomena, save for the most fleeting of trends. Furthermore, stars live in the present, not in the past. Some fans may think that today's stars are no match for those of yesteryear, but any precedent that present-day stars set would not quite hark back to primordial time. Consequently, getting close to the stars does not require going back in time. Indeed, the divide between ordinary folks and movie stars is more spatial than temporal, and our connection to stars involves more rituals than myths. We seek out the places where they live—for example, maps and tours of stars' homes—more than any precedents that they have forged. In short, movie stars do not accord with Eliade's claim of modern myths.

For some theorists of myth—notably, E. B. Tylor and J. G. Frazer—myth is a wholly primitive or at least pre-modern phenomenon, and "modern myth" is an oxymoron. For other theorists, including Jung and Campbell as well as Eliade, myth is eternal. Yet Eliade's claim that moderns have myths is less convincing than Jung's or Campbell's. Where they allow for fully secular myths, in which case modern adherents need not be religious to employ them, Eliade insists that seemingly secular myths are really religious, in which case modern adherents must themselves be religious to use them. Where Jung and Campbell read myth symbolically and can thereby interpret it in ways that are palatable to moderns, Eliade reads myth literally and is thereby stuck with the incredulity that accompanies many modern myths—for example, that of Superman, to note one of his favorites.

Jung and Campbell take myth to be an expression of the human mind, in which case both the function and the subject matter of myth run askew to those of science. Eliade takes myth to be foremost an explanation of the physical world, in which case it clashes with natural science, which Eliade no less than Jung and Campbell equates with modernity. Even as an explanation of the social world, which Eliade allows for, myth still clashes with social science. Above all, where Jung and Campbell deem secular myths, and especially for Jung private myths, the equal in power to religious ones, Eliade deems or must deem seemingly secular myths hapless inferiors to overtly religious ones. He thereby faces a key dilemma that Jung and Campbell avoid: to be acceptable to moderns, myths must be secular, yet to function as myths, they must be religious. Failing to overcome this dilemma, Eliade fails to show that modern myths exist.

Chapter 8

Eliade on Myth and Science

Mircea Eliade is a typical, if also would-be atypical, twentieth-century theorist of myth. In contrast to nineteenth-century theorists, who set myth against science, Eliade, like other twentieth-century theorists, sought to reconcile myth with science. He maintained that moderns can consistently have both. After summarizing the nineteenth-century approach to myth, I will turn to the twentieth-century one. I will compare Bronislaw Malinowski's position with Eliade's, on which I will then concentrate. Whether Eliade, like Malinowski, succeeds in reconciling myth with science is the main issue I will consider.

Myth and Science

The challenge to myth may be almost as old as myth itself. In ancient Greece the main challenge was on moral grounds. Plato rejected the myths of Homeric gods because those gods, rather than being models for humans, behaved shamefully. In the *Timaeus* and other works Plato created his own myths. Alternatively, the Stoics reinterpreted popular myths as moral and metaphysical allegories.

In modern times the main modern challenge to myth has been on intellectual grounds. Myth, it has been asserted, is incompatible with natural science as an explanation of the physical world. Since modernity is taken to be almost identical with science, the question is whether myth is compatible with science. The question is not whether science, which is the given, is compatible with myth.

Science is assumed to do so well what myth, taken to have existed from ancient times, does: explain the origin and operation of the physical world. Where myth attributes events in the world to the decisions of gods, science ascribes events to impersonal, mechanical processes. To accept the scientific explanation of the world is automatically to reject the mythic one. The two explanations are assumed to be incompatible.

The most facile response to the gauntlet thrown down by science has been to ignore science. An only slightly less facile response has been to pronounce science itself mythic. A more credible response has accepted science as the reigning explanation of the world and has then either "surrendered" or "regrouped." Surrendering means simply replacing myth with science. Regrouping means recharacterizing myth as compatible with science.

The nineteenth-century response to myth, exemplified by the pioneering anthropologists E. B. Tylor and J. G. Frazer, was that of surrendering. The twentieth-century response, with far more exemplars, was that of regrouping, which itself took various forms. One form was to recharacterize the *subject matter* of myth. Now myth was no longer about the physical world. It was instead about the social world, about human nature, or about the experience of living in the physical world, which was different from being about the physical world itself. The exemplars of this form of regrouping were at once existentialists—Rudolf Bultmann, Hans Jonas, and Albert Camus—and psychologists—Sigmund Freud and C. G. Jung.

A second form of regrouping was to recharacterize the *function* of myth. No longer serving to explain—or, for Frazer, also to control—the physical world, myth now served to do almost anything else. Myth could comfort, could command, could evaluate, or could justify. The function now served reflected the subject matter. The subject matter could now be the social world, though it could also remain the physical world—the physical world itself and not merely the experience of the physical world. For example, a myth about mortality could serve to justify it. A myth about the hierarchy in society could serve to command acceptance of that hierarchy. The exemplars of this approach were the anthropologist Bronislaw Malinowski and the historian of religions Mircea Eliade, with Freud and Jung also altering the function, not just the subject matter, of myth.

The recharacterization of the subject matter of myth often involved the translation of myth from a literal reading—the reading assumed by both Tylor and, with some qualification, Frazer—into a symbolic one. A myth about Zeus was now taken to be a myth about a king, a father, the father archetype, or thunder itself. The recharacterization of the function of myth did not always require any translation, so that myth was often still read literally.

Nineteenth-century Theories of Myth: Tylor and Frazer

The leading exponents of the nineteenth-century view of myth were Tylor, whose main work, *Primitive Culture*, was published in 1871, and Frazer, whose key work, *The Golden Bough*, was first published in 1890. For Tylor, myth provides knowledge of the world as an end in itself. For Frazer, the knowledge that myth provides is a means to controlling the world, above all to secure food. For both Tylor and Frazer, the events explained or effected by myth are physical—either ones in the external world, such as rainfall and death, or ones in the human world, such as reproduction and death. Myth is not about social events, such as marriage and war. Myth is the primitive counterpart to natural, not social, science. It is the counterpart to biology, chemistry, or physics rather than to sociology, anthropology, psychology, or economics. For Tylor, myth is the exact counterpart to scientific theory. For Frazer, myth is the exact counterpart to applied science.

Myth, which is part of religion, attributes rain to either a decision by a god (Tylor) or the physical state of a god (Frazer). For Tylor, rain falls because a god decides to send it, and the reason can be anything. For Frazer, rain falls because a god either urinates or is incontinent. In science rain falls because of impersonal, meteorological processes.

For Tylor and Frazer, mythic and scientific explanations are incompatible because both are direct. In myth gods operate not behind or through impersonal forces but in place of them. God does not set meteorological processes in motion but instead likely dumps accumulated buckets of water on a designated spot below. For Tylor and Frazer alike, one therefore cannot stack the mythic explanation atop the scientific explanation, crediting science with the direct explanation and crediting myth with the indirect explanation. Rather, one must choose between them. Because moderns by definition have science, the choice has already been made. They must give up myth, which is not merely outdated but outright false. Moderns who still cling to myth have failed either to recognize or to concede the incompatibility of it with science.

Twentieth-century Theories of Myth: Malinowski and Eliade

In the twentieth century myth was reconciled with science. Moderns, while still defined as scientific, could now retain myth. Tylor's and Frazer's theories were spurned on many grounds: for ignoring myths about other than the physical world, for precluding modern myths, for subsuming myth under religion and thereby precluding secular myths, for deeming the function of myth scientific-like, and for deeming myth false. Even a myth in which a god sends rain was seen as about other than rain.

Yet twentieth-century theorists did not try to reconcile myth with science by challenging science. They did not take any of the easy steps: "relativizing" science, "sociologizing" science, making science "masculine," or making science "mythic." No less than their nineteenth-century predecessors did they accept science as the prevailing explanation of the physical world. Rather, they recharacterized *myth* as other than a literal explanation of the physical world. Myth was, then, made compatible with science, but only by removing myth from competition with science.

To be sure, for both Malinowski (see his "Magic, Science and Religion" [1954a] and "Myth in Primitive Psychology" [1954b]) and Eliade (see his 1959a and 1975), myth is an explanation in part, but the explanation is only a means to a nonscientific end rather than the end itself. For Malinowski, that end is to reconcile humans to disease, death, and other brute aspects of the physical world. For Eliade, the end is to carry humans back to the time of the myth, which is always the past, in order to encounter god. Myth is like a magic carpet, but a carpet that goes in only one direction.

For both Malinowski and Eliade, myth is about social phenomena—customs, laws, and institutions—as well as about physical ones. For Malinowski, myths about social phenomena serve to reconcile members to impositions that they might otherwise reject, such as class division. The beneficiary is society, not the individual. For Eliade, myths about social phenomena serve the same magic carpet-like function as myths about physical ones. The beneficiary is the individual.

Insofar as myth for Malinowski deals with the social world, it turns its back on the physical world. But even when myth deals with the physical world, its connection to that world is limited and so still evinces the twentieth-century approach to myth. Myth may explain how flooding arose—a god or a human brought it about—but science, not myth, explains why flooding occurs whenever it does. And science, not myth, says what, if anything, to do about it. Myth assumes that nothing can be done about it and espouses resigned acceptance of a largely uncontrollable world.

Unlike Tylor and Frazer, Malinowski maintains that primitive peoples, not just moderns, have science as well as myth, however rudimentary their science is. Myth and science are compatible because their functions are distinct. But Malinowski never tries to reconcile the mythic explanation of the origin of physical phenomena like flooding with the scientific explanation of the recurrence of the phenomena. He never ventures beyond function to content. He simply assumes that because the functions of myth and science for primitive peoples are distinct, the contents must be compatible. (He also distinguishes religion from both myth and science on the same grounds: function.) Whether for him moderns even have myth he never makes clear. It may be that they have ideology in place of social myths.

By contrast to Malinowski, Eliade, like Tylor and Frazer, assumes that primitive peoples have just myth and not also science, so that the issue of the compatibility of myth with primitive science does not arise. But unlike Malinowski, Tylor, and Frazer alike, Eliade argues that moderns have myth as well as science. Whether he, unlike Malinowski, actually tries to reconcile myths of the physical world with science, we will see. At the least, he appeals to the fact of the co-existence of myth and science for moderns to argue that the two must be compatible, just as Malinowski does for "primitives." At the same time he concentrates on distinctively modern myths, which are of social rather than physical phenomena. Modern myths attribute events not to gods but to merely exceptional human beings—to culture heroes. For Malinowski, even the creation of physical events, such as mortality, can be the work of humans, and those humans need hardly be heroic. Eliade ventures far beyond Malinowski, not to say Tylor and Frazer, in making myth universal and not, as presumably for Malinowski, merely primitive.

Neither Malinowski nor Eliade challenges Frazer's and especially Tylor's literal reading of myth. Whatever their break with Tylor and Frazer on the function and subject matter of myth, they continue to read myth literally. By contrast, fellow twentieth-century theorists Bultmann, Jonas, and Camus reject a literal reading of myth. For them, myth read literally means Tylor's and Frazer's nineteenth-century approach. They insist that the key to understanding myth is to read it symbolically, which thereby removes it from competition with science. By contrast, Malinowski and Eliade reconcile myth with science by recharacterizing the function of myth.

Eliade

Eliade does not reject the explanatory function of myth. For him, as for Tylor, myth serves to explain how gods created and control the world:

> Myth narrates a sacred history; it relates an event that took place in pri-
> mordial Time, the fabled time of the "beginnings." In other words, myth
> tells how, through the deeds of Supernatural Beings, a reality came into
> existence, be it the whole of reality, the Cosmos, or only a fragment of
> reality—an island, a species of plant, a particular kind of human behav-
> ior, an institution. (Eliade 1975: 5–6)

> Myths, that is, narrate not only the origin of the World, of animals, of
> plants, and of man, but also all the primordial events in consequence
> of which man became what he is today—mortal, sexed, organized in a
> society, obliged to work in order to live, and working in accordance with
> certain rules. (Eliade 1975: 11)

Clearly, myth is about more than the physical world. Seemingly, it can
be about anything in the world and so far exceeds the scope of myth for
nineteenth-century theorists.

Most other twentieth-century theorists—Freud, Jung, Bultmann,
Jonas, and Camus—reconcile myth with science by cutting off myth from
the physical world. They substitute the human mind, society, or the experience of the physical world as the subject matter of myth. Eliade does
not. For him, as also for Malinowski, the physical world remains a subject
matter of myth, and any other subject matter supplements, not replaces,
it. Eliade is thus bolder than most of his fellow twentieth-century theorists because he refuses to concede the physical world to science.
Like Malinowski, he refuses to concede the physical world to moderns
exclusively.

Eliade meets the challenge of science by, like Malinowski, proposing
functions served by myth in addition to the explanatory one. Myth for
Eliade justifies as well as explains phenomena, and does so in the same
way that it does for Malinowski. Myth does not pronounce phenomena
good. It pronounces them inevitable and in that restricted sense seeks
to reconcile humanity to them. For example, myth justifies death less
by postulating an afterlife, though Eliade notes myths that do, than by
rooting death in an event in primordial time, when the world was still
malleable but when any action made permanent whatever it effected. In
primordial, or mythic, time the cosmic clay was soft. By subsequent, historical, ordinary time it had hardened. According to myth, human beings
die because "a mythical Ancestor stupidly lost immortality, or because
a Supernatural Being decided to deprive him of it, or because a certain
mythical event left him endowed at once with sexuality and mortality,
and so on" (Eliade 1975: 92). Myth makes the present less arbitrary and

therefore more tolerable by locating its origin in the hoary past, just as for Malinowski.

But Eliade goes beyond Malinowski to maintain that myth does more than explain and justify. It also regenerates. To hear, to read, and especially to reenact a myth is magically to return to the time when the myth took place, the time of the origin of whatever phenomenon it explains and justifies: "But since ritual recitation of the cosmogonic myth implies reactualization of that primordial event, it follows that he for whom it is recited is magically projected *in illo tempore*, into the 'beginning of the World'; he becomes contemporary with the cosmogony" (Eliade 1959a: 82).

In returning one to primordial time, myth reunites one with the gods, who were nearest just after creation, as the biblical case of "the Lord God['s] walking in the garden in the cool of the day" typifies (Genesis 3:8). That "reunion" reverses the post-lapsarian separation from the gods, a separation that is equivalent to the fall, and renews one spiritually: "What is involved is, in short, a return to the original time, the therapeutic purpose of which is to begin life once again, a symbolic rebirth" (Eliade 1959a: 82).

The American bank robber Willie Sutton, continually caught and imprisoned, was asked why he continued to rob banks. His reply: because that's where the money is. For Eliade, humans go back in time because that's where the gods are. They enlist myth, which for Eliade is always about the origin of something in the past, to do so. The ultimate payoff is experiential: encountering divinity. The ultimate payoff of ritual is the same, but ritual involves space rather than time.

Clearly, science offers no regenerative or even justificatory function. Science merely explains. Myth can do things that science cannot, in which case science does not compete with myth, at least not altogether.

But Eliade argues more. For him, myth not only serves functions that transcend the function served by science but also serves them for moderns as well as for "primitives." Moderns for Eliade fancy themselves scrupulously rational, intellectual, unsentimental, and forward-looking—in short, scientific. Nothing could veer farther from their collective self-image than adherence to myth, which they dismiss as egregiously backward and irrational. Yet even they, according to Eliade, cannot dispense with myth:

> A whole volume could well be written on the myths of modern man, on the mythologies camouflaged in the plays that he enjoys, in the books that he reads. The cinema, that "dream factory," takes over and employs countless mythical motifs—the fight between hero and monster,

initiatory combats and ordeals, paradigmatic figures and images (the maiden, the hero, the paradisal landscape, hell, and so on). Even reading includes a mythological function … because, through reading, the modern man succeeds in obtaining an "escape from time" comparable to the "emergence from time" effected by myths. Whether modern man "kills" time with a detective story or enters such a foreign temporal universe as is represented by any novel, reading projects him out of his personal duration and incorporates him into other rhythms, makes him live in another "history." (Eliade 1959a: 205)[1]

Plays, movies, and books are the genres that express modern myths because they reveal the existence of another world alongside the everyday one—a world of extraordinary figures and events akin to those found in traditional myths, which are myths about gods. The figures in modern myths are, strictly, human, but they have one or more god-like qualities. They are therefore akin to gods. Eliade, zealous to maintain that all humans are religious, wants to make the humans in modern myths god-like in order to make modern myths religious.

The difference for sophisticated theologians between humans and God is one of kind. For example, God has no body. But the popular difference between humans and gods is one of degree: a god's body is bigger. Not only "pagan" gods but also the biblical God has a body. Otherwise, to cite a single instance, Moses at the burning bush (Exodus 3) would not have to look away to avoid seeing God and would not have to stop at the perimeter to avoid stepping on the ground where God has walked. Myths evince the popular, not the sophisticated, characterization of God.

Furthermore, the actions of those figures account for the present state of the everyday world. For example, in the movie *Braveheart*, if not only in the movie, William Wallace is celebrated as the founding father of Scotland, even if he did not live to see an independent nation. In the movie, as in legend, Wallace is credited with almost superhuman charisma, military prowess, and courage. In one scene in the movie several members of his army are discussing their leader when he passes by. When one of the soldiers says that there goes Wallace, another, who has never seen him close up, denies that that person can be he. Why? Because that person is not tall enough.

Most of all, moderns get so absorbed in plays, movies, and books that they imagine themselves to be back in the world before their eyes. Spectators and readers get "lost" in a play, a movie, or a book. They get "carried away." They travel from present, profane time back to the sacred time of the story. They do not identify themselves with the characters of the stories. They do not deify themselves. They retain the divide between heroes and ordinary persons—a divide more rigid than that between heroes and gods. They imagine themselves not to be William Wallace but simply to be in his presence. They do not think that they can change history. They yearn only to witness it. They fantasize about being in the presence of Wallace. This is what Eliade means by an encounter with god.

It is celebrities in all walks of life who are the heroes of modern myths, though indisputably only a few of them are credited with establishing any custom, law, or institution. The most elevated of celebrities are Hollywood stars, and it is they who loom closest to gods. On screen, stars, like gods, are greater than ordinary folks in degree. To begin with, they are gargantuan in size. Merely human virtues are magnified into superhuman ones: bravery becomes fearlessness, kindliness becomes saintliness, beauty becomes incandescence, strength becomes omnipotence, wisdom becomes omniscience.

But there are also differences of kind. Like gods, film stars are rarely seen in person. When beheld on screen, film stars, like gods, can do anything and can take on disguises—their roles. And of course, stars are immortalized in their films. In all of these ways film stars far surpass sport and rock celebrities, whose prime appearances are live and are thereby limited to what talent and special effects can concoct. Compare Michael Jackson's moonwalk with the mobility of Spider-Man.

Going to the movies is going to a sacred space. The cinema blocks out the outside world and substitutes a world of its own. The more effective the movie, the more the audience forgets where it is and finds itself in the time and place of the movie. Things are permitted in movies that never happen in the proverbial "real world." In the movies, as in heaven, anything is possible. The phrase "only in the movies" is telling. To go to the movies is to suspend disbelief. It is to agree to "play along." The ultimate payoff of moviegoing is encountering the actors themselves, even if only on the screen. Going to the movies is like going to church—to a set-off, self-contained place where god is likeliest to be found.

If, argues Eliade, even moderns, who are self-professed scientific atheists, actually have their own myths, then science does not preclude myth. Therefore myth and science are compatible. Where for Malinowski myth and primitive science are compatible, for Eliade myth and modern science are.

Questions

However appealing, Eliade's dual counterargument to Tylor and Frazer—that myth serves functions that science cannot duplicate and that even moderns cherish myth—is dubious. First, the nonexplanatory functions of myth depend on the explanatory one, as Eliade himself recognizes in always characterizing myth, as quoted, as at least an explanation: "In other words, myth tells how, through the deeds of Supernatural Beings, a reality came into existence." But then myth can serve its other functions only if it can fend off science in serving its explanatory function. How it can do so, Eliade never says.

Perhaps Eliade is assuming that the phenomena explained by modern myths are entirely social—for example, the origin of tools, marriage, government, and nationhood—and not at all natural—for example, the origin of the sun and the moon. But then his distinctiveness among fellow twentieth-century theorists dissolves. They too reconcile myth with science by removing myth from the physical world.

Furthermore, if not natural science, then social science seeks to account for social phenomena. Mythic explanations of customs, laws, and institutions attribute them to heroics rather than to economic, social, and political processes. Mythic explanations are of the "Great Man" variety, epitomized by Thomas Carlyle's *On Heroes, Hero-Worship and the Heroic in History* (1847).

It was the pioneering Victorian sociologist Herbert Spencer who offered the classic dismissal of this romantic brand of explanation. Rather than the cause of society, a great man is the product of society. In Spencer's famous summary phrase, "Before he [the great man] can re-make his society, his society must make him" (Spencer 1874: 35). The changes any great man makes are marginal and are merely the direct causes of change. The underlying causes are the ones that produced the great man himself: "So that all those changes of which he is the proximate initiator have their chief causes in the generations he descended from" (Spencer 1874: 35). Mocking Carlyle, Spencer declares that if you wish to understand social change, "you will not do it though you should read yourself blind over the biographies of all the great rulers on record" (Spencer 1874: 37). Biographies are the myths of modern heroes.

Nothing has changed since Spencer's day. The social scientific position is still that individuals, however great, do not make history. Impersonal processes do, just as in natural science. In short, mythic explanations of even social phenomena seem at odds with science—here social science.

Second, modern myths do not always go backward in time. They may instead go forward, as in science fiction, or go sideways, such as to other cultures around the world. Even myths that do move backward by no means always go back to the occasion on which present-day customs, rules, or institutions were created. Of course, Eliade can reply that these kinds of "myths" thereby do not qualify as myths and so do not challenge his theory. But this reply would then make the theory nonfalsifiable.

Third, moderns travel back in time only in their imaginations, not in reality. In seeing a play or movie or reading a book about George Washington, Americans may feel *as if* they are present at the Revolution, and may especially feel so during celebrations of independence on July 4. But Americans hardly claim to be whisked back on a mythic time machine. Or if they do, it is only for the duration of the activity. Once the play, movie, or book is over, so is the myth. The experience of sacred time ceases abruptly. One may remember a stirring story long afterward, but as a memory or an inspiration only.

Above all, Eliade, like Malinowski, simply declares that myth is compatible with science without working out how. The science that, for Malinowski, "primitives" have is rudimentary, and there may be no primitive social science. The science that moderns have is far more developed, and there is also social science.

Eliade is so eager to show that moderns, despite themselves, harbor myth that he misses the burden of figuring out *how* moderns, whose culture is overwhelmingly scientific, can still have myth. For Tylor and Frazer, moderns who apparently have both have simply failed to recognize the clear-cut incompatibility of them. Surely Eliade does not want to leave the presence of myth alongside science as a contradiction. But then he must work out how a mythic explanation is consistent with a scientific one. He never does so. His overall claim that moderns have myth demands a sturdier argument.

Chapter 9

Dubuisson on Twentieth-Century Theorists of Myth: Foreword to Daniel Dubuisson, *Twentieth Century Mythologies: Dumézil, Lévi-Strauss, Eliade*

Daniel Dubuisson's *Twentieth Century Mythologies: Dumézil, Lévi-Strauss, Eliade* was originally published in 1993 as *Mythologies du XXe siècle: Dumézil, Eliade, Lévi-Strauss*. Note the change in the order of the three figures in the titles. As Dubuisson reports in his preface to the present, expanded, English edition, the original edition caused a stir, but mainly over the exposé of the unsavory political views underlying Mircea Eliade's theory of myth and of religion. As important as that exposé continues to be, more important here is the project that unites his study of the trio.

Dubuisson is intent on working out the basic assumptions of the three theories. He wants to show that the theories are theories not merely of myth but of something larger, of which myth is an expression. Georges Dumézil's theory of myth rests on a view of society. Claude Lévi-Strauss' theory of myth rests on a view of the mind. Eliade's theory of myth rests on a political ideology. Dubuisson does not merely lay out the fundamental tenets of each theory but also evaluates them. Rigorously and relentlessly, he subjects them all to criticism.

The typical way to evaluate theories is by applying them: if they work, the theories are confirmed. Here the tenets of the theories are presupposed, and the test is whether the theories fit the myths to which they are applied. For example, the applicability of Freud's theory to a particular myth presupposes the existence of the Oedipus complex. This approach is still a test of theories, for if the theory does not fit, the theory must explain why. Of course, the theory must accept as myth the case to which it is applied. But this test is tamer than that about the theory itself. The difference is, in one use of the terms, that between *interpretation* and *explanation*.[1]

Dubuisson's evaluation of theories falls under explanation: are the theories convincing in their own right, their applicability aside? Dubuisson actually mentions few myths. Instead, he lays out the main assumptions of each theory. The test for him is whether those assumptions make internal sense. In evaluating the theories, he is as attentive to incompleteness as to contradictoriness. Thus he rightly faults theories for their failure to answer either or both of the key questions about myth: what is its origin, and what is its function? Dubuisson examines each theory with his four-step "comparative epistemology," which is intended to unify the modern study of myth altogether.

In his introduction Dubuisson explains that he chooses his three theorists because "their exemplary works dominated the field of mythological study from the end of the Second World War." If "twentieth century theories" is extended to the first half of the century, surely the theories of Freud, Jung, Malinowski, and Bultmann have been at least as influential, though Dubuisson himself refuses to confer on Freud and Jung the status of theorists.

One might insist that theories, as theories, must be universal. By that criterion Dumézil, whose comparisons are limited to Indo-European myths, would not qualify as a theorist. Dumézil even insists on the uniqueness and therefore on the incomparability of Indo-European mythology. Still, his importance for the study of myth is incontestable, and his brand of a "structuralist" approach to myth per se is set against that developed by Lévi-Strauss.

Twentieth-century theories as a whole—those of not only Dubuisson's threesome but also Freud, Jung, Malinowski, and Bultmann—are distinct from nineteenth-century theories, such as those of Tylor and Frazer (see Segal 2015: 3). Nineteenth-century theories tended to see myth as the "primitive" counterpart to natural science, which was considered to be wholly modern. Myth and science alike were taken to be explanations of all events in the physical world. Science rendered myth not merely redundant but outright impossible. For both offer direct explanations of events. The mythic explanation is personalistic: rain falls because a god decides to send it. The scientific explanation is impersonal: rain falls because of meteorological processes. Because in myth the god does not set meteorological processes in motion but instead, say, dumps accumulated buckets of water on the designated spot below, one cannot reconcile the explanations by stacking the mythic explanation atop the scientific explanation, crediting science with the direct explanation and crediting myth with the indirect explanation. Rather, one must choose between them. Because moderns by definition have science, the choice has been made for them. They must give up myth.

By contrast, twentieth-century theories tended to see myth as almost anything but the counterpart to natural science. Either myth was not an explanation, or it was not even about the physical world. Or both. For Malinowski and Eliade, for example, myth is in part an explanation, but explanation is only a means to a nonscientific end. For Malinowski, that end is to reconcile humans to disease, death, and other brute aspects of the physical world. For Eliade, the end is to carry humans back to the time of the creation of physical phenomena and thereby back to the time when the gods were near. Furthermore, for both Malinowski and Eliade, myth is as much about social phenomena—customs, laws, and institutions—as about physical ones. For Bultmann, myth is not about the physical world itself but about the human experience of the world, and myth serves not to explain that experience but simply to capture it. For both Freud and Jung, myth is as far removed from the domain of natural science as can be. Myth is about the human unconscious, which projects itself onto the world in the form of gods and heroes but which must be disentangled from the world. Myth serves as a means of encountering not the world but the unconscious.

For Malinowski, "primitives" have science as well as myth, so that myth is not incompatible with science. But for Malinowski, myth is still an exclusively primitive enterprise. For Eliade, all human beings have and must have myth, and he writes to show moderns that they, too, have myth. For Bultmann, all human beings can and should have myth, and he writes to enable moderns to retain myth alongside science. For Freud, moderns do not need myth, which harms those who have it by perpetuating neurosis. Those who still have myth should recognize its true nature and give it up. For Jung, everyone needs myth, and moderns must find a substitute for traditional, religious myth, which has been bested by science.

Of Dubuisson's three theorists, the one who most clearly qualifies, in my terms, as a twentieth-century theorist is Dumézil. Myth for him is not about the physical world but about the social world. It is about the tripartite structure of Indo-European society. Myth serves not to explain that structure but to express and perhaps thereby to reinforce it. In neither subject matter nor function does myth encroach on natural science.

Eliade never tries to reconcile myths about the physical world with natural science, which for him no less than for Tylor and Frazer moderns by definition have. Instead, he offers examples of what for him amount to modern myths. Insofar as these myths are modern—they are about culture heroes rather than gods, and are about the creation of the human, not the physical, world—myth must be compatible with science.

Lévi-Strauss seems to fit least well my characterization of twentieth-century theorists. Myth for him is part of primitive thinking, which for him is not pre-scientific, let alone anti-scientific, but fully scientific. "Primitives" no less than moderns seek to categorize, whether or not also to explain, physical phenomena. Primitive thinking is systematically taxonomic. Lévi-Strauss deems the ordering of things the heart of science, and "primitives" organize their world no less thoroughly than moderns. The difference between primitive and modern thinking is only the level at which each works: primitive science works at the observable, sensory level; modern science, at the unobservable, nonsensory level, such as at the microscopic level. Myth is concrete: it is about particular characters or events. Modern science is abstract: it is about generalizations. At the same time the particularities of myth are symbols of generalizations.

For Lévi-Strauss, ordering takes the form of not merely categorizing phenomena but categorizing them into sets of logical oppositions—for example, into the opposition between food eaten raw and food first cooked. Lévi-Strauss credits myth with not merely presenting these oppositions, which are actually experienced, but also resolving or at least tempering them. Myth solves intellectual problems. Still, myth is really about the human mind, not about the world. More precisely, as Dubuisson recognizes, it is about both. For Lévi-Strauss maintains that while the human mind is structured to think "oppositionally" and to project oppositions onto the world, the world itself is structured oppositionally as well. To understand myth is not, as for Freud and Jung, to withdraw projections and to recognize the hiatus between the mind and the world. Jung does veer close to Lévi-Strauss with his concept of synchronicity, which argues for a parallel between the mind and the world.

Dubuisson, refreshingly, does not raise the question raised by most writers on myth: can moderns still have myth? He is concerned with the question only insofar as his subjects are. Of his three, Eliade is by far the one most concerned. Whomever Eliade is writing about, he is writing *to* moderns, and he is writing to show that, despite their professed scorn for supposedly long outdated, pre-scientific myth, they remain mythic at heart. For Eliade, myth is part of religion. To prove that religion is panhuman, he looks for cases of myth, if also of ritual, among purported nonbelievers. For Eliade, moderns have myths and rituals despite themselves.

Their myths and rituals are typically private and camouflaged, but myths and rituals they still are.

Lévi-Strauss restricts myth to "primitives" and suggests that the modern counterpart to myth is, of all things, politics. But he uses myth to show that myths are a logical, intellectual phenomenon rather than the expression of flighty imagination. If myths are exclusively primitive, the mind that creates them is panhuman. Like Eliade, Lévi-Strauss wants to narrow the assumed divide between "primitives" and moderns, but by showing that the two *think* the same rather than by showing that the two *believe* the same.

Because Dumézil restricts himself to ancient Indo-European mythology, he scarcely attends to the issue of the universality of myth. Ironically, some critics argue against him that the tripartite structure of Indo-European mythology is not limited to Indo-European culture and may even be universal. But Dumézil himself insists on the uniqueness of the structure, which he attributes to a unique convergence of historical factors.

Dubuisson has unbounded admiration for both Dumézil and Lévi-Strauss. He sees Dumézil as a consummate scholar and sees Lévi-Strauss as an extraordinary thinker. For Eliade, by contrast, Dubuisson has contempt, even while acknowledging his influence. Dubuisson sees Eliade as an intellectual charlatan, who bandies vague, empty slogans and invokes sources that he may never have understood or even read.

Worse, Dubuisson sees Eliade's theory of myth and of religion as a whole as a coverup—a coverup for a fascistic, racist, and antisemitic political ideology. Dubuisson asserts that, far from leaving behind his sordid political positions from his native Romania, Eliade simply translated them into high-sounding religious terms. Where Dubuisson discusses at length the wholly intellectual influences on the theories of Dumézil and Lévi-Strauss, he takes the influences on Eliade to be wholly political. Others have argued that Eliade espoused the views of the Iron Guard in the 1930s and 1940s, and Dubuisson acknowledges the work that has preceded his own. But he goes beyond others in matching up these views with Eliade's later writings on myth and religion. Where Dubuisson is eager to show how the views of both Dumézil and Lévi-Strauss changed—for example, Dumézil was first influenced mostly by Frazer but later by Durkheim—he is equally eager to show how the views of Eliade remained the same.

The result is a divide in the tone and content of Dubuisson's book. Undeniably, the intensity and the passion which drive Dubuisson's scholarship are evident on every page, just as they are in his other books. No mere academic is he. He is a genuine intellectual. But where he zealously works to reconstruct the fundamental principles girding the theories of Dumézil and Lévi-Strauss, he zealously strives to expose the fraud and bigotry at work in the theory of Eliade. The juxtaposition of admiration with disdain is not, for me, unsettling. On the contrary, it is invigorating. Dubuisson writes to show why we should cherish the theories of two celebrated twentieth-century theorists of myth but should scorn the theory of a third one.

Chapter 10

Myth and Literature

The relationship between myth and literature has taken varying forms. The most obvious form has been the use of myth in works of literature. A standard theme in literature courses has been the tracing of classical figures, events, and themes in Western literature. Courses begin with the Church Fathers, who utilized classical mythology even while warring on paganism, and proceed through Petrarch, Boccacio, Dante, Chaucer, Spenser, Shakespeare, Milton, Goethe, Byron, Keats, and Shelley, and then on to Joyce, Eliot, Gide, Cocteau, Anouilh, and O'Neill. The same has commonly been done for biblical myths. Both classical and biblical myths have alternatively been read literally, been read symbolically, been rearranged, and been outright rewritten. And they are to be found in all of the arts, including music and film. Freud used the figures Oedipus and Electra to name the most fundamental human drives—though it was, to be precise, C. G. Jung who coined the name Electra complex—and he took from other psychiatrists the figure Narcissus to name self-love.

The pervasiveness of classical, or pagan, mythology is even more of a feat than that of biblical mythology. For classical mythology has survived the demise of the religion of which, two thousand years ago, it was originally a part. By contrast, biblical mythology has been sustained by the nearly monolithic presence of Christianity. Indeed, classical mythology has been preserved by the culture tied to the religion that killed off classical religion.[1] Until recently, the very term "paganism" has had a negative connotation.

The Mythic Origin of Literature

Myth is commonly taken to be words, usually in the form of a story. A myth is read or heard. It says something. Yet there is an approach to myth that finds this view of myth artificial. According to the myth and ritual, or "myth ritualist," theory, myth does not stand by itself but is tied to ritual.

Myth is not just a statement but an action. It is acted out. The pioneering myth ritualist was the Scottish biblicist and Arabist William Robertson Smith, though for him myth explains a ritual that is no longer understood. It was, rather, his fellow Scot, the classicist and anthropologist J. G. Frazer (1854–1941), who in *The Golden Bough* developed the theory into its standard form.[2] For him, myth is the script of ritual. He himself was concerned with the myth-ritualist theory of religion alone, but others applied his theory to literature, deriving literature from myth.

Frazer offers two versions of myth ritualism, versions that he fails to disentangle. In one version the king is a mere human being and simply plays the role of the god. The dramatic enactment of the death and rebirth of the god, who is the god of vegetation, magically causes the rebirth of the presently dead god and in turn of the presently dead vegetation. The ritual is performed annually at the end, or would-be end, of winter.

In the other version of the ritual the king is himself divine, with the god of vegetation residing in him, and is actually killed and replaced. The soul of the god is thereby transferred to the new king. The killing of the king does not magically induce the killing of the god but instead simply preserves the health of the god, for the king is killed at the first sign of weakness or at the end of a fixed term so short as to minimize the chance of illness or death in office. The state of the king determines the state of the god of vegetation and in turn the state of vegetation itself. What part myth actually plays in this second version of myth ritualism is not easy to see. The myth of the death and rebirth of the god is not enacted. Instead, the residence of the god is simply changed! Nevertheless, this second version of myth ritualism has proved the more influential by far.

The most notable application of the myth-ritualist theory outside of religion has been to literature. The English classicist Jane Ellen Harrison (1850–1928), who had already applied the first version of Frazer's myth ritualism to ancient Greek religion, proceeded to derive all art, not just literature, from the same version. In *Ancient Art and Ritual* (1913) she speculates that gradually people ceased believing that the imitation of an action caused that action to occur. Yet rather than abandoning ritual, they now practiced it as an end in itself. Ritual for its own sake became art, her clearest example of which is drama. More modestly than she, her fellow classicists Gilbert Murray and F. M. Cornford rooted specifically Greek epic, tragedy, and comedy in myth ritualism. Murray then extended the theory to Shakespeare.[3]

Other standard-bearers of the theory have included Jessie Weston on the Grail legend, E. M. Butler on the Faust legend, C. L. Barber on

Shakespearean comedy, Herbert Weisinger on Shakespearean tragedy and on tragedy per se, Francis Fergusson on tragedy, Lord Raglan on hero myths and on literature as a whole, and Northrop Frye and Stanley Edgar Hyman on literature generally.[4] As literary critics, these myth ritualists have understandably been concerned less with myth itself than with the mythic origin of literature. Works of literature are interpreted as the outgrowth of myths once tied to rituals. For those literary critics indebted to Frazer, as the majority are, literature harks back to Frazer's second myth-ritualist scenario. "The king must die" becomes the familiar summary line.

For literary myth ritualists, myth becomes literature when myth is severed from ritual. Myth tied to ritual is religious literature. Myth cut off from ritual is secular literature, or plain literature. When tied to ritual, myth can serve the explanatory and, even more, magical functions ascribed to it by myth ritualists. Myth can even change the world. Bereft of ritual, myth is demoted to mere commentary.

Literary myth ritualism is a theory not of myth and ritual themselves, both of which are assumed, but of their impact on literature. Yet it is a not a theory of literature either, for it refuses to reduce literature to myth. Literary myth ritualism is an explanation of the transformation of myth and ritual into literature. Let us consider a few examples.

In *From Ritual to Romance* (1920) the English medievalist Jessie Weston (1850–1928) applied Frazer's second myth-ritualist version to the Grail legend. Following Frazer, she maintains that, for ancients and "primitives" alike, the fertility of the land depended on the fertility of their king, in whom resided the god of vegetation. But where for Frazer the key ritual was the sacrifice of an ailing king for the rejuvenation of the god, for Weston the aim of the Grail quest was the *rejuvenation* of the ailing king and *thereby* of the god. Furthermore, Weston adds an ethereal, spiritual dimension that transcends Frazer. The aim of the quest turns out to have been mystical oneness with god and not just food from god. It is this spiritual dimension of the legend that inspired T. S. Eliot to use Weston in "The Waste Land." Weston is not reducing the Grail legend to primitive myth and ritual but is merely tracing the legend back to primitive myth and ritual. The legend itself is literature, not myth. Because Frazer's second myth-ritualist scenario is not about the enactment of a myth of the god of vegetation but about the condition of the reigning king, the myth giving rise to the Grail legend is not the life of a god like Adonis but the life of the Grail king himself.

In *The Idea of a Theater* (1949) Francis Fergusson (1904–86), an esteemed American theater critic, applied Frazer's second myth-ritualist version to the whole genre of tragedy.[5] He argues that the story of the suffering and redemption of the tragic hero derives from Frazer's scenario of the killing and replacement of the king. For example, Oedipus, King of Thebes, must sacrifice his throne, though not his life, for the sake of his subjects. Only with his abdication will the plague cease. But for Fergusson, as for Weston, the renewal sought is less physical than spiritual. And Oedipus seeks it for himself as well as for his people.

More than most other literary myth ritualists, Fergusson is concerned as much with the product—drama—as with the source—myth and ritual. He even criticizes Harrison and especially Murray for taking the meaning of tragedy to be the Frazerian act of regicide rather than, say, the theme of self-sacrifice. For Fergusson, as for Weston, the Frazerian scenario provides the background to literature but is itself myth and ritual rather than literature.

In *Anatomy of Criticism* (1957) famed Canadian literary critic Northrop Frye (1912–91) argued that not just one genre but all genres of literature derive from myth—specifically, the myth of the life of the hero.[6] Frye associates the life cycle of the hero with several other cycles: the yearly cycle of the seasons, the daily cycle of the sun, and the nightly cycle of dreaming and awakening. The association with the seasons comes from Frazer. The association with the sun, never attributed, perhaps comes from Max Müller. The association with dreaming comes from C. G. Jung. The association of the seasons with heroism, while again never attributed, may come from Lord Raglan, author of *The Hero* (1936). Frye offers his own heroic pattern, which he calls the "quest-myth." But unlike some other heroic patterns, it consists of just four broad stages: the birth, triumph, isolation, and defeat of the hero.

For Frye, each main genre of literature parallels at once a season, a stage in the day, a stage of consciousness, and above all a stage in the heroic myth. Romance parallels at once spring, sunrise, awakening, and the birth of the hero. Comedy parallels summer, midday, waking consciousness, and the triumph of the hero. Tragedy parallels autumn, sunset, daydreaming, and the isolation of the hero. Satire parallels winter, night, sleep, and the defeat of the hero. The literary genres do not merely parallel the heroic myth but derive from it. The myth itself derives from ritual—from the version of Frazer's myth ritualism in which divine kings are killed and replaced.

Like most other literary myth ritualists, Frye does not reduce litera-ture to myth. On the contrary, he, most uncompromisingly of all, insists on the autonomy of literature. Like Fergusson, he faults Murray and Cornford not for speculating about the myth-ritualist origin of tragedy (Murray) and comedy (Cornford)—a nonliterary issue—but for inter-preting the meaning of either as the enactment of Frazer's scenario of regicide—the literary issue.

Yet Frye proceeds to enlist both Frazer and Jung to help extricate the meaning, not just the origin, of literature. For he takes their key works to be themselves works of literary criticism and not merely or even chiefly works of anthropology or psychology: "the fascination which *The Golden Bough* and Jung's book on libido symbols [i.e., *Symbols of Transformation* (Jung's Collected Works, vol. 5)] have for literary critics is ... based ... on the fact that these books are primarily studies in literary criticism" (Frye 1963: 17). "*The Golden Bough* isn't really about what people did in a remote and savage past; it is about what the human imagination does when it tries to express itself about the greatest mysteries, the mysteries of life and death and afterlife" (Frye 1978: 89). Similarly, Jung's *Psychology and Alchemy* (Jung's Collected Works, vol. 12), which Frye also singles out, "is not a mere specious paralleling of a defunct science [i.e., alchemy] and one of several Viennese schools of psychology, but a grammar of literary symbolism which for all serious students of literature is as important as it is endlessly fascinating" (Frye 1978: 129).

Frye surely goes too far in characterizing Frazer and Jung as at heart collectors of myths like the ancient Apollodorus. Both Frazer and Jung intend to be accounting for the origin and the function, not merely the meaning, of myth, and the "grammars" they provide are intended as arguments, not as compendia of symbols. Frazer claims that ritualistic regicide did occur, even if for Harrison and others it later got watered down to mere drama. Jung claims that archetypes really exist in the mind and even in the world.

Because Frye brings myth and literature so closely together, even without collapsing literature into myth, his literary criticism is confus-ingly called "myth criticism," of which he himself is often considered the grandest practitioner. Equally commonly, his literary criticism is called "archetypal criticism" because in innocently calling the genres of literature "archetypes," he is mistaken for a Jungian and, again, for the grandest of Jungian practitioners. His being called Jungian here is sepa-rate from his use of Jung's *Symbols of Transformation* as a sourcebook of myths. To compound the confusion, there *are* outright Jungian literary critics who are properly called archetypal critics, beginning with Maud Bodkin in *Archetypal Patterns in Poetry* (1934).[7] To compound the confusion yet further, there are *post*-Jungians who call themselves "archetypal psychologists" *rather than* Jungians. The most prominent are James Hillman and David Miller, both of whom write voluminously on myth.[8]

In *Violence and the Sacred* (1977) and other works the French literary critic René Girard (1923–2015) offers the sharpest break between myth and literature.[9] Like Fergusson and Frye, Girard faults Harrison and Murray for conflating myth and ritual with tragedy. But he faults the two even more sternly for domesticating tragedy. For Harrison and Murray, myth merely *describes* the Frazerian ritual, and tragedy merely *dramatizes* it. Worse, tragedy turns an actual event into a mere theme (see Girard 1977: 6). For Girard, myth *covers up* the ritual, and tragedy, as in Sophocles' plays about Oedipus, *uncovers* it. But Girard's criticism of Harrison and Murray is directed at Frazer's second myth-ritualist scenario, in which the king is killed outright. Harrison and Murray use instead Frazer's first myth-ritualist scenario, in which the king merely plays the part of the god of vegetation. Here the god dies but the king does not, and the god may die without being killed. Girard's charge that Harrison, Murray, and even in part Frazer miss the human killing that underlies all tragedy is thus embarrassingly misdirected.

Myth as Story

Tylor

Another aspect of myth as literature has been the focus on a common story line. Yet not all theorists of myth focus on myth as story. For example, neither Frazer nor the pioneering English anthropologist E. B. Tylor (1832–1917), his fellow theorist of myth as the primitive counterpart to science, considers myth as story.[10] It is not that either would deny that a myth is a story.[11] It is, rather, that they deem myth a causal explanation of events in the physical world that merely happens to take the form of a story. Their paralleling of myth to science requires the downplaying of the story form and the playing up of the explanatory content.

Of course, myth for both Frazer and Tylor tells the story of how, for example, Helius or Apollo becomes responsible for the sun and exercises that responsibility. But what interests the two is the information itself, not the way it is conveyed. Standard literary considerations such as characterization, time, voice, point of view, and reader response are ignored, just as they would be in the analysis of a scientific law. Because myth for them is intended to explain recurrent events, it can be rephrased as a law. Whenever rain falls, it falls because the god of rain has decided to send it, and always for the same reason. When the sun rises, it rises because the sun god has, say, chosen to mount his chariot, to which the sun is attached, and to ride across the sky, and again always for the same reason.

For Tylor in particular, who reads myth literally and rails against contemporaries who read it symbolically, as Frazer himself sometimes does, myth is anything but literature, and to approach myth as literature is to trivialize it, to turn its explanatory truth claims about the world into merely poetic descriptions. Where Frye and others argue that literature is not reducible to myth, Tylor argues that myth is not reducible to literature. In the wake of postmodernism, in which arguments in all fields, including science and law, are recharacterized as stories, Tylor's indifference to the story aspect of myth is notable.

As much as Tylor stresses the role of reason in myth and religion, he accords a place to imagination, at least in myth. Like the rest of religion, of which it is a part, myth functions to explain the world. But unlike the rest of religion, myth does so in the form of stories, which are in part the product of imagination.

It is thus imagination which partly creates the sun god and then transforms the belief in the sun god into the fantastic story of Helius' or Apollo's daily driving a chariot across the sky. What Tylor does vigorously decry is the view that myth stems from *unrestrained* imagination:

> Among those opinions which are produced by a little knowledge, to be dispelled by a little more, is the belief in an almost boundless creative power: the human imagination. The superficial student, mazed in a crowd of seemingly wild and lawless fancies, which he thinks to have no reason in nature nor pattern in this material world, at first concludes them to be new births from the imagination of the poet, the tale-teller, and the seer. (Tylor 1871, vol. 1: 273)

Tylor even maintains that his dual symbolist nemeses, the euhemerists and the moral allegorizers, fail to take myth seriously *because* they attribute it to unbridled imagination, which he equates with "poetic fancy" (see, for example, Tylor 1871, vol. 1: 285, 289–90). For Tylor, to attribute myth to imagination is invariably to make its subject other than the physical world and its function other than explanatory.

Still, Tylor accords a commodious place to *restrained* imagination—imagination restrained by reason. The comparative approach, which he takes for granted neither the euhemerists nor the moral allegorizers employ (see Tylor 1871, vol. 1: 280-82), "makes it possible to trace in mythology the operation of imaginative processes recurring with the evident regularity of mental law" (Tylor 1871, vol. 1: 282; see also 274-75). Tylor assumes that untethered imagination would never yield the patterns he finds in myths, so that regularities constitute *ipso facto* evidence of the subordination of imagination to reason. The stories may be fantastic, but they are fantastic in uniform ways. Tylor asks rhetorically, "What would be popularly thought more indefinite and uncontrolled than the products of the imagination in myths and fables?" (Tylor 1871, vol. 1: 18). Here he anticipates Claude Lévi-Strauss.

Tylor's subordination of imagination to reason is symptomatic of the central limitation of his overall theory of myth: his overemphasis on myth as akin to science and his underemphasis on it as akin to literature. Myth for him is a scientific-like hypothesis that merely happens to take the form of a story. Like Lévi-Strauss, he downplays the format in order to uphold the content. He assumes that myth, like the rest of religion, is an explanation of the physical world, is taken seriously only when it is taken as an explanation of the physical world, and is taken as an explanation of the physical world only when the form is taken as merely a colorful way of presenting the content. Form and content are separable, and content alone counts. To treat the form as anything more is to reduce a set of would-be truth claims about the world, true or false, to fiction.

Burke

Tylor's opposition between myth and literature seems particularly artificial when seen from the standpoint of the American literary critic Kenneth Burke (1897-1993). In, above all, *The Rhetoric of Religion* (1961) Burke argues that myth is the transformation of metaphysics into story. Myth expresses symbolically, in terms of temporal priority, what "primitives" cannot express literally: metaphysical priority.[12] In Burke's famous phrase, myth is the "temporizing of essence." For example, the first creation story in Genesis puts in the form of six days what in fact is the "classification" of things in the world into six classes: "Thus, instead of saying 'And that completes the first broad division, or classification, of our subject matter,' we'd say: 'And the evening and the morning were the first day'" (Burke 1961: 202). While myth for Burke is ultimately the expression of nontemporal truths, it is still the expression of them in story form, so that even if the meaning needs to be extricated from the form, story is still what, contrary to Tylor, makes myth myth.[13] Here Burke is like Lévi-Strauss. What Burke calls "essence," Lévi-Strauss calls "structure."

Blumenberg

Antithetical to Tylor stands the German philosopher Hans Blumenberg (1920–96), author of, above all, *Work on Myth* (1985).[14] Blumenberg would classify Tylor as a conspicuous representative of the Enlightenment approach to myth—one of the two approaches that he castigates. (The other is the Romantic approach.[15]) While Blumenberg cites Tylor only once, and in passing (see Blumenberg 1985: 151), it is clear how he would respond to Tylor's view of myth as the primitive counterpart to science.

Blumenberg rejects this supposedly Enlightenment view of myth on the grounds that myth continues to exist in modernity (see Blumenberg 1985: 263–64, 274). The survival of living myth in the wake of science supposedly proves that its function was never scientific.

By a scientific explanation Blumenberg means a genetic, or etiological, one. As he writes in criticism of the Enlightenment view, "That the relationship between the 'prejudice' called myth and the new science should [for the Enlightenment] be one of competition necessarily presupposes the interpretation of individual myths as etiological" (Blumenberg 1985: 265).

Blumenberg offers four arguments for the view of myth as nonetiological. It is the middle two of the four that bear on myth as story. Blumenberg asserts that myths tell stories *rather than* give reasons: "In the [erroneous] etiological explanation of myth ... the recognition of myth as an archaic accomplishment of reason has to be justified by its having initially and especially given answers to questions, rather than having [in actuality] been the implied rejection of those questions by means of storytelling" (Blumenberg 1985: 166; see also 184–85, 257–59).

Furthermore, within a myth anything can derive from anything else, in which case there must be scant interest in accurate derivation and therefore in derivation itself: "When anything can be derived from anything, then there just is no explaining, and no demand for explanation. One just tells stories" (Blumenberg 1985: 127). Indeed, myth presents mere "sequences" rather than "chronology," by which he means causality (Blumenberg 1985: 126; see also 128).

Blumenberg's arguments for myth as nonetiological are tenuous. Undeniably, myths tell stories rather than give arguments. But this difference in form need scarcely mean a difference in function. Tylor, for his part, disregards the form for the content and sees myth as presenting arguments in the form of stories. Plato, Plotinus, and other ancient critics of myth *as* story take for granted that the function of myth is the same as that of philosophy, which Blumenberg rightly associates with science. Insofar as Thales and other Presocratics succeed Homer and Hesiod, Homer and especially Hesiod must be providing etiologies of their own.

Undeniably as well, in myth anything can derive from anything else. Indeed, nearly anything at all can happen. But even the most fantastic etiologies are not therefore less etiological. Even if anything can happen in myth, myth is still reporting how it did happen.

Whether Tylor is more convincing than Blumenberg or Blumenberg more convincing than Tylor, they constitute the opposing positions on the nature of myth as story. For Tylor, myth is an explanation that merely takes the form of a story. For Blumenberg, myth is a story and therefore not an explanation.

Hero Myths

Myths collectively are too varied to share a plot, but common plots have been proposed for specific kinds of myths, most often for hero myths. Other categories of myths, such as creation myths, flood myths, myths of paradise, and myths of the future, have proved too disparate for all but the broadest commonalities.

In 1876 the Austrian scholar Johann Georg von Hahn used fourteen cases to argue that all "Aryan" hero tales follow an "exposure and return" formula more comprehensive than Tylor's.[16] In each case the hero is born illegitimately, out of the fear of the prophecy of his future greatness is abandoned by his father, is saved by animals and raised by a lowly couple, fights wars, returns home triumphant, defeats his persecutors, frees his mother, becomes king, founds a city, and dies young. Though himself a solar mythologist, von Hahn tries only to establish a pattern for hero myths. He does not offer any origin or function. In other words, he does not theorize.

Similarly, in 1928 the Russian folklorist Vladimir Propp sought to demonstrate that Russian fairy tales follow a common plot, in which the hero goes off on a successful adventure and upon his return marries and gains the throne.[17] Propp's pattern skirts both the birth and the death of the hero. While himself a Marxist, Propp here, in his earlier, formalist phase, attempts no more than von Hahn: to establish a pattern for hero stories. He offers no origin or function.

Of the scholars who have theorized about the patterns that they have delineated in hero myths, the most important have been the Viennese-born psychoanalyst Otto Rank (1884–1939), who eventually settled in the United States; the American mythographer Joseph Campbell (1904–87); and the English folklorist Lord Raglan (1885–1964). Rank later broke irreparably with Sigmund Freud, but when he wrote *The Myth of the Birth of the Hero* (1909), he was a Freudian apostle. While Campbell was never a full-fledged Jungian, he wrote *The Hero with a Thousand Faces* (1949) as a kindred soul of C. G. Jung.[18] Raglan wrote *The Hero* (1936) as a Frazerian.

Rank

For Rank, following Freud, heroism deals with what *Jungians* call the first half of life. The first half—birth, childhood, adolescence, and young adult-hood—involves the establishment of oneself as an independent person in the external world. The attainment of independence expresses itself con-cretely in the securing of a job and a mate. The securing of either requires both separation from one's parents and mastery of one's instincts. Freudian problems involve a lingering attachment to either parents or instincts. To depend on one's parents for the satisfaction of instincts or to satisfy instincts in anti-social ways is to be stuck, or fixated, at a childish level of psychological development.

Rank's pattern, which he applies to thirty hero myths, is limited to the first half of life. It goes from the hero's birth to his attainment of a "career." Literally, or consciously, the hero, who is always male, is a his-torical or legendary figure like Oedipus. The hero is heroic because he rises from obscurity to the throne. Literally, he is an innocent victim of either his parents or, ultimately, fate. While his parents have yearned for a child and abandon him only to save the father, they nevertheless do abandon him. The hero's revenge, if the parricide is even committed knowingly, is, then, understandable: who would not consider killing one's would-be killer?

Symbolically, or unconsciously, the hero is heroic not because he dares to win a throne but because he dares to kill his father. The killing is definitely intentional, and the cause is not revenge but sexual frus-tration. The father has refused to surrender his wife—the real object of the son's efforts. Too horrendous to face, the true meaning of the hero myth gets covered up by the concocted story. Rather than the culprit, the hero becomes an innocent victim or at worst a justified avenger. What the hero seeks gets masked as power, not incest. Most of all, who the hero is becomes some third party, a historical or legendary figure, rather than either the creator of the myth or anyone stirred by it. Identifying himself with the literal hero, the myth maker or reader vicariously revels in the hero's triumph, which in fact is his own. *He* is the real hero of the myth.

Literally, the myth culminates in the hero's attainment of a throne. Symbolically, the hero gains a mate as well. One might, then, conclude that the myth fittingly expresses the Freudian goal of the first half of life. In actuality, it expresses the opposite. The wish it fulfills is not for detachment from one's parents and from one's anti-social instincts but, on the contrary, for the most intense possible relationship to one's parents and the most anti-social of urges: parricide and incest, even rape.

The myth maker or reader is an adult, but the wish vented by the myth is that of a child of three to five. The fantasy is the fulfillment of the Oedipal wish to kill one's father in order to gain access to one's mother. The myth fulfills a wish never outgrown by the adult who either invents or uses it. That adult is psychologically an eternal child. Having never developed an ego strong enough to master his instincts, he is neurotic. Since no mere child can overpower his father, the myth maker imagines being old enough to do so. In short, the myth expresses not the Freudian goal of the first half of life but the fixated childhood goal that keeps one from accomplishing it.

On the one hand the myth expresses the Oedipal wish mentally rather than physically, symbolically rather than literally, and unconsciously rather than consciously. The fulfillment of the wish of myth, like that of dream, does not lie on the surface and must be reconstructed. On the other hand the fulfillment of the wish depends on the plot—the reconstructed plot. Indeed, the plot *is* the fulfillment of the wish.

Campbell

Where for Freud and Rank heroism is limited to the first half of life, for Jung it involves the second half—adulthood—even more. For Freud and Rank, heroism involves relations with parents and instincts. For Jung, heroism in even the first half involves, in addition, relations with the unconscious. Heroism here means separation not only from parents and anti-social instincts but even more from the unconscious: every child's managing to forge consciousness is for Jung a supremely heroic feat.

The goal of the uniquely Jungian second half of life is likewise consciousness, but now consciousness of the Jungian unconscious rather than, as in the first half, of the external world. One must return to the unconscious, from which one has invariably become severed. But the ultimate aim is to return in turn to the external world. The ideal is a balance between consciousness of the external world and consciousness of the unconscious.

Where Rank's hero returns to his birthplace, Campbell's marches forth to a strange, new, divine world, which the hero has never visited or even known existed. Where Rank's hero *returns* home to encounter his father and mother, Campbell's hero *leaves* home to encounter a male and a female god, who are neither his parents nor necessarily even a couple. When Campbell writes that myths "reveal the benign self-giving aspect of the archetypal father," he is using the term *archetypal* in its Jungian sense (Campbell 1972: 139–40). The father and the mother are but two of the archetypes of which the Jungian, or collective, unconscious is composed. Archetypes are unconscious not because they have been repressed but because they have never been conscious. For Jung and Campbell, myth originates and functions not, as for Freud and Rank, to satisfy neurotic urges that cannot be manifested openly but to express normal sides of the personality that have just not had a chance at realization.

By identifying himself with the hero of a myth, Rank's myth maker or reader vicariously lives out in his mind an adventure that, if ever directly fulfilled, would be acted out on his parents themselves. While also identifying himself—or herself—with the hero of a myth, Campbell's myth maker or reader vicariously lives out in the mind an adventure that even when directly fulfilled would still be taking place in the mind. For parts of the mind are what the myth maker or reader is really encountering.

For Campbell, just as for Rank, a myth works through the plot, which again is mental rather than physical, symbolic rather than literal, and unconscious rather than conscious. The plot is the expression of the journey from ordinary consciousness to the unconscious and back.

Raglan

Raglan applies Frazer's second myth-ritualist version to hero myths. Where Frazer identifies the king with the god of vegetation, Raglan in turn identifies the king with the hero. For Frazer, the king's willingness to die for the community may be heroic, but Raglan outright labels the king a hero. Frazer presents a simple pattern for the myth of the god: the god dies and is reborn. Raglan works out a detailed, twenty-two-step pattern for the myth of the hero—a pattern that he then applies to twenty-one myths. That pattern covers the whole life of the hero and not just, as for Propp, Rank, and Campbell, a portion of it.

But Raglan does more: he links up the myth with the ritual. In Frazer's second version of myth ritualism, as noted, the ritual enacted is not the myth of the death and rebirth of a god but the sheer transfer of the soul of the god from one king to another. There is really no myth at all. Raglan, by making the heart of hero myths not the attainment of the throne but the loss of it, matches the myth of the hero with the Frazerian ritual of the removal of the king. The king in the myth who loses his throne and later his life parallels the king in the ritual who loses his life. The myth that Raglan links to ritual is not that of a god but that of a hero—some legendary figure whose selflessness real kings are expected to emulate. Strictly, then, the myth is less the script for the ritual, as in Frazer's first myth-ritualist scenario, than the inspiration for the ritual.

The plot is central to Raglan's theory of myth. He appeals to the commonness of the plot to argue that the meaning of hero myths lies in that plot, that the heart of the plot is the loss of the throne, and that only an accompanying ritual of regicide makes sense of the focus in the myth on the toppling of the king. Raglan's myth ritualism does not merely make the plot the scenario for the ritual but argues for the ritual from the plot.

Chapter 11

Hell and Paradise for Milton and Others

In Genesis 3 the fall is both spatial and temporal. On the one hand Adam and Eve get evicted from Eden and must settle outside it. On the other hand the shift is from a time before the fall to the time thereafter. Modern interpreters of the Bible focus more on the fall in time than on the fall in space, which seems hopelessly literal and hopelessly unscientific. A spatial fall places Eden in a place on earth, at the meeting point of four rivers, two of them known. But Eden has still yet to be discovered. By contrast, a temporal fall allows for a nonphysical event. The fall can be mental—for example, a fall "into" consciousness. And it can occur any time and any place. It can more readily be taken symbolically, as a depiction of the transformation that everyone undergoes. Here I will consider the fall both spatially and temporally. Milton's own characterization of hell and paradise is at once spatial and temporal.

Both space and time always get divided up. Just as there is the temporal division into past, present, and future, so there is the spatial division into near and far. Spatial divisions can be up or down or sideways. And they can exist simultaneously: up does not preclude down or sideways. By contrast, temporal divisions cannot co-exist: the past cannot simultaneously be the present or the future. What counts is that space and time are each knowable only by division—division into this space rather than another, into this time rather than another. There cannot be up in and of itself or the past in and of itself.

But even if space and time are inherently divisible, they are not inherently divisible into sacred and profane space or into sacred and profane time. Religion takes spatial and temporal divisions and classifies them as divine and human.

Durkheim and Eliade

Among theorists of religion, Emile Durkheim (1915) gives the division into sacred and profane its classic expression. The sacred for him is the group. The profane is the individual. What constitutes the experience of the sacred is the gathering of the group, which is to say in one place, if also at the same time. Durkheim contrasts the isolation of members of the aboriginal totemic clan *between* gatherings to the euphoria experienced *during* gatherings. The group that gathers experiences its god, which in fact is itself. The group that gathers together stays together.

For Mircea Eliade (1959a), myth deals with time, and ritual deals with space. Both are means of reaching the sacred. Because the sacred is hard to reach, both myths and rituals are indispensable, and they can work together. Gods, who are part of the sacred, have gradually become "otiose," which means ever harder to reach. Yet in principle even Adam and Eve would have needed myths and rituals to reach God.

The issue at hand is what happens to sacred space when space ceases to be physical—a place—and becomes mental, or spiritual—a state of mind. How can there still be sacred space? I turn to William Robertson Smith on the Hebrew Bible. Then I consider a more extreme scenario: what happens when space is made mental yet remains physical. I turn here to John Milton.

Smith on Primitive and Ancient Religion versus Modern Religion

In his classic work *Lectures on the Religion of the Semites* (1894) Smith draws many sharp differences between "primitive" and ancient religion on the one hand—he lumps the two together—and modern religion on the other. Primitive and ancient religion is ritualistic, mythic, partly amoral, and collectivist. Modern religion is creedal, nonritualistic, nonmythic, wholly moral, and individualistic. The key difference is that primitive and ancient religion is materialist, whereas modern religion is spiritual.

One consequence of the materialist nature of primitive and ancient religion is that the sacredness, or "holiness," of a god, person, or place stems from other than character. To moderns, holiness is "an ethical idea" and is based on character: "God, the perfect being, is the type of holiness; men are holy in proportion as their lives and character are god-like; places and things can be called holy only by a figure, on account of their association with spiritual things" (Smith 1894: 140). By contrast, to ancients, "holy persons were such, not in virtue of their character but in virtue of their race, function, or mere material consecration" (Smith 1894: 141). Persons practicing the worst immoralities could still be labeled "holy."

In primitive and ancient religion the attribute "holy" was applied less to persons than to gods, seasons, things, and most of all places. While persons, things, and times were, as in modern religion, holy because of their association with gods, their holiness was tied to the places—the physical spots—where the gods were present: "Holy persons things and times, as they are conceived in antiquity, all presuppose the existence of holy places at which the persons minister, the things are preserved, and the times are celebrated." In fact, the holiness of the gods themselves "is an expression to which it is hardly possible to attach a definite sense apart from the holiness of their physical surroundings" (Smith 1894: 141). So, for Smith, the sacredness of space lies in the place itself. His tying of sacredness to the place itself does not, however, explain the cases of the burning bush and Mt. Sinai.

Because of the materialist conception of religion among "primitives" and ancients, the physical world was divided into two domains: the demonic and the divine, or wilderness and civilization.

Generalizing from the case of the Arabian *jinn* to that of early Semitic religion, Smith distinguishes the domains:

> In fact the earth may be said to be parcelled out between demons and wild beasts on the one hand, and gods and men on the other. To the former belong the untrodden wilderness with all its unknown perils, the wastes and jungles that lie outside the familiar tracks and pasture grounds of the tribe, and which only the boldest men venture upon without terror; to the latter belong the regions that man knows and habitually frequents, and within which he has established relations, not only with his human neighbours, but with the supernatural beings that have their haunts side by side with him. And as man gradually encroaches on the wilderness and drives back the wild beasts before him, so the gods in like manner drive out the demons, and spots that were once feared, as the habitation of mysterious and presumably malignant powers, lose their terrors and either become common ground or are transformed into the seats of friendly deities. From this point of view the recognition of certain spots as haunts of the gods is the religious expression of the gradual subjugation of nature by man. (Smith 1894: 121–22)

The "triumph" of gods over demons is gradual and is "finally sealed and secured" only in the post-nomadic, agricultural stage, "when the god of the community became also the supreme lord of the land and the author of all the good things therein" (Smith 1894: 122).

The demons who had formerly occupied the land either were driven out into uninhabited land or "were reduced to insignificance as merely subordinate beings of which private superstition might take account"— perhaps as magic—"but with which public religion had nothing to do" (Smith 1894: 122-23). In the land now "frequented by the community of men the god of the community was supreme." Now "every place that had special supernatural associations was regarded, not as a haunt of unknown demons, but as a holy place of the known god" (Smith 1894: 123).

By the "wilderness" Smith means both literal location and religious state. Taken literally, Smith means the land between Egypt and the Promised Land. He means above all the desert. The wanderings in the desert for forty years are associated with thirst, hunger, disease, earthquakes, and snakes.

Yet wilderness means not just unoccupied land but also land inhabited by all of the "heathen" cultures that Israel encounters. With the wilderness is associated continual fighting. (On the Israelites' wanderings see Exodus 13:17-22 and 15:22-17:15; Numbers 10:11-14:45, 16:1-17:13, 20:1-25:18, 27:12-23, and 31:1-34:29.)

If in ancient Israelite religion the wilderness for Smith means geographical location and is to be contrasted to the Promised Land, in modern religion the wilderness for Smith means "spiritual" location. Now the wilderness is mental. It is the state of separation from God. It is the state of sin. As decisive as the demarcation of the physical world between wilderness and home is for ancient Israelites, once the division between material and spiritual emerges in religion, as it does in the Israelite Prophets, in Christianity, and most fully in Protestantism, any distinctions within the physical world become pointless, if not incoherent. How can any division between sacred and profane space count when space per se has been spiritualized?

Milton

It is in John Milton's *Paradise Lost* (1667) that one finds the illogical finale to trying to make space, profane as well as sacred, at once physical and spiritual, which is to say at once outer and inner.

Milton combines riveting descriptions of hell and paradise as places "out there" in the world with characterizations of them as states of mind. On the one hand Hell, into which Satan and his retinue land after their fall from heaven, is a lake of fire, the light from which only makes the place darker. The beach is itself on fire and offers no respite from the heat:

> At once as far as Angels' ken he [Satan] views
> The dismal Situation waste and wild,
> A Dungeon horrible, on all sides round
> As one great Furnace flam'd, yet from those flames
> No light, but rather darkness visible
> Serv'd only to discover sights of woe,
> Regions of sorrow, doleful shades, where peace
> And rest can never dwell, hope never comes
> That comes to all; but torture without end
> Still urges, and a fiery Deluge, fed
> With ever-burning Sulphur unconsum'd:
> Such place Eternal Justice had prepar'd
> For those rebellious, here thir Prison ordained
> In utter darkness, and thir portion set
> As far remov'd from God and light of Heav'n
> As from the Center thrice to th' utmost Pole. (I.59–74)

On the other hand hell is a state of mind. Satan, upon awakening in hell, boasts that both heaven and hell are the product of mind and can therefore be established anywhere at will:

> Is this the Region, this the Soil, the Clime,
> Said then the lost Arch-Angel, this the seat
> That we must change for Heav'n, this mournful gloom
> For that celestial light? Be it so, since he
> Who now is Sovran can dispose and bid
> What shall be right: ...
>
> Farewell happy Fields
> Where Joy for ever dwells: Hail horrors, hail
> Infernal world, and thou profoundest Hell
> Receive thy new Possessor: One who brings
> A mind not to be chang'd by Place or Time.
> The mind is its own place, and in itself
> Can make a Heav'n of Hell, a Hell of Heav'n. (I.241–55)

Later, Satan says the same, but now in self-doubt rather than in arrogance, as he recognizes what he has lost and recognizes that, as evil, he turns everything into hell:

> Me miserable! which way shall I fly
> Infinite wrath, and infinite despair?
> Which way I fly is Hell; myself am Hell; (IV.73–75)

It is not just Satan the character who makes hell and paradise into mental states. As author, Milton writes of Satan that

> from the bottom stir
> The Hell within him, for within him Hell
> He brings, and round about him, nor from Hell
> One step no more than from himself can fly
> By change of place .... (IV.19–21)

What for Milton is true of hell is also true of paradise. On the one hand it is a place "out there," lovingly and lushly described:

> Beneath him with new wonder now he [Satan] views
> To all delight of human sense expos'd
> In narrow room Nature's whole wealth, yea more,
> A Heaven on Earth: for blissful Paradise
> Of God the Garden was, by him in the East
> Of Eden planted; Eden stretch'd her Line
> From Auran Eastward to the Royal Tow'rs
> Of Great Seleucia, built by Grecian Kings,
> Or where the Sons of Eden long before
> Dwelt in Telassar: in this pleasant soil
> His far more pleasant Garden God ordain'd;
> Out of the fertile ground he [God] caus'd to grow
> All Trees of noblest kind for sight, smell, taste;

> Thus was this place,
> A happy rural seat of various view:
> Groves whose rich Trees wept odorous Gums and Balm,
> Others whose fruit burnisht with Golden Rind
> Hung amiable, Hesperian Fables true,
> If true, here only, and of delicious taste: (IV.205–51)

On the other hand the archangel Michael, having consoled Adam with knowledge of the virtues that human beings can acquire only in the wake of the fall—Faith, Patience, Temperance, Love, and Charity—concludes:

> then wilt thou not be loath
> To leave this Paradise, but shalt possess
> A paradise within thee, happier far. (XII.586–87)

This psychologizing of the world is to be found even earlier than Milton, most famously in the description of hell by Mephistopheles in Christopher Marlowe's *Doctor Faustus* (1592):

Hell hath no limits, nor is circumscribed
In any one self place; for where we are is hell,
And where hell is, there must we ever be. (1604 ed., Act I.553–55)

But Milton, in contrast to Marlowe, wants to retain space—hell and paradise alike—as physical and not merely mental, as outer and not merely inner. But can he do so? When Satan declares that he himself creates hell—because hell is mental—he is denying that hell is also physical, for otherwise he could not create it himself. Yet Milton seems to spurn this consequence.

Freud and Jung

By contrast to Milton, modern depictions of heaven and hell have differentiated the outer from the inner. Two of the most celebrated cases are those of C. G. Jung and Sigmund Freud. Jung is especially eager to trace the psychologizing of the world all the way back to ancient Gnostics and in turn to medieval alchemists. But for him and Freud alike, the twentieth century has been distinctive in its separation of the psychological from the physical and also from the metaphysical—the separation of the inner from the outer rather than, as for Milton, the juxtaposition of the two.

Freud and Jung assert that what had previously been taken as physical is in fact a projection of the mental. For neither, has the psychologizing of the world meant the reduction of the world to the mind, as in idealism. Nor has it meant the reduction of the world to a human creation, as in constructionism. On the contrary, it has meant the differentiation of the world "out there"—a world independent of humans—from the imposition onto the world of elements belonging to humans *rather than* to the world. The physical world remains, but sacred space goes.

Projections onto the outer world, which had taken the form of gods, have been largely withdrawn by moderns. The outer world has come to be recognized as a natural rather than a supernatural domain, to be explained by impersonal scientific laws rather than by the decisions of gods. Writes Freud:

> Let us consider the unmistakable situation as it is to-day. We have heard the admission that religion no longer has the same influence on people that it used to.... Let us admit that the reason—though perhaps not the only reason—for this change is the increase of the scientific spirit in the higher strata of human society. Criticism has whittled away the evidential value of religious documents, natural science has shown up the errors in them. (Freud 1961: 38)

Writes Jung: "Only in the following centuries, with the growth of natural science, was the projection withdrawn from matter and entirely abolished altogether with the psyche.... Nobody ... any longer endows matter with mythological properties. This form of projection has become obsolete" (Jung 1968e: 300).

Jung's concept of synchronicity, developed with the physicist Wolfgang Pauli, does not restore sacredness to the physical world. Rather, it restores a symmetry *between* humans and the world. What is found in humans is also found in the world. But what are found in the world are not gods.

The differentiation of the physical from the psychological has meant the removal of any sacredness from the physical world. There is no longer any sacred space in the world.

Winnicott

In between Freud and Jung comes D. W. Winnicott, the English psychoanalyst and child psychiatrist. Winnicott analyzes the continuation of children's play in adult make-believe.

For Winnicott, play is *acknowledged* by children as other than reality: children grant that they are just playing. But play is no mere escapism. It involves the appropriation of reality for oneself. It involves the construction of a reality that has personal meaning. To pretend that a spoon is a train is to take a spoon and to turn it into a train. Far from projecting oneself onto the world, as for Freud and Jung, play is the construction of a world. As Winnicott continually declares, play is "creative." Far from confusing itself with reality, play demarcates the difference. Play grants itself the right to treat a spoon as a train, and a parent is barred from asking whether the spoon really is a train. Once play is over, the train is again a mere spoon. Sacred space is again profane space.

To use Winnicott's famous term, play is a "transitional" activity. It provides a transition not merely from childhood to adulthood but also from the inner world of fantasy to outer reality: "play can easily be seen to link the individual's relation to inner reality with the same individual's relation to external or shared reality" (Winnicott 1987: 145). Play links the realms by taking items from the external world and constructing a reality—a set-off space, if also time—to fit the fantasy: play takes a spoon and transforms it into a train. Yet play does not deny the difference between the inner and the outer worlds, for only during play is the spoon a train. On the one hand play is recognized as make-believe: outside of play the spoon is conceded to be only a spoon. On the other hand the make-believe is taken seriously: within play the spoon really is a train.

As adult extensions of play, Winnicott, in stereotypically English fashion, names gardening and cooking, in both of which one creates a world with personal meaning out of elements from the external world. Winnicott also names art and religion, in both of which as well one constructs a world, though with a far deeper meaning to it:

> It is assumed here that the task of reality-acceptance is never completed, that no human being is free from the strain of relating inner and outer reality, and that relief from this strain is provided by an intermediate area of experience which is not challenged (arts, religion, etc.). This intermediate area is in direct continuity with the play area of the small child who is "lost" in play. (Winnicott 1982: 13)

I suggest adding myth, itself not discussed by Winnicott, as another case of adult play. The world of myth is like that of a novel or a film. It is real while the novel is read or the film watched. Interrupting the novel or the film is disruptive and breaks the reality of the experience. The novel or film is not assumed to be real outside itself, but within it anything can happen, and whatever happens is accepted.

Winnicott is not reconciling space as outer with space as inner. Rather, he is forging an in-between reality, which is neither exclusively outer nor exclusively inner. This in-between, play-like reality circumvents rather than solves the problem that faces those who want to spiritualize sacred space. Even with Winnicott, they still cannot do so. Space cannot be both physical and nonphysical. When it becomes nonphysical, it ceases to be space.

I am not swayed by the notion of symbolic space. Physical space as symbolizing something nonphysical is one thing. Nonphysical space is something else.

Chapter 12

Must Mythic Heroes Be Male?

The study of hero myths goes back at least to 1871, when the Victorian anthropologist E. B. Tylor argued that many of them follow a uniform plot, or pattern: the hero is exposed at birth, is saved by other humans or animals, and grows up to become a national hero (see Tylor 1871, vol. 1: 254-55).[1] All of his examples are of male heroes. Tylor did not apply to hero myths his theory of myth per se, which itself allows for female as well as male gods. He sought only to establish a pattern for hero myths, not to answer any of the theoretical questions: their origin, function, or subject matter.

Of the scholars who have not only delineated patterns but also analyzed the origin, function, and subject matter of hero myths, by far the most important have been the Viennese psychoanalyst Otto Rank (1884–1939), the American mythographer Joseph Campbell (1904–87), and the English folklorist Lord Raglan (1885–1964). Rank later broke irreparably with Sigmund Freud, but when he wrote *The Myth of the Birth of the Hero* (1909 [trans. 1914]), he was a Freudian apostle.[2] While Campbell was never a full-fledged Jungian, he wrote *The Hero with a Thousand Faces* (1949) as a kindred soul of C. G. Jung's. Raglan wrote *The Hero* (1936) as a theoretical ally of J. G. Frazer.

Rank

Freudians analyze all kinds of myths, not just hero myths. Still, they often turn other kinds of myths into hero myths. Rank himself turns birth and survival into heroic feats. His heroes are exclusively male. Even creation myths have been seen by Freudians as accomplishing the feat of giving birth to the world—by males as well as by females.[3]

For Rank, following Freud, heroism deals with what *Jungians* call the "first half of life." The first half—birth, childhood, adolescence, and young adulthood—involves the establishment of oneself as an independent person in the external world. The attainment of independence expresses itself concretely in the securing of a job and a mate. The securing of either requires both separation from one's parents and mastery of one's instincts. Independence of one's parents means not the rejection of them but self-sufficiency. Similarly, independence of one's instincts means not the denial of them but control over them. When Freud says that the test of happiness is the capacity to work and love, he is clearly referring to the goals of the first half of life, which for him hold for all of life. Freudian problems involve a lingering attachment to either parents or instincts. To depend on one's parents for the satisfaction of instincts, or to satisfy instincts in anti-social ways, is to be stuck, or fixated, at childhood.

Rank's pattern, which he applies to over thirty hero myths, falls within the first half of life. It goes from the hero's birth to his attainment of a "career":

> The hero is the child of most distinguished parents, usually the son of a king. His origin is preceded by difficulties, such as continence, or prolonged barrenness, or secret intercourse of the parents due to external prohibition or obstacles. During or before the pregnancy, there is a prophecy, in the form of a dream or oracle, cautioning against his birth, and usually threatening danger to the father (or his representative). As a rule, he is surrendered to the water, in a box. He is then saved by animals, or by lowly people (shepherds), and is suckled by a female animal or by an [sic] humble woman. After he has grown up, he finds his distinguished parents, in a highly versatile fashion. He takes his revenge on his father, on the one hand, and is acknowledged, on the other. Finally he achieves rank and honors. (Rank et al. 1990: 57)

Literally, or consciously, the hero is a historical or legendary figure like Oedipus. He is heroic because he rises from obscurity to, typically, the throne. Literally, he is an innocent victim of either his parents or, ultimately, Fate. While his parents have yearned for a child and sacrifice him only to save the father, they nevertheless do sacrifice him. The hero's revenge, if the parricide is even committed knowingly, is, then, understandable: who would not consider killing one's would-be killer?

Symbolically, or unconsciously, the hero is heroic not because he dares to win a throne but because he dares to kill his father. The killing is definitely intentional, and the cause is not revenge but sexual frustration. The father has refused to surrender his wife—the real object of the son's efforts: "as a rule the deepest, generally unconscious root of the dislike of the son for the father, or of two brothers for each other, is referrable to the competition for the tender devotion and love of the mother" (Rank et al. 1990: 74). Too horrendous to face, the true meaning of the hero myth gets covered up by the concocted story, which makes the father, not the son, the culprit. The pattern is simply "the excuse, as it were, for the hostile feelings which the child harbors against his father, and which in this fiction are projected against the father" (Rank et al. 1990: 68–69). What the hero seeks gets masked as power, not incest. Most of all, who the hero is becomes some third party—the named hero—rather than either the creator of the myth or anyone stirred by it. Identifying himself with the named hero, the myth maker or reader vicariously revels in the hero's triumph, which in fact is his own. *He* is the real hero of the myth, which at heart is not biography but autobiography.

Literally, the myth culminates in the hero's attainment of a throne. Symbolically, the hero gains a mate as well. One might, then, conclude that the myth fittingly expresses the Freudian goal of the first half of life. In actuality, it expresses the opposite. The wish fulfilled is not for detachment from one's parents and from one's anti-social instincts but, on the contrary, for the most intense possible relationship to one's parents and for the most anti-social of urges: parricide and incest, even rape. Taking one's father's job and one's mother's hand does not quite spell independence of them.

The myth maker or reader is an adult, but the wish vented by the myth is that of a child of three to five: "Myths are, therefore, created by adults, by means of retrograde childhood fantasies, the hero being credited with the myth-maker's personal infantile [i.e., childhood] history" (Rank et al. 1990: 82). The fantasy is the fulfillment of the male's Oedipal wish to kill his father in order to gain access to his mother. The myth fulfills a wish never outgrown by the adult who either invents or uses it. That adult is psychologically an eternal child.

To be sure, the fulfillment provided by myth is symbolic rather than literal, mental rather than physical, disguised rather than overt, unconscious rather than conscious, and vicarious rather than direct. By identifying himself with the named hero, the creator or reader of the myth acts out in his mind deeds that he would never dare act out in the world. Even the Oedipal deeds of the *named* hero are disguised, for the heroic pattern operates at or near the manifest, not the latent, level. Still, the myth does provide fulfillment of a kind.

In order for the manifest level to hide, if also to reveal, the latent one, the pattern deciphered by Rank makes the feud between father and son one over power, not sex. Hence the pattern culminates not merely in the killing of the father but also in the supplanting of him as, usually, king:

"Finally he [the son] achieves rank and honors." Rank never explains why the manifest conflict is over the throne. Yet that manifest motive need not skew hero myths toward males. For there can be fights over a queen's throne as readily as over a king's—for example, the fight to the death between Queen Elizabeth I and Mary, Queen of Scots.

Rather, Rank, following Freud, may be assuming that the fight between father and son is more intense than that between mother and daughter because of the threat of castration. Hero myths are fantasies concocted by adult males in which the hero gets to do as an adult what the myth maker or reader dared not even attempt as a child: take on the father. At the same time Rank may be assuming that fathers are simply more imposing than mothers. Certainly, he associates heroism with bravery. In any event Rank confines hero myths to male heroes—above all in *The Incest Theme in Literature and Legend* (1992), which is even more Oedipal than *The Myth of the Birth of the Hero*, and even more strikingly after his break with Freud, beginning with *The Trauma of Birth* (1929).

While Freud was prepared to grant that "the act of birth is the first experience of anxiety, and thus the source and prototype of the affect of anxiety" (Freud 1953, vol. 5: 400 n. 3), he was never prepared to make birth the main, let alone the sole, source of anxiety and neurosis. He refused to subordinate the Oedipus complex, which centers on the father, to the trauma of birth, which necessarily centers on the mother. For Rank, who broke with Freud over this issue, the infant's anxiety at birth is the source of all subsequent anxiety. Conflict with the father remains, but because he blocks the son's yearning to return to the mother's womb rather than because he blocks the son's Oedipal yearning.

While Rank's *The Myth of the Birth of the Hero* already evinces the hiatus between his subsequent, post-Freudian focus on the hero's birth and his original, Freudian focus on the hero's deeds, the real shift comes with *The Trauma of Birth*. There Rank systematically interprets all of human life to fit the birth trauma. He continues to see myth as wish fulfillment, but the wish now fulfilled is, like the rest of culture, either to undo birth or to create a second womb. Where in *The Myth of the Birth of the Hero* the father is the culprit for *opposing* birth, in *The Trauma of Birth* the mother is the culprit for *giving* birth. Oedipus' blinding of himself upon discovering that he has committed incest represents not guilt for his Oedipal deeds but "a return into the darkness of the mother's womb, and his final disappearance through a cleft rock into the Underworld expresses once again the same wish tendency to return into the mother earth" (Rank 1929: 43).

With Rank begins the change of focus among psychoanalysts from the Oedipal stage to the pre-Oedipal one. Now the key relationship is not that between father and son but that between mother and child—of either sex. Yet even here Rank confines himself to males, whose heroism now is the overcoming of the opposition from the mother, with the father allying himself with the mother rather than, as in the Oedipal stage, the reverse.

Campbell

Though commonly called one, Joseph Campbell was never a straightfor-ward Jungian.[4] Still, Campbell stands close to Jung and stands closest in *The Hero with a Thousand Faces* (1949), which remains the classic Jungian analysis of hero myths. Where for Freud and Rank heroism is limited to the first half of life, for Jung it involves the second half even more. For Freud and Rank, heroism involves relations with parents and instincts. For Jung, heroism in even the first half involves, in addition, relations with the unconscious. Heroism here means separation not only from par-ents and anti-social instincts but even more from the unconscious. For Jung, managing to forge consciousness is a supremely heroic feat, and one as imperative for females as for males.

Just as classical Freudian problems involve the failure to establish one-self in the outer world, in the form of working and loving, so distinc-tively Jungian problems involve the failure to re-establish oneself in the inner world, in relation to the unconscious. Freudian problems stem from excessive attachment to the world of childhood; Jungian problems, from excessive attachment to the world one enters upon breaking free of the childhood world: the external world. To be severed from the internal world is to feel empty and lost.

Jung allows for heroism in both halves of life, and again by females as well as by males.[5] Yet the image that he uses to characterize heroism in both halves is that of a mother and her son. For Freud and Rank, both Freudian and post-Freudian, the mother is one's actual mother. For Jung, the mother is a symbol of one's unconsciousness. Called the Great Mother or the Terrible Mother, she symbolizes everyone's primordial uncon-scious. For Freud and Rank, the son means a male. For Jung, the son is a symbol of everyone's ego consciousness, or consciousness of the external world, which is to say, of the external world as separate from oneself: "the mother corresponds to the collective unconscious, and the son to con-sciousness" (Jung 1967 [1956]: 259). In the first half of life the son seeks to break free of the mother and become independent of her. In the second half of life the son, now independent, seeks to return to the mother to reconnect with her, but in turn to return to ordinary consciousness to form the self. Jung compares this two-part process with the course of the sun: from sunrise to sunset and back to sunrise (see Jung 1967 [1956]: 171).

Jung calls the accomplishment of the tasks of both halves of life heroic because of the difficulty involved. In the first half the son is as tempted to remain with the mother as the mother is to keep him with her. Breaking free of her requires courage and will. In the second half the son is as tempted never to leave the mother again as the mother is to keep him back with her. Managing to resist her allure also demands discipline and determination.

Jung associates masculinity with consciousness, ego, and culture, and associates femininity with the unconscious, egolessness, and instincts. Still, the ultimate goal is, rather than the replacement of femininity by masculinity, the harmonizing of the two. But it is the ego, symbolized by the son, that accomplishes this task. Psychological development is the work of one's—anyone's—masculine side.

Jung reinterprets the incest taboo as that established by society not to keep an adult male from acting out a yearning for sex with the mother but to keep anyone's ego consciousness from reunion with the unconsciousness and thereby dissolution altogether (see Jung 1967 [1956]: 235–36, 255, 259, 271, 417-18). The male unable to forge independence of the unconscious—that is, unable to achieve the goal of even the first half of life—is an eternal youth, who is under the sway of the *puer* archetype. The female counterpart to the puer is the *puella* archetype. Jung writes far more on the puer than on the puella.[6] His best examples of those dominated by the puer archetype are Adonis (or Tammuz) and Attis—the first two of Frazer's main examples of the god of vegetation (see Jung 1967 [1956]: 258).

The opposite of the puer is the hero archetype: where the puer eventually succumbs to the allure of the unconscious and so dies once and for all, the hero manages to resist the allure and is reborn (see Jung 1967 [1956]: 259). That rebirth makes the hero psychologically immortal. Hence Jung declares that "He who stems from two mothers is the hero: the first birth makes him a mortal man, the second an immortal half-god" (Jung 1967 [1956]: 322). The female counterpart to the hero is the heroine, who is the opposite of the puella.

On what data does Jung base his key analysis of hero myths—that in *Symbols of Transformation* (1967 [1956])? On the fantasies of an American—not a patient of his—whose pseudonym was "Frank Miller." Yet Frank Miller was in fact a woman, so that for Jung heroism as symbolically male comes from the fantasies of a woman, not of a man![7]

Where Jung allows for heroism in both halves of life, Erich Neumann focuses on heroism in the first half of life.[8] While Jung himself certainly correlates kinds of myths with stages of psychological development, Neumann, in above all *The Origins and History of Consciousness* (1970), works out the stages, beginning with the "uroboric" stages of sheer unconsciousness, and proceeding to the incipient emergence of the ego out of the unconscious, the development of an independent ego consciousness, and—in the second half of life—the eventual return of the ego to the unconscious to create the self. Following Jung, whose outright disciple he was, Neumann characterizes the course of psychological development as one of continuing heroism—with each stage posing a Herculean-like task. Also following Jung, Neumann characterizes heroism for all as symbolically masculine. Like Jung, he associates masculinity with consciousness, ego, and culture, and associates femininity with the unconscious, egolessness, and instincts.

Where Neumann, like Rank, limits himself to heroism in the first half of life, Campbell, in *The Hero with a Thousand Faces*, confines himself to heroism in the second half. Rank's scheme begins with the hero's birth; Campbell's, with the hero's adventure. Where Rank's scheme ends, Campbell's begins: with the adult hero ensconced at home. Rank's hero must be young enough for his father and in some cases even his grandfather still to be in power. Campbell does not specify the age of his hero, but the hero must be no younger than the age at which Rank's hero myth therefore ends: young adulthood. While some of Campbell's own examples are of child heroes, they violate his scheme, according to which heroes must be willing to leave behind all that they have accomplished at home. Even more, these cases violate his Jungian meaning, according to which heroes must be fully developed egos ready to encounter the unconscious from which they have long been severed. Campbell's heroes should, then, be in the second half of life. Campbell does acknowledge heroism in the first half of life and even cites Rank's monograph, but he demotes this youthful heroism to mere preparation for adult heroism: he calls it the "childhood of the human hero."[9]

Where Rank's hero returns to his birthplace, Campbell's marches forth to a strange, new world, which the hero has never visited or even known existed. This extraordinary world is the world of the gods, and the hero must hail from the human world precisely to be able to experience the distinctiveness of the divine one.

In this exotic, supernatural world the hero encounters above all a supreme female god and a supreme male god. The maternal goddess is loving and caring. By contrast, the male god is tyrannical and merciless. The hero has sex with the goddess and marries her. He competes with the male god and then kills him. Yet with both gods, not just the goddess, the hero becomes mystically one and thereby becomes divine himself.

Where Rank's hero *returns* home to encounter his father and mother, Campbell's hero *leaves* home to encounter a male and a female god, who are neither his parents nor a couple. Yet the two heroes' encounters are much alike: just as Rank's hero kills his father and, if usually only latently, marries his mother, so Campbell's hero, in reverse order, first marries the goddess and then kills the god. The differences, however, are even more significant. Because the goddess is not the hero's mother, sex with her does not constitute incest. Despite appearances, the hero's relationship to the male god is for Campbell no less positive and so no less non-Oedipal.

Because Campbell enlists myths of female heroes as often as those of male ones—his opening example is that of the Grimms' "The Princess and the Frog"—it is seemingly inappropriate for me to refer to Campbell's hero as "he." Yet in fact Campbell restricts heroism to males—once the three-part heroic journey moves from the stage of departure to the stage of initiation. Without notice or explanation Campbell abruptly narrows his focus from heroes of either gender to exclusively male ones. While he does include female heroes in the first subsection of the stage of initiation, or the "road of trials," once he gets to the heart of initiation—the encounter with the god and the goddess—all of his heroes are male. More precisely, most are male, for Campbell still cites some female examples, even though they clearly are not "meeting with the goddess," facing "woman as the temptress," or achieving "atonement with the father." It is because encounters with the god and the goddess are exclusively undertaken by male heroes that the pattern here can so easily be mistaken as Freudian.

Yet nothing in the overall journey at either the manifest or the latent level in fact demands exclusively male initiation: the encounter is with the masculine and feminine, or father-like and mother-like, sides of the personality, which both sexes harbor. And the Princess does encounter a male frog, though their encounter is not quite what Campbell's pattern prescribes. Straight-laced Campbell, one can take for granted, never envisions other than heterosexual relations with the goddess, and even the reconciliation with the male god—called by Campbell "atonement with the father"—assumes a male hero. In short, Campbell could effortlessly have widened the substages to allow for encounters on the part of either female or male heroes. But he does not.

Understandably, then, others have offered a feminine counterpart to what they take to be Campbell's exclusively masculine brand of heroism. Carol Pearson and Katherine Pope in *The Female Hero in American and British Literature* (1981) write: "The great works on the hero—such as Joseph Campbell's *The Hero with a Thousand Faces*, Dorothy Norman's *The Hero: Myth/Image/Symbol*, and Lord Raglan's *The Hero: A Study in Tradition, Myth and Drama*—all begin with the assumption that the hero is male" (Pearson and Pope 1981: vii). Writes Carol Pearson in *The Hero Within* (1989): "The great books on the hero, such as Joseph Campbell's *The Hero with a Thousand Faces*, assumed either that the hero was male or that male heroism and female heroism were essentially the same" (Pearson 1989: xx).[10] Pearson and Pope note that Campbell declares at the outset that the hero may be either male or female, but they maintain that he "then proceeds to discuss the heroic pattern as male and to define the female characters as goddesses, temptresses, and earth mothers" (Pearson and Pope 1981: 4). They fault Jung as well on the same grounds (see Pearson and Pope 1981: 4).

In *The Hero Within* Pearson follows Campbell in deeming the heart of heroism a journey, but she proposes six archetypes, or roles, that male and female heroes follow in their journeys with different orders and different emphases. The traditional male progresses from Orphan to Warrior to Wanderer to Martyr to Magician. The traditional female moves from Orphan to Martyr to Wanderer to Warrior to Magician. Furthermore, most contemporary men's values "are very much defined by the Warrior ethic" (Pearson 1989: 9). By contrast, most contemporary women either are Martyrs or "have moved quickly through the Wanderer and Warrior stages and are beginning to experiment with being Magicians" (Pearson 1989: 9). Pearson adds that "conservatives" assert that the Martyr archetype is distinctly female and the Warrior archetype distinctly male, where many feminists argue that "the Magician mode is the new emerging female system in contrast to the old patriarchal Warrior way of being in the world" (Pearson 1989: 9).

In the process of proposing a new heroic journey to counter the male proclivity of Campbell's, Pearson abandons Campbell's Jungian approach.

The roles she delineates are not innate predispositions, as for Jung, but choices. Her "archetypes" are more Sartrean: they are chosen identities.

Raglan

Lord Raglan's brand of myth ritualism derives ultimately from J. G. Frazer: myth provides the script for ritual. Frazer in fact presents two versions of the myth and ritual scenario.[11] In one version the king is a mere human being and simply plays the role of the god. The dramatic enactment of the death and rebirth of the god, who is the god of vegetation, magically causes the rebirth of the presently dead god and in turn of the presently dead vegetation. The ritual is performed annually at the end—the would-be end—of winter. In the other form of the ritual the king is himself divine, with the god of vegetation residing in him—and is actually killed and replaced. The soul of the god is thereby transferred to the new king. The killing of the king does not magically induce the killing of the god but instead simply preserves the health of the god, for the king is killed at the first sign of weakness or at the end of a fixed term so short as to minimize the chance of illness or death in office. The state of the king determines the state of the god of vegetation and in turn the state of vegetation.

Frazer's key examples of gods of vegetation are from Western Asia and Egypt: Adonis (Greek) (or Tammuz [Babylonian]), Attis (Syrian), Osiris (Egyptian), and Dionysus (Greek)—and also Jesus. All are male. To be sure, he does write that "a great Mother Goddess,"

> the personification of all the reproductive energies of nature, was worshipped under different names but with a substantial similarity of myth and ritual by many peoples of Western Asia; that associated with her was a lover, or rather series of lovers, divine yet mortal, with whom she mated year by year, their commerce being deemed essential to the propagation of animals and plants, each in their several kind; and further, that the fabulous union of the divine pair was simulated and, as it were, multiplied on earth by the real, though temporary, union of the human sexes at the sanctuary of the goddess for the sake of thereby ensuring the fruitfulness of the ground and the increase of man and beast. (Frazer 1922: 385)

But the male god of vegetation remains the more important, for in Frazer's first version of myth ritualism it is primarily the myths of male gods that are ritually enacted to revive them, not their consorts. His fullest female counterpart to Adonis, Attis, Osiris, and Dionysus is Persephone.

Raglan adopts Frazer's second version of myth ritualism.[12] Here the king *is* the god of vegetation rather than plays the part of the god. Consequently, the killing and replacement of the king do not magically cause the death and rebirth of the god but *are* the death and rebirth— better, the weakening and reinvigoration—of that god and therefore of vegetation.[13] For Raglan, as for Frazer, the myth describes the life of the figure and the ritual enacts it. The function of the ritual, which is performed either at the end of the king's fixed term or upon his weakening, is, as for Frazer, to aid the community.

Venturing beyond Frazer, Raglan equates the king with the hero. For Frazer, the king may in effect be a hero to his community, but only Raglan labels him one. It is Raglan who turns a theory of myth in general into a theory of hero myths in particular. Moreover, Raglan introduces his own detailed hero pattern, which he applies to twenty-one hero myths. That pattern extends all the way from the hero's conception to his death. In contrast to Rank's and Campbell's patterns, it therefore covers both halves of life:

(1) The hero's mother is a royal virgin;
(2) His father is a king, and
(3) Often a near relative of his mother, but
(4) The circumstances of his conception are unusual, and
(5) He is also reputed to be the son of a god.
(6) At birth an attempt is made, usually by his father or his maternal grandfather, to kill him, but
(7) He is spirited away, and
(8) Reared by foster-parents in a far country.
(9) We are told nothing of his childhood, but
(10) On reaching manhood he returns or goes to his future kingdom.
(11) After a victory over the king and/or a giant, dragon, or wild beast,
(12) He marries a princess, often the daughter of his predecessor, and
(13) Becomes king.
(14) For a time he reigns uneventfully, and
(15) Prescribes laws, but
(16) Later he loses favour with the gods and/or his subjects, and
(17) Is driven from the throne and city, after which
(18) He meets with a mysterious death,
(19) Often at the top of a hill.
(20) His children, if any, do not succeed him.
(21) His body is not buried, but nevertheless
(22) He has one or more holy sepulchres. (Rank et al. 1990: 138)

Clearly, parts one to thirteen correspond roughly to Rank's entire scheme, though Raglan himself never read Rank. Six of Raglan's cases duplicate Rank's, and the anti-Freudian Raglan nevertheless also takes the case of Oedipus as his standard. The victory that gives the hero the throne is not, however, Oedipal, for the vanquished is not necessarily his father, even if, as for Rank, the father is usually the one who had sought his son's death at birth. Parts fourteen to twenty-two do not correspond at all to Campbell's scheme. The hero's exile is loosely akin to the hero's journey, but for Raglan there is no return. The hero's sepulchres do serve as a kind of boon, but not for his native community. For Rank, the heart of the hero pattern is gaining kingship—or other title. For Raglan, the heart is losing kingship. Wherever Campbell's heroes are kings, the heart is their journey while king.

Raglan's preoccupation with the king obviously dictates male heroes only. For Raglan, kingship ties the myth to the ritual: what for Raglan is the core of the myth—the toppling of the king—corresponds to the undeniable core of the ritual—the killing of the king. Strictly, the myth, which describes the life of a past hero, is less the script, as for Frazer, than the inspiration for the ritual, which involves the killing of the present king. The myth is intended to spur the incumbent to submit to the ritual and thereby be a hero to his subjects.

For Raglan, kingship also ties the hero to the god: heroes are kings, and kings are gods. True, the hero must die and must therefore be literally a mere mortal, but the hero's death accomplishes a superhuman feat: it ensures the revival of vegetation and thereby the survival of the kingdom, though Raglan does not, like Frazer, automatically make the god the god of vegetation. Raglan's heroes have the power to affect the physical world, even if only by dying. They are the saviors of their subjects. Somehow queens cannot do the same.

In "Traits of the Female Hero" (1984) Mary Ann Jezewski proposes a female hero pattern as the counterpart to Raglan's. But her proposal is not nearly so damning as Pearson's, for Raglan, unlike Campbell, never presumes to be considering other than male heroes.[14] Jezewski's pattern breaks with Raglan's in not insisting that female heroes either rule or be removed before they die. But then Jezewski severs the link between hero and god. Moreover, she limits herself to the mythic pattern and so ignores any link to ritual. What she offers is a whittled-down version of Raglan. The price she pays for a female hero à la Raglan is the elimination of the heart of Raglan's theory. Her very attempt to "feminize" Raglan's theory shows how male-centered his is.

In conclusion, myths of female heroes need to start from scratch.

Chapter 13

Does Synchronicity Bring Myth Back to the World?

There is a clear-cut divide between nineteenth- and twentieth-century theories of myth. In the nineteenth century myth was taken to be the "primitive" counterpart to science, which was assumed to be entirely modern. Myth originated and functioned to do for primitive peoples what science now did for moderns: account for all events in the physical world. One could not consistently hold both kinds of explanations, and moderns, who were *defined* as scientific, were logically obliged to abandon myth. The rise of science spelled the death of myth.

The leading exponents of the nineteenth-century view of myth were the pioneering anthropologist E. B. Tylor, whose main work, *Primitive Culture*, was published in 1871, and the classicist and fellow pioneering anthropologist J. G. Frazer, whose key work, *The Golden Bough*, was first published in 1890. For Tylor, myth provides knowledge of the world as an end in itself. For Frazer, the knowledge that myth provides is a means to control over the world, above all for securing food. For both, myth is the primitive counterpart to natural, not social, science. It is the counterpart to biology, chemistry, and physics rather than to sociology, anthropology, psychology, and economics. For Tylor, myth is the exact counterpart to scientific theory. For Frazer, myth is the exact counterpart to applied science.

Myth, which is part of religion, attributes rain to a decision by a god; science attributes it to impersonal, meteorological processes. For Tylor and Frazer, the explanations are incompatible because both are direct. In myth, gods operate not behind or through impersonal forces but in place of them. Therefore one cannot stack the mythic explanation atop the scientific explanation, crediting science with the direct explanation and crediting myth with the indirect explanation. Rather, one must choose between them. Because moderns by definition have science, the choice has been made for them. They must give up myth, which is not merely outdated but false. Moderns who still cling to myth have failed either to recognize or to concede the incompatibility of it with science.

Twentieth-Century Theories of Myth

In the twentieth century myth was reconciled with science. Moderns, still defined as scientific, could now retain myth. Tylor's and Frazer's theories were spurned on many grounds: for precluding modern myths, for subsuming myth under religion and thereby precluding secular myths, for deeming the function of myth scientific-like, and for deeming myth false. Yet twentieth-century theorists did not try to reconcile myth with science by challenging science. They did not take any of the easy steps: "relativizing" science, "sociologizing" science, making science "masculine," or making science "mythic." No less than their nineteenth-century predecessors did they accept science as the reigning explanation of the physical world. Rather, they recharacterized *myth* as other than a literal explanation of events in the physical world.

Twentieth-century theories of myth can, accordingly, be divided into three groups. First are those theories which maintain that myth, while still about the world, is not an explanation of the world, in which case its function diverges from that of science. The true function of myth can range from acceptance of the world to escape from the world. The preeminent theorists here are the anthropologist Bronislaw Malinowski and the historian of religions Mircea Eliade.

Second are those theories which maintain that myth is not to be read literally, in which case the subject matter of myth is not the physical world. The true subject matter of myth can range from the impact of the physical world on human beings to human beings themselves. The leading theorists here are the New Testament scholar Rudolf Bultmann and the philosopher Hans Jonas. Also fitting here is the existentialist writer Albert Camus.

Third and most radical are those theories which maintain both that myth is not an explanation and that myth is not to be read literally. Here fall, above all, Freud and Jung. As much as the two differ from each other, they both deem the subject matter of myth the human mind and deem the function of myth the experience of that mind.

For both Malinowski (1954b) and Eliade (1959a), myth is, to be sure, an explanation in part, but explanation is only a means to a nonscientific end rather than the end itself. For Malinowski, that end is to reconcile humans to disease, death, and other brute aspects of the physical world. For Eliade, the end is to carry humans back to the time of the myth, which is always the past, in order to encounter god. Myth is like a magic carpet.

For both Malinowski and Eliade, myth is as much about social phenomena—customs, laws, and institutions—as about physical ones. The subject matter of myth is thus more than the physical world. For Malinowski, myths about social phenomena serve to reconcile members to impositions that they might otherwise reject. The beneficiary is society, not the individual. For Eliade, myths about social phenomena serve the same magic carpet-like function as myths about physical ones.

Insofar as myth for Malinowski deals with the social world, it turns its back on the physical world. But even when myth deals with the physical world, its connection to that world is limited. Myth may explain how flooding arose—a god or a human brought it about—but science, not myth, explains why flooding occurs whenever it does. And science alone says what to do about it. Indeed, myth assumes that nothing can be done about it. Myth and science are compatible because their functions are distinct.

So, too, for Eliade. But he goes beyond Malinowski and certainly Tylor and Frazer in proclaiming myth universal and not merely primitive. Where for Malinowski primitive peoples have both myth and science and moderns have only science, for Eliade, as for Tylor and Frazer, primitive peoples have only myth. But for Eliade, in contrast to Malinowski, Tylor, and Frazer alike, moderns have myth as well as science, in which case myth must be universal.

Where neither Malinowski nor Eliade challenges Frazer's and especially Tylor's literal reading of myth, Bultmann and Jonas do. While they limit themselves to their specialties, Christianity and Gnosticism, they apply a theory of myth per se—a theory that comes from the early, existentialist philosophy of Martin Heidegger.

Bultmann (1953) acknowledges that, read literally, myth is about the physical world and is incompatible with science. It should therefore rightly be rejected as uncompromisingly as Tylor and Frazer reject it. But unlike both Malinowski and Eliade as well as both Tylor and Frazer, Bultmann proposes reading myth symbolically. In his celebrated, if excruciatingly confusing, phrase, myth should be "demythologized," which means not eliminating, or "demythicizing," myth but instead extricating its true, existential meaning. To seek evidence of an actual worldwide flood, while dismissing the miraculous notion of an unsinkable ark containing all species, would be to *demythicize* the myth of Noah. To interpret the flood as a symbolic statement about the precariousness of human life would be to *demythologize* the myth.

Demythologized, myth ceases to be about the world itself and turns out to be about the human *experience* of the world. Demythologized, myth ceases to be an explanation at all and becomes an expression, an expression of what it "feels" like to live in the world. The New Testament, when demythologized, contrasts the alienation from the world felt by those who have not yet found God to the at-homeness in the world felt by those who have found God. Myth ceases to be merely primitive and becomes universal. It ceases to be false and becomes true. It still speaks to humans because it depicts the eternal human condition.

Like Bultmann, Jonas (1963) seeks to show that ancient myths retain a message for moderns. For Jonas, as for Bultmann, myth read symbolically describes the alienation of humans from the world as well as from their true selves prior to their acceptance of God. Because ancient Gnosticism, unlike mainstream Christianity, sets the soul against the body and sets immateriality against matter, humans remain alienated from the material world and from their bodies even after they have found the true God. In fact, the true God can be found only by rejecting the false god of the material world. Gnostics overcome alienation from this world only by transcending the world. Gnostic mythology can still speak to moderns because, correctly understood, it addresses not the nature of the world but, like Christian mythology according to Bultmann, the nature of the experience of the world. Hence for Jonas, as for Bultmann, myth and science do not compete.

Freud (1953, 1958) and Jung (1971) offer the most extreme departure from Tylor and Frazer. For they transform both the literal meaning and the explanatory function of myth. The subject matter of myth—the human unconscious—is as far removed from the outer world as can be. In myth the unconscious projects itself onto the world in the form of gods and heroes, so that the analysis of myth requires the disentangling of myth from the world. Myth functions as a means of encountering not the world but the unconscious.[1]

In "The Theme of the Three Caskets" Freud comments snippily on an interpretation made by E. Stucken of the choice of the caskets in *The Merchant of Venice*:

> He [Stucken] writes: "The identity of Portia's three suitors is clear from their choice: the Prince of Morocco chooses the gold casket—he is the sun; the Prince of Arragon chooses the silver casket—he is the moon; Bassanio chooses the leaden casket—he is the star youth."

> Thus our little problem has led us to an astral myth! The only pity is
> that with this explanation we are not at the end of the matter. The ques-
> tion is not exhausted, for we do not share the belief of some investiga-
> tors that myths were read in the heavens and brought down to earth;
> we are more inclined to judge with Otto Rank that they were projected
> on to the heavens after having arisen elsewhere under purely human
> conditions. It is in this human content that our interest lies. (Freud
> 1958: 291–92)

Rather than originating in the experience of the natural world, myth for
Freud originates in the experience of the family and is then projected
onto the world.

Toward nature mythologists, Jung is at least as dismissive as Freud. For
him, humans lack the creativity to invent the idea of god. Rather, they
are born with that idea and project it onto vegetation and other natural
phenomena:

> This latter analogy [between god and natural phenomenon] explains
> the well-attested connection between the renewal of the god and sea-
> sonal and vegetational phenomena. One is naturally inclined to assume
> that seasonal, vegetational, lunar, and solar myths underlie these anal-
> ogies. But that is to forget that a myth, like everything psychic, cannot
> be solely conditioned by external events. Anything psychic brings its
> own internal conditions with it, so that one might assert with equal
> right that the myth is purely psychological and uses meteorological or
> astronomical events merely as a means of expression. The whimsicality
> and absurdity of many primitive myths often makes the latter explana-
> tion seem far more appropriate than any other. (Jung 1971: 193–94)

Bringing Myth Back to the World

Where theorists of the nineteenth century assumed that myth could not
be dislodged from the world and therefore could not be saved from science, theorists of the twentieth century saved myth from science either
by removing myth altogether from the world or by removing it as an
explanation of the world. The question for the twenty-first century is
whether myth can be returned to the world, but in a way still compatible
with science. The postmodern dismissal of the authority of science, often
evinced by labeling science itself mythic, cheapens both myth and science. My admiration for twentieth-century theorizing lies in its attempt
to accommodate myth *to* science rather than to spurn science in the
name of myth.

There have been several attempts to bring myth back to the world. Most notable is the work of the scientist James Lovelock, beginning with his 1979 book *Gaia*. He sees the earth, or Gaia, as a personality that figures out ways to keep itself healthy. Gaia becomes a virtual god.[2]

Very differently, Jung, despite his relentless psychologizing of myth, waxes romantic about the existential function of myth: that is, the meaning it gives life in the outer world. This function of myth is the same as that for Bultmann and Jonas. To cite Jung's favorite example: "The Pueblo Indians believe that they are the sons of Father Sun, and this belief gives their life a perspective and a goal beyond their individual and limited existence. It leaves ample room for the unfolding of their personality, and is infinitely more satisfactory than the certainty that one is and will remain the underdog in a department store" (Jung 1976: 247).

But Jung's appreciation is of the existential power of myth for primitive peoples only. The meaningfulness that myth offers Pueblo Indians works only by personifying the external world. This pre-scientific option is not available to moderns. And even existentialist theorists of myth, especially Bultmann, have difficulty offering moderns a comforting world without resurrecting God as an active agent in that world.

Synchronicity

A more promising Jungian way of bringing myth back to the world—the outer world—doubtless lies in the concept of synchronicity (see Jung 1969: 419–519 and 520–31).[3]

The term refers to the coincidence between our thoughts and the behavior of the world, between what is inner and what is outer. As Jung writes of his favorite example of synchronicity, that of a resistant patient who was describing a dream about a golden scarab when a scarab beetle appeared: "at the moment my patient was telling me her dream a real 'scarab' tried to get into the room, as if it had understood that it must play its mythological role as a symbol of rebirth" (Jung 1973–76, vol. 2: 541). Here the world apparently responds to the patient's dream. But understood synchronistically, the world merely, if most fortuitously, *matches* the patient's dream, not *causes* it or is caused by it. Synchronicity is not like astrology, in which the planets determine personality. The patient's conscious attitude, which dismisses the notion of an unconscious, is "out of sync" with the world. The unconscious is using this coincidence to impress on the patient the kinship between humans and the world—exactly the kind of kinship that myth, as a person-like account of the world, provides the Pueblos.

With the concept of synchronicity the world regains meaningfulness even without personalization. The world regains the meaningfulness that had been lost with the withdrawal of mythic projections. Furthermore, that meaningfulness is now inherent in the world rather than projected onto it: "synchronistic experiences serve our turn here. They point to a latent meaning which is independent of [our] consciousness" (Jung 1973-76, vol. 2: 495). Meaningfulness now stems not from the existence of god, or personality, in the world but from the symmetry between human beings and the world. Rather than alien and indifferent to humans, the world proves to be akin to them—not because gods respond to human wishes or because human wishes directly affect the world but because human thoughts correspond to the nature of the world.

But in the case of the patient, what exactly is the "mythological role" of the beetle as "a symbol of rebirth"? The patient's experience of synchronicity is not itself myth, which would be an account of that experience. But an account means a causal account. Can there be a causal account of noncausality? Can there be a myth of synchronicity—a myth accompanying a case of synchronicity?

Roderick Main (2007) takes this example of synchronicity and argues that it constitutes "myth beyond projection." He teases out the association for Jung, whether or not for the patient, of the scarab with ancient myths of rebirth, of creation, and of heroic rescue. He suggests that the incident with the scarab aroused in Jung his notion of himself as the heroic rescuer of not merely his psychologically imprisoned patient but the whole psychologically locked-up modern West.

The first question is whether the mythological associations really deal with the world. Even if synchronicity itself ties the inner world to the outer one, do the myths it stirs themselves deal with the outer world? If what is being rescued is the unconscious side of humanity, then surely the outer world is a mere steppingstone to the inner one. Undeniably, synchronicity, as a noncausal phenomenon, circumvents the issue that in the nineteenth century pitted myth against science: the cause of events in the outer world. But are myths tied to synchronicity really connected to the outer world? Main has explained to me that for Jung they are. Synchronicity enhances the meaningfulness of myths about the outer world but does not create it. The myth of the rebirth of the scarab is to be found in the outer world as well as in the world of the patient's dream.

The outer myth is not a projection of the inner one and thereby does not need to be withdrawn.

With synchronicity, Jungian psychology offers an extraordinary vehicle for carrying myth back to the world—and without leaving science behind. Still, one question, not to be answered here, lingers: is the myth of the rebirth of the scarab explaining the appearance of the scarab or merely being invoked upon the appearance of the scarab? Unless the myth explains the scarab, the myth may lie more in the background than in the foreground. Myth, then, may not yet be fully back in the world.

Chapter 14

The Bible as Myth, Science, Religion, and Philosophy

The modern study of myth has tied myth to science, religion, and philosophy. I here trace the varying relationships among these categories and then consider how the story of Noah would fare in each case.

Definition of Myth

I have attended many a conference in which speakers fervently propound on "the nature of myth" in novel X or movie Y or religion Z. Yet so much of the argument depends on the definition of myth. Let me make clear my own.

To begin with, I propose defining myth as a story. That myth, whatever else it is, is a story may seem self-evident. After all, when asked to name myths, most of us think first of *stories* about Greco-Roman gods and heroes. Yet myth can also be taken more broadly as a belief or credo—for example, the American "rags to riches myth" or the American "myth of the frontier." Horatio Alger wrote scores of popular novels illustrating the rags to riches myth, but the credo itself does not rest on any myth. The same is true of the myth of the frontier.

All of the approaches to myth, or theories of myth, discussed in this chapter and in this book deem myth a story, or a plot—with a beginning, middle, and end. Indeed, only the theory of Claude Lévi-Strauss (1955, 1966, 1970) does not deem myth a story. Theories that read myth symbolically rather than literally still take the subject matter to be the unfolding of the story.

If, then, myth is to be taken here as a story, what is the story about? For folklorists above all, myth is about the creation of the world. In the Hebrew Bible only the two creation stories (Genesis 1 and 2), the Garden of Eden story (Genesis 3), and the Noah story (Genesis 6–9) would qualify as myths. All other stories would instead constitute either legends or folktales. I am not so rigid and instead define myth as simply a story about something significant. The story can take place in the past, as it must for Mircea Eliade and for Bronislaw Malinowski, or in the present or the future.

For theories from, above all, religious studies, the main characters in myth must be gods. Here, too, I am not so rigid. If I were, I would have to exclude most of the Hebrew Bible, for example, where all the stories may *involve* God but apart from only the first two chapters of Genesis are at least as much about human beings as about God. I insist only that the main figures be personalities—divine, human, or even animal. Excluded would be impersonal forces like Plato's Good, but not Plato's divine craftsman in the *Timaeus*. Among theorists, Tylor is the most preoccupied with the personalistic nature of myth, but all the other theorists to be discussed assume it—with the exception, again, of Lévi-Strauss. At the same time the personalities need not be the agents of action and can also be the objects of action.

Save for Rudolf Bultmann and Hans Jonas, who ignore the issue, all of the theorists considered in this chapter tend to the function of myth, and Malinowski focuses on it almost exclusively. Theorists differ sharply over what the function of myth is. I do not presume to dictate what the function of myth must somehow be. I note only that for all the theorists the function is weighty—in contrast to the lighter functions of legend and folktale. I thereby assert that myth accomplishes something significant for adherents, but I leave open-ended what that accomplishment might be.

In today's parlance myth is considered false. Myth is "mere" myth. For example, in 1997 historian William Rubinstein published *The Myth of Rescue: Why the Democracies Could Not Have Saved More Jews from the Nazis*. The title says it all. The book challenges the common conviction that many Jewish victims of the Nazis could have been saved if only the Allies had committed themselves to rescuing them. Rubinstein is challenging the assumption that the Allies were indifferent to the fate of European Jews and were indifferent because they were antisemitic. For him, the term "myth" captures the sway of the conviction about the failure to rescue more fully than would tamer phrases like "erroneous belief" and "popular misconception." A "myth" is a conviction that is false yet tenacious.

By contrast, the phrase "rags to riches myth" uses the term myth neutrally or even positively, while still conveying the hold of the conviction.

A blatantly false conviction might seem to have a stronger hold than a true one, for the conviction remains firm even in the face of its transparent falsity. But a cherished conviction that is true can be clutched as tightly as a false one, especially when supported by persuasive evidence. Ironically, some Americans who continue to espouse the rags to riches credo may no longer refer to it as a "myth" *because* the term has come to connote falsity. I suggest that, to qualify as a myth, a story, which can of course express a conviction, be held tenaciously by adherents. But I leave unanswered whether the story is in fact true, literally or otherwise.

Myth as True Science

In the West the chief *ancient* challenge to myth came from philosophy. Plato above all rejected Homeric myth on ethical grounds. The chief *modern* challenge to myth has come from science. Here myth is assumed to explain how gods control the physical world rather than, as for Plato, how they behave among themselves. Where Plato bemoans myths for presenting the gods as exemplars of immoral behavior, modern critics dismiss myths for explaining the world unscientifically.

One form of the modern challenge to myth has been to the scientific credibility of myth. Did creation really occur in a mere six days, as the first of two creation stories in Genesis (1:1–2:4a) claims? Was there really a worldwide flood? Is the earth truly but six or seven thousand years old? Could the ten plagues on the Egyptians actually have happened?

The most unrepentant defense against this challenge has been to claim that the biblical account of all these events is correct. For after all, the Hebrew Bible was revealed to Moses by God. Myth is here subsumed under religion. To be sure, this position, known as "creationism," assumes varying forms, ranging, for example, from taking the days of creation to mean exactly six days to taking them to mean "ages." But the biblical stories, including their miraculous elements, are deemed true. They do not require interpretation, only appreciation. We do not turn to Philo to enable us to fathom the literal content. Creationism arose in reaction to Darwin's *Origin of Species* (1859), which contends that species gradually emerged out of one another rather than having been created separately and virtually simultaneously. Surprisingly, creationism has become ever more, not ever less, uncompromisingly literalist in its rendition of the biblical account of creation.[1]

To take creationists as pitting religion, and therefore myth, against science would be to misconstrue their position. Creationists of all stripes tout their views as scientific *as well as* religious. "Creationism" is short-hand for "creation science," which appropriates scientific evidence of any kind both to bolster its own claims and to refute those of secular rivals like evolution. Doubtless "creation scientists" would object to the term "myth" to characterize the view they defend, but only because the term has come to connote false belief. If the term is used neutrally for a firmly held conviction, creationism is a myth that claims to be scientific. For creation scientists, it is evolution that is untenable scientifically. In any clash between the Bible and modern science, modern science must give way to biblical science, not vice versa. Here myth is subsumed under both religion and true science. What is pitted against myth is atheistic science, which is false.

Myth as Modern Science

A much tamer defense of myth against the challenge of modern science has been to reconcile myth with modern science. Here elements at odds with modern science are either removed or, more cleverly, reinterpreted as in fact scientific. Myth is credible scientifically because it *is* science—modern science. There might not have been a Noah singlehandedly able to gather up all living species and to keep them alive in a wooden boat sturdy enough to withstand the strongest seas that ever arose, but a worldwide flood did occur. What thus remains in myth is true because it is scientific. Here myth is removed from religion, which is set against science, and is moved to the camp of science. The often miraculous details of myth are discarded as dross. Underneath lies gold, which is to say scientifically credible fact. This approach to myth is the opposite of that called "demythologizing," which separates myth from science.[2]

In their comment on the first plague, the turning of the waters of the Nile into blood (Exodus 7:14-24), the editors of the Protestant *Oxford Annotated Bible* epitomize this rationalizing approach: "The plague of blood apparently reflects a natural phenomenon of Egypt: namely, the reddish color of the Nile at its height in the summer owing to red particles of earth or perhaps minute organisms" (May and Metzger 1977: 75). Of the second plague, that of frogs (Exodus 8:1-15), the editors declare similarly: "The mud of the Nile, after the seasonal overflowing, was a natural place for frogs to generate. Egypt has been spared more frequent occurrence of this pestilence by the frog-eating bird, the ibis" (May and Metzger 1977: 75). How fortuitous that the ibis must have been away on holiday when Aaron stretched out his hand to produce the plague and must have just returned when Moses wanted the plague to cease! Instead of setting myth *against* science, this tactic turns myth *into* science—and not, as is fashionable today, science into myth.[3]

Myth as Primitive Science

By far the most common response to the challenge of science has been to reject myth for science. Here myth, while still an explanation of the world, is now taken as an explanation of its own kind, not a scientific explanation in mythic guise. The issue is therefore not the scientific credibility of myth but the compatibility of myth with science. Myth is considered to be "primitive" science—or, more precisely, the pre-scientific counterpart to science, which, at least as the commonplace explanation of physical events, is assumed to be exclusively modern. Myth is here part of religion. Where religion apart from myth provides the sheer belief in gods, myth fills in the details of how gods cause events.

Religion and science are incompatible—not because they serve the same function but because they do so incompatibly. Both religion and science offer direct, or immediate, explanations of events. Thunder occurs not because the creator god has set up meteorological laws or turned on a switch but because the god has taken a thunder bolt from his collection and thrust the bolt in the direction in which he wants it to go. God does not operate behind the scenes. Rather, God operates in place of any meteorological principle—though admittedly some tacit scientific-like laws are being assumed in explaining why the bolt attains the velocity that it does and reaches its target.

Because moderns by definition accept science, they cannot also have myth, and the phrase "modern myth" is self-contradictory. Myth is a victim of the process of secularization that constitutes modernity.

The myth of the Flood would be a pre-scientific explanation of a physical event. The event need hardly have happened. It need only be believed to have happened. Most likely by far, there never was a worldwide flood. Or there was never one that covered all land and wiped out all living things. Certainly no one would have managed to survive a flood of this severity. Probably, some local or regional flood got exaggerated into a global event. The cause of any flood that did occur was in fact geological, not religious. No deity was involved, so that there was no retribution for human misdeeds. The event had nothing to do with humans. Taken pre-scientifically, the story has no scientific core, to which religion has been attached. There is nothing scientific and everything religious about it. Want to learn about the history of the earth? Study geology, not the Bible.[4]

The relationship between religion and science has actually been anything but uniform, and works with tendentious titles like Andrew Dickson White's *A History of the Warfare of Science with Theology in Christendom* (1896) express a one-sided viewpoint.[5] Still, religion and science, and therefore myth and science, were indisputably more regularly opposed in the nineteenth century than in the twentieth century, where they were more regularly reconciled.

Tylor

The pioneering English anthropologist E. B. Tylor (1832–1917), author of *Primitive Culture* (1871), remains the classic exponent of the nineteenth-century view that myth and science are at odds.[6] With Tylor comes the issue of the relationship of myth to philosophy, not just of myth to science and to religion. For Tylor subsumes myth under religion and in turn subsumes both religion and science under philosophy. He divides philosophy into "primitive" and "modern." Primitive philosophy is identical with primitive religion. There is no primitive science. Modern philosophy, by contrast, has two divisions: religion and science. Of the two, science is by far the more important and is the modern counterpart to primitive religion, which is akin to science but is not scientific.

Modern religion is composed of two elements—metaphysics and ethics—neither of which is present in primitive religion. Metaphysics deals with nonphysical entities, of which "primitives" have no conception. Ethics is not absent from primitive culture, but it falls outside primitive religion: "the conjunction of ethics and Animistic philosophy, so intimate and powerful in the higher culture, seems scarcely yet to have begun in the lower" (Tylor 1871, vol. 2: 11). Tylor uses the term "animism" for religion per se, modern and primitive alike, because he derives the belief in gods from the belief in souls ("anima" in Latin means soul). In primitive religion souls occupy all physical entities, beginning with the bodies of humans. Gods are the souls in all physical entities *except* humans, who themselves are not gods.

For Tylor, primitive religion is the counterpart to science because both are explanations of the physical world. He thus characterizes primitive religion as "savage biology" (Tylor 1871, vol. 2: 20) and maintains that "mechanical astronomy gradually superseded the animistic astronomy of the lower races" and that today "biological pathology gradually supersedes animistic pathology" (Tylor 1871, vol. 2: 229). The religious explanation is personalistic: the decisions of gods explain events. The scientific explanation is impersonal: mechanical laws explain events.

For Tylor, the sciences as a whole have replaced religion as the explanation of the physical world, so that "animistic astronomy" and "animistic pathology" refer only to primitive, not modern, animism. Modern religion has surrendered the physical world to science and has retreated to the immaterial world, especially to the realm of life after death—that is, of the life of the soul after the death of the body. Where in primitive religion souls are deemed material and are found in all things, in modern religion they are deemed immaterial and are limited to human beings:

> In our own day and country, the notion of souls of beasts is to be seen dying out. Animism, indeed, seems to be drawing in its outposts, and concentrating itself on its first and main position, the doctrine of the human soul.... The soul has given up its ethereal substance, and become an immaterial entity, "the shadow of a shade." Its theory is becoming separated from the investigations of biology and mental science, which now discuss the phenomena of life and thought, the senses and the intellect, the emotions and the will, on a ground-work of pure experience. There has arisen an intellectual product whose very existence is of the deepest significance, a "psychology" which has no longer anything to do with "soul." The soul's place in modern thought is in the metaphysics of religion, and its especial office there is that of furnishing an intellectual side to the religious doctrine of the future. (Tylor 1871, vol. 2: 85)

Similarly, where in primitive religion gods are deemed material, in modern religion they are deemed immaterial. Gods thereby cease to be agents in the physical world—Tylor assumes that physical effects must have physical causes—and religion ceases to be an explanation of the physical world. Gods are relocated from the physical world to the social world. They become models for humans, just as they should be for Plato. One now reads the Bible not for the story of creation but for the Ten Commandments, just as for Plato a bowdlerized Homer would enable one to do. Jesus is to be emulated as the ideal human, not as a miracle worker.

This irenic position is also like that of the evolutionary biologist Stephen Jay Gould, who in his *Rock of Ages* (2002) argues that science, above all evolution, is compatible with religion because the two never intersect. Science explains the physical world; religion prescribes ethics and gives meaning to life: "Science tries to document the factual character of the natural world, and to develop theories that coordinate and explain these facts. Religion, on the other hand, operates in the equally important, but utterly different, realm of human purposes, meanings, and values" (Gould 2002: 4). But where for Gould religion has *always* served a function different from that of science, for Tylor religion has been forced to retrain upon having been made compulsorily redundant by science. And its present function is a demotion. Tylor is closer to biologist Richard Dawkins, though Dawkins, unlike Tylor, is unprepared to grant religion even a lesser function in the wake of science.

For Tylor, the demise of religion as an explanation of the physical world has meant the demise of myth altogether, which for Tylor is thus confined to primitive religion. Even though myth is an elaboration on the belief in gods, the belief itself can survive the rise of science where somehow myth cannot. Apparently, myths are too closely tied to gods as agents in the world to permit any comparable transformation from physics to metaphysics. Where, then, there is "modern religion," albeit religion shorn of its key role as explanation, there are no modern myths.

Tylor subsumes both primitive religion and science under philosophy because for him both are speculative. The creators of primitive religion, and therefore of myth, are "savage philosophers." True, science is testable, where myth is not. But the heart of both is not the observations that lead to hypothesized causes but the hypothesizing itself.

In pitting myth against science, as in pitting religion *qua* explanation against science, Tylor epitomizes the nineteenth-century view of myth. In the twentieth century the trend has been to reconcile myth as well as religion with science, so that moderns can retain myth as well as religion.

For Tylor, myth and science are not merely redundant but incompatible. Why? Because the explanations they give are. It is not simply that the mythic explanation is personalistic and the scientific one impersonal. It is that both are direct explanations, and of the same events.

One reason Tylor pits myth against science is that he subsumes myth under religion. For him, there is no myth outside religion, even though modern religion is without myth. Because primitive religion is the counterpart to science, myth must be as well. Because religion is to be taken literally, so must myth be.

A Tylorian approach to the story of Noah would see the tale not as a mere record of a flood believed to have been worldwide but as an explanation of that flood. Something striking, to put it mildly, had been observed. The reason for God's causing the flood could be anything and would not have to be punishment. It could be caprice or accident. God would be taken as directly intervening to cause the event. God would not have set in place laws of nature and be observing their effect. God would be assumed to be acting like Zeus in throwing thunder bolts. Myth for Tylor is less about one-time or irregular events than about recurrent ones. He would want to read the myth as an explanation not just of why a flood came once but why floods come whenever they do and with whatever severity they do, even if this flood is uniquely severe. The uniform explanation would be a decision by a divine personality. The motive—say, punishment—would ideally always be the same but could vary.

The most conspicuous part of the story that would fall outside Tylor's theory is the moralizing. For Tylor, myth, as the counterpart to science, explains, not evaluates. God's motive in causing the flood may be judgmental, but the subject of myth is God's motive itself, not the justice of his action.

Frazer

Tylor's is but one view of the relationship between myth and science and between religion and science. Closest to Tylor stands J. G. Frazer (1854–1941), the Scottish classicist and fellow pioneering anthropologist, and the author of *The Golden Bough* (1890).[7] For Frazer, as for Tylor, myth is part of primitive religion; primitive religion is part of philosophy, itself universal; and primitive religion is the counterpart to natural science, itself entirely modern. Primitive religion and science are, as for Tylor, mutually exclusive and not merely redundant. Primitive religion is false, science true. But where for Tylor primitive religion, including myth, functions as the counterpart to scientific *theory*, for Frazer it functions even more as the counterpart to *applied* science, or technology. Where for Tylor primitive religion, including myth, serves to *explain* the physical world, for Frazer it serves even more to *effect* the world, above all by spurring the crops to grow. Where Tylor treats myth as a sheer text, Frazer ties myth to ritual, which enacts it.

For example, the myth of Adonis is one of Frazer's main examples of, for him, the central myth of all mythologies: the biography of the chief god, the god of vegetation. For Frazer, the myth of Adonis would have been acted out, and that ritualistic enactment would have been believed to work magically to effect whatever was acted out. To act out the resurfacing of Adonis would have been to effect it and thereby the resurfacing of the crops. The myth would have served not simply to explain why the crops had died—they had died because Adonis, in descending to the land of the dead, had died—but, more, to revive the crops. For Frazer, the payoff of myth could scarcely be more practical: avoiding starvation.

It is not easy to see how Frazer's theory would apply to the myth of Noah, even if Frazer did compile a three-volume *Folk-Lore in the Old Testament* (1918). For Frazer, the chief god is the god of vegetation, not of the sky. Only insofar as crops depend on rain would his theory be relevant to flooding. The loss of crops to worldwide cold or heat—another ice age or global warming—would work, but the story of Noah is of the death of those dependent on crops and not just of the crops themselves. In Frazer's stage of religion the god of vegetation could withhold crops or rain for any reason, of which punishment would be just one. In Frazer's stage of magic and religion combined the crops would suffer as the automatic consequence of a weakened or dead god, not of any decision by a god. Clearly, God in the story of Noah is not physically tied to the physical world, which is controlled by him from above. And as with Tylor, so with Frazer, the moral element of the story would fall outside the theory. In his *Folk-Lore in the Old Testament* Frazer interprets biblical customs as cases of "primitive" religion or of magic and religion combined, even if he acknowledges the presence in the Hebrew Bible of higher, ethical religion.

Frazer does discuss the case of Noah in his tome. But he focuses on the two documentary sources that underlie the story: P and J. He is interested more in the differences between the sources than in the combined story of the flood. His discussion puts the story wholly in the stage of religion—with God's punishment as the cause of the flood and not with any attempt by Noah to control the world, not least the flood.

The biggest difficulty for Tylor's and Frazer's view of myth as the primitive counterpart to science is that it conspicuously fails to account for the retention of myth in the wake of science. If myth functions to do no more than science, why is it still around? Tylor and Frazer would surely reply that whatever remains is not myth, and exactly because it is not serving a scientific-like function.

By contrast, the contemporary German philosopher Hans Blumenberg (1920–96), author of *Work on Myth* (1985), maintains that the survival of myth alongside science proves that myth has *never* served the same function as science.[8] Yet neither Blumenberg nor Tylor and Frazer explain why myth, or religion as a whole, is still invoked *alongside* science to explain physical events.

For example, whenever a handful of passengers survives a plane crash, the crash itself gets explained scientifically, but the survival often gets credited to intervention by God and not to, say, the location of the seats. Tylor and Frazer would doubtless reply that the survivors have simply not faced up to the incompatibility of their religious explanation with a scientific one. But they have not accepted science over religion.

Lucien Lévy-Bruhl

Reacting against the views of Tylor and Frazer and other members of what he imprecisely calls "the English school of anthropology," the French philosopher and armchair anthropologist Lucien Lévy-Bruhl (1857–1939), the author of *How Natives Think* (1966), insisted on a much wider divide between myth and science. Where for Tylor and Frazer "primitives" think like moderns, just less rigorously, for Lévy-Bruhl "primitives" think differently from moderns. Where for Tylor and Frazer primitive thinking is logical, just erroneous, for Lévy-Bruhl primitive thinking is plainly other than logical.

According to Lévy-Bruhl, "primitives" believe not, as for Tylor, that all natural phenomena harbor individual, human-like souls, or gods, but that all phenomena, including humans and their artifacts, are part of an impersonal sacred, or "mystic," realm pervading the natural one. "Primitives" believe, further, that the "participation" of all things in this mystic reality enables phenomena not only to affect one another magically but also to become one another, yet somehow remain what they are: "objects, beings, phenomena can be, though in a way incomprehensible to us [moderns], both themselves and something other than themselves" (Lévy-Bruhl 1966: 61). The Bororo of Brazil declare themselves red araras, or parakeets, yet still human beings. Lévy-Bruhl calls this belief "prelogical" because it violates the law of noncontradiction: the notion that something can simultaneously be both itself and something else.

Where for Tylor and Frazer myth involves the same processes of observation, inference, and generalization as science, or at least of science as they think of it, for Lévy-Bruhl mythic thinking is the opposite of scientific thinking. Where for Tylor and Frazer "primitives" *perceive* the same world as moderns but simply *conceive* of it differently, for Lévy-Bruhl "primitives" see and in turn conceptualize the world differently from moderns—namely, as identical with themselves.

For Lévy-Bruhl, as for Tylor and Frazer, myth is part of religion, religion is primitive, and moderns have science rather than religion. But where Tylor and Frazer subsume both religion and science under philosophy, Lévy-Bruhl associates philosophy with thinking freed from mystical identification with the world. Primitive thinking is nonphilosophical because it is not detached from the world. "Primitives" have a whole mentality of their own, one evinced in their myths.

Even the use to which myth is put is for Lévy-Bruhl one of involvement rather than, as for Tylor and Frazer, one of detachment. "Primitives" use religion, especially myth, not to explain or to control the world but instead to commune with it—more precisely, to restore the "mystic" communion that has gradually begun to fade:

> Where the participation of the individual in the social group is still directly felt, where the participation of the group with surrounding groups is actually lived—that is, as long as the period of mystic symbiosis lasts—myths are meagre in number and of poor quality.... Can myths then likewise be the products of primitive mentality which appear when this mentality is endeavouring to realize a participation no longer felt—when it has recourse to intermediaries, and vehicles designed to secure a communion which has ceased to be a living reality? (Lévy-Bruhl 1966: 330)

Presented with the myth of Noah, Lévy-Bruhl would presumably focus on the dissolution of distinctions that the flood causes—notably, that between water and dry land and as a consequence all the distinctions among living things on dry land. Everything returns to the undifferentiated state of oneness with which the first of the two biblical creation stories (P) begins. For Lévy-Bruhl, primitive consciousness at once makes and denies distinctions. The story of Noah retains several key distinctions: that between God and humans and that between Noah and the physical world. But the ease with which it at once effaces yet restores many other distinctions evinces a level of consciousness not far beyond the primitive one. Still, is there any evidence that the recitation or enactment of the myth served to restore any sense of identity with the world?

Bronislaw Malinowski

One reaction to Lévy-Bruhl was to accept his separation of myth from philosophy but not his characterization of myth as pre-philosophical or pre-scientific. The key figure here was the Polish-born anthropologist Bronislaw Malinowski (1884–1942), who early on moved to England. His key essays on myth were collected in his book *Magic, Science and Religion and Other Essays* (1954).[9] Where Lévy-Bruhl asserts that "primitives" seek to commune with nature rather than to explain it, Malinowski asserts that "primitives" seek to control nature rather than to explain it. Both associate a philosophical approach with an explanatory, or intellectualist, one. Both attribute this contrived notion of myth and, in general, of religion to a contrived notion of "primitives."

Invoking Frazer, for whom myth and religion are the primitive counterpart to applied science, Malinowski argues that "primitives" are too busy scurrying to survive in the world to have the luxury of reflecting on it. Where for Frazer "primitives" use myth *in place of* science, which, again, is exclusively modern, for Malinowski "primitives" use myth as a *fallback* to science. "Primitives" possess not just the counterpart to science but science itself: "If by science be understood a body of rules and conceptions, based on experience and derived from it by logical inference, embodied in material achievements and in a fixed form of tradition and carried on by some sort of social organization—then there is no doubt that even the lowest savage communities have the beginnings of science, however rudimentary" (Malinowski 1954a: 34). "Primitives" use science to control the physical world. Where science stops, they turn to magic.

Where magic stops, "primitives" turn to myth—not to secure further control over the world, as Frazer would assume, but the opposite: to reconcile themselves to aspects of the world that cannot be controlled, such as natural catastrophes, illness, aging, and death. Myths, which are not limited to religion, root these woes in the irreversible, primordial actions of either gods or humans. According to a typical myth, humans age because two forebears did something foolish that introduced old age irremediably into the world: "The longed-for power of eternal youth and the faculty of rejuvenation which gives immunity from decay and age, have been lost by a small accident which it would have been in the power of a child and a woman to prevent" (Malinowski 1954b: 137). Myth explains how, say, flooding arose—a god or a human brought it about—but primitive science and magic try to do something about it. By contrast, myth says that nothing can be done about it. Myths that serve to resign "primitives" to the uncontrollable are about physical phenomena. Myths about *social* phenomena, such as customs and laws, serve to persuade "primitives" to accept what *can* be resisted.

Almost certainly, Malinowski would read the myth of Noah not as a reassuring tale of the justice of God's actions but as a scary reminder of the uncontrollability of nature. That Noah survives would be secondary; that the rest of humanity does not would be primary. If the myth can be taken as considering this the first case of severe flooding, then the myth would fit Malinowski's view that myth is always of origin. Subsequent cases of flooding, even if never so severe, would be repetitions of the first case. Myth would be serving not to philosophize about human frailty but simply to emphasize it. Myth would arise at the point of human helplessness before the world.

The myth of Noah would also surely be taken as establishing social regulations, the power of which would come from their antiquity, not from their self-evident propriety. God forges a covenant with Noah. Forbidden is murder (Genesis 9:6), and commanded is reproduction (9:7). Ham's seeing his father naked is deemed unnatural (9:21-27). The myth would serve to bolster prohibitions and commandments of the time by making them so old.

Claude Lévi-Strauss

Reacting both against Malinowski's view of "primitives" as practical rather than intellectual and against Lévy-Bruhl's view of "primitives" as emotional rather than intellectual, the French anthropologist Claude Lévi-Strauss (1908-2009), author of *The Savage Mind* (1966), *Structural Anthropology* (1967), *The Raw and the Cooked* (1970), and *Myth and Meaning* (1978),[10] boldly sought to revive an intellectualist view of "primitives" and of myth. At first glance he seems a sheer throwback to Tylor. In declaring that "primitives," "moved by a need or a desire to understand the world around them, ... proceed by intellectual means, exactly as a philosopher, or even to some extent a scientist, can and would do" (Lévi-Strauss 1978: 16) Lévi-Strauss seems indistinguishable from Tylor.

Yet in fact Lévi-Strauss is severely critical of Tylor, for whom "primitives" concoct myth rather than science because they think less critically than moderns. For Lévi-Strauss, "primitives" create myth because they think *differently* from moderns—but, contrary to Lévy-Bruhl, still think and still think rigorously. For both Tylor and Lévi-Strauss, myth is the epitome of primitive thinking.

Where for Tylor primitive thinking is personalistic and modern thinking impersonal, for Lévi-Strauss primitive thinking is concrete and modern thinking abstract. Primitive thinking deals with phenomena qualitatively rather than, like modern thinking, quantitatively. It focuses on the observable, sensible aspects of phenomena rather than, like modern thinking, on the unobservable, insensible ones:

> For these men [i.e., "primitives"] ... the world is made up of minerals, plants, animals, noises, colors, textures, flavors, odors.... What separates the savage thought from [modern] scientific thought is perfectly clear— and it is not a greater or lesser thirst for logic. Myths manipulate those qualities of perception that modern thought, at the birth of modern science, exorcised from science. (Lévi-Strauss, in Akoun et al. 1972: 39)

Yet antithetically to Tylor, Lévi-Strauss considers myth no less scientific than modern science. Myth is simply part of the "science of the concrete" rather than of the science of the abstract: "[T]here are two distinct modes of scientific thought. These are certainly not a function of different stages of the human mind but rather of two strategic levels at which nature is accessible to scientific enquiry: one roughly adapted to that of perception and the imagination: the other at a remove from it" (Lévi-Strauss 1966: 15). Where for Tylor myth is the primitive counterpart to science per se, for Lévi-Strauss myth is the primitive counterpart to *modern* science. Myth *is* primitive science, but not thereby inferior science.

If myth is an instance of primitive thinking because it deals with concrete, tangible phenomena, it is an instance of thinking itself because it classifies phenomena. Lévi-Strauss maintains that all humans think in the form of classifications, specifically pairs of oppositions, and project them onto the world. Many cultural phenomena express these oppositions. Myth is distinctive in resolving or, more accurately, tempering the oppositions it expresses. Where for Tylor myth is scientific-like precisely because it goes beyond observation to explanation, for Lévi-Strauss myth is outright scientific because it records and categorizes observations, even while actually tempering, not merely recording, observed contradictions. Those contradictions are to be found not in the plot but in what Lévi-Strauss famously calls the "structure."

A structuralist analysis of the myth of Noah would break down the plot into a series of distinctions, which would be taken as oppositions. The oppositions would not just be physical. God versus humanity, life versus death, obedience versus disobedience, creation versus destruction—these pairs would be juxtaposed with water versus dry land, heaven versus earth, male versus female, and dry versus wet. Either an in-between third factor would be found to "mediate" between the opposing items in each pair, or else one group of opposing pairs would be claimed to mediate the oppositions in the other pairs. The myth would be seen as an intellectual exercise—as a means of diminishing, not dissolving, oppositions, which would be experienced in life. The oppositions experienced would stem on the one hand from the projection of the structure of the mind onto the world and on the other hand from the actual nature of the world. The projection and that onto which it was projected would conveniently coincide. This coincidence is what the psychologist C. G. Jung calls "synchronicity." The myth would be admired for its intellectual rigor. It would be akin to a mathematical proof.

Karl Popper

In *Conjectures and Refutations* (1962) Karl Popper (1902–94), the Viennese-born philosopher of science who eventually settled in England, breaks even more radically with Tylor. First, Tylor never explains how science ever emerged, for religion, including myth, provides a comprehensive and seemingly nonfalsifiable explanation of all events in the physical world. Second, science for Tylor does not build on myth but simply replaces it. For Popper, science emerges *out of* myth—not, however, out of the *acceptance* of myth but out of the *criticism* of it: "Thus, science must begin with myths, and with the criticism of myths ..." (Popper 1974: 50). By "criticism" Popper means not rejection but assessment, which becomes scientific when it takes the form of attempts to falsify the truth claims made. To be scientific is to be testable, not necessarily to be true.

Going even further, Popper maintains that there are scientific as well as religious myths—antithetical to Tylor, himself never cited by Popper. For Popper, the difference between scientific and religious myths is not in their content but in the attitude toward them. Where religious myths are accepted dogmatically, scientific myths are questioned:

> My thesis is that what we call "science" is differentiated from the older myths not by being something distinct from a myth, but by being accompanied by a second-order tradition—that of critically discussing the myth. Before, there was only the first-order tradition. A definite story was handed on. Now there was still, of course, a story to be

> handed on, but with it went something like a silent accompanying text
> of a second-order character: "I hand it on to you, but tell me what you
> think of it. Think it over. Perhaps you can give us a different story."... We
> shall understand that, in a certain sense, science is myth-making just as
> religion is. (Popper 1974: 127)

Popper even maintains that scientific theories *remain* myth-like, for
theories, like myths, can never be proved, only disproved, and therefore
"remain essentially uncertain or hypothetical" (Popper 1998: 116). Still,
myths are not scientific-like unless they can be tested.

The myths that grab Popper are creation myths, for they make bold
conjectures about the origin of the world and thereby pave the way for
scientific theorizing. He would, then, presumably, approve of the myth
of Noah for its speculations about the origin of flooding, but he would
expect criticism to spur the eventual rejection of a personalistic, religious explanation for an impersonal, scientific one.

Paul Radin

To review: Tylor and Frazer alike subsume both myth and science under
philosophy. In reaction, Lévy-Bruhl sets myth against both science and
philosophy. For him, primitive identification with the world, as evinced
in myth, is the opposite of the detachment from the world demanded
by science and philosophy alike. In reaction in turn to Lévy-Bruhl,
Malinowski recharacterizes myth as a reaction to the experience of helplessness before the world. The reaction of Lévi-Strauss is to assert the
philosophical character of myth.

The reaction of Paul Radin (1883–1959), a Polish-born anthropologist who came to America as an infant, is the same: making myth philosophical. The title of his key work is self-explanatory: *Primitive Man as
Philosopher* (1957 [1927]).[11]

Though oddly Radin never mentions Tylor here, he is best understood
vis-à-vis Tylor. He in effect revives Tylor's intellectualist view, according
to which myth seeks to explain as an end in itself, while at once qualify-
ing and extending that view. Radin grants that *most* "primitives" are far
from philosophical but observes that so are most persons in any culture.
He distinguishes between the average person, the "man of action," and
the exceptional person, the "thinker":

> The former [i.e., the man of action] is satisfied that the world exists and
> that things happen. Explanations are of secondary consequence. He is

ready to accept the first one that comes to hand. At bottom it is a matter of utter indifference. He does, however, show a predilection for one type of explanation as opposed to another. He prefers an explanation in which the purely mechanical relation between a series of events is specifically stressed. His mental rhythm—if I may be permitted to use this term—is characterized by a demand for endless repetition of the same event or, at best, of events all of which are on the same general level.... Now the rhythm of the thinker is quite different. The postulation of a mechanical relation between events does not suffice. He insists on a description couched either in terms of a gradual progress and evolution from one to many and from simple to complex, or on the postulation of a cause and effect relation. (Radin 1957: 232–33)

Both "types of temperament" are to be found in all cultures, and in the same proportion. If, for Radin, Lévy-Bruhl is therefore wrong to deny that any "primitives" are reflective, Tylor is equally wrong to assume that all are. But those "primitives" who are reflective get credited by Radin with a philosophical prowess keener than that granted even myth makers by Tylor, who calls them "savage philosophers." For Radin, primitive speculations, found most fully in myths, do more than account for events in the physical world. Myths deal with metaphysical topics of all kinds, such as the ultimate components of reality. Contrary to Tylor, for whom religious and mythic assumptions are never questioned, "primitives" for Radin are capable of rigorous criticism: "it is manifestly unfair to contend that primitive people are deficient either in the power of abstract thought or in the power of arranging these thoughts in a systematic order, or, finally, of subjecting them and their whole environment to an objective critique" (Radin 1957: 384). Likely for Radin, as definitely for Popper, the capacity for criticism is the hallmark of thinking.

Radin would seek to read the myth of Noah as metaphysics. The issues raised by the myth would include the nature of classification, the nature of time, and the nature of substance. The myth could also be read theologically, as a theodicy. Myth would here be philosophy, just presented in the genre of a story. The key theorist who likewise sees myth as the transformation of metaphysics into story is the American literary critic Kenneth Burke, above all in *The Rhetoric of Religion* (1961).

Ernst Cassirer

A far less dismissive reaction to Lévy-Bruhl than Radin's came from the German philosopher Ernst Cassirer (1874-1945), especially in his

Philosophy of Symbolic Forms, volume 2 (1955). For Cassirer, wholly follow-ing Lévy-Bruhl, mythic, or "mythopoeic," thinking is primitive, is laden with emotion, is part of religion, and is the projection of mystical one-ness onto the world. But Cassirer claims to be breaking sharply with Lévy-Bruhl in asserting that mythic thinking has its own brand of logic. In actuality, Lévy-Bruhl says the same and invents the term "prelogi-cal" exactly to avoid labeling mythic thinking "illogical" or "nonlogical." Applied to the myth of Noah, Cassirer's theory would doubtless focus on the same dissolution and retention of distinctions as Lévy-Bruhl's.

Cassirer also claims to be breaking with Lévy-Bruhl in stressing the autonomy of myth as a form of knowledge—language, art, and science being the other main forms:

> But though a subordination of myth to a general system of symbolic forms seems imperative, it presents a certain danger…. [I]t may well lead to a leveling of the intrinsic [i.e., distinctive] form of myth. And indeed there has been no lack of attempts to explain myth by reducing it to another form of cultural life, whether knowledge [i.e., science], art, or language. (Cassirer 1955, vol. 2: 21)

Yet Cassirer simultaneously maintains, no differently than Lévy-Bruhl, that myth is incompatible with science and that science succeeds it: "Science arrives at its own form only by rejecting all mythical and metaphysical ingredients" (Cassirer 1955, vol. 2: xvii). For both Cassirer and Lévy-Bruhl, myth is exclusively primitive and science exclusively modern. Still, Cassirer's characterization of myth as a form of *knowledge*— as one of humanity's symbol-making, world-creating enterprises—puts myth in the same genus as science—the opposite of where Lévy-Bruhl puts it. Myth for Cassirer is quasi-philosophical, where for Lévy-Bruhl it is anything but.

The Frankforts

The fullest application to myth of the theories of Lévy-Bruhl and of Cassirer came in a 1946 book by a group of Near Eastern specialists entitled *The Intellectual Adventure of Ancient Man: An Essay on Speculative Thought in the Ancient Near East*. When republished in paperback in 1949, this title and subtitle were relegated to a double subtitle, and the book was given a new main title that is a give-away: *Before Philosophy*. According to Henri and H. A. Frankfort, who provide the theory, ancient Near Eastern peoples lived at a primitive stage of culture that is properly labeled "pre-philosophical."

The subsumption of ancient under primitive harks back to Tylor and Frazer—and also to the nineteenth-century Semiticist William Robertson Smith. Moderns, contend the Frankforts, think "philosophically," which means abstractly, critically, and unemotionally. The field of philosophy is only one area that employs philosophical thinking, and the true exemplar of "philosophical" thinking is science. Tylor, Lévy-Bruhl, and others likewise use the term "philosophical" this broadly, as almost synonymous with "intellectual," and likewise deem science the purest manifestation of it. Antithetically to moderns, assert the Frankforts, "primitives" think "mythopoeically," which means concretely, uncritically, and emotionally. Mythology is but one, if the richest, expression of mythopoeic thinking.

Philosophical and mythopoeic ways of thinking are more than different conceptions of the world. They are different *perceptions* of the world, just as for Lévy-Bruhl. The "fundamental difference" is that for moderns the external world is an "It," where for "primitives" it is a "Thou"—terms taken from the Jewish philosopher Martin Buber (1958 [1946]). An I-It relationship is detached and intellectual. An I-Thou one is involved and emotional—the original title of the Frankforts' book aside. The paradigmatic I-Thou relationship is love.

To say that "primitives" experience the world as Thou rather than as It is to say that they experience it as a person rather than a thing. The coming of rain after a drought is ascribed not to atmospheric changes but to, say, the defeat of a rival god by the rain god, as described in myth. To understand the world as Thou is to efface various everyday, I–It distinctions. "Primitives" fail to distinguish between the merely subjective and the objective: they see the sun rise and set, not the earth circling it. They see colors, not wave lengths. They fail to distinguish between appearance and reality: the stick *is* crooked in the water rather than merely seemingly so; dreams are real because they are experienced as real. "Primitives" fail to distinguish between a symbol and the symbolized. A name is identical with its possessor, as in Frazer's magical Law of Similarity. The reenactment of a myth means its recurrence, as in Frazer's first version of myth ritualism.

Ancient Egyptians and Mesopotamians, argue the Frankforts, lived in a wholly mythopoeic world. The move from mythopoeic to philosophical thinking began with the Israelites, who fused many gods into one god and placed that god outside of nature. Israelites thereby paved the way for the Greeks, who transformed that personal god into one or more impersonal forces underlying nature, or appearance. The final "demythicizing" of nature awaited only the transformation of pre-Socratic imagination into experimental science.

There are many problems with the Frankforts' thesis. First, at times mythopoeism for them amounts to no more than Tylor's personalistic explanation of physical events rather than to any distinctive mentality. Second, Buber's I-Thou is limited to the experience of persons, not of things. Third, any phenomenon can surely be experienced as both an It and a Thou. Fourth, no culture could engage nature exclusively as Thou yet be detached enough to, say, raise crops. Fifth, the characterization of ancient Near Eastern cultures as wholly mythopoeic, of Israel as largely nonmythopoeic, and of Greece as wholly scientific is embarrassingly simplistic, as, notably, F. M. Cornford on Greek science makes clear.[12]

Still, the Frankforts deserve praise for trying to apply Lévy-Bruhl's abstract theory to specific cases. Their main claim, following that of Lévy-Bruhl and Cassirer, is that myths, while themselves stories, presuppose a distinctive mentality. Ironically, the Frankforts' strongest criticism of Lévy-Bruhl is the same as Cassirer's and is equally misplaced: it is Lévy-Bruhl himself who insists that primitive thinking is distinctive but not illogical. If one were to disregard the Frankforts' pious near-exclusion of ancient Israel from mythopoeism, one would look there for the same primitive level of consciousness that Lévy-Bruhl and Cassirer would seek.

Rudolf Bultmann

As philosophical as Cassirer's approach to myth is, he never contends that myth *is* philosophy. The theorists who do so are the German theologian Rudolf Bultmann (1884–1976) and the German-born philosopher Hans Jonas (1903–93), who eventually settled in the United States.[13] The two not only take the meaning of myth from philosophy—from early, existentialist Heidegger—but also confine themselves to the issue of meaning. Neither the origin nor the function of myth interests them. Like some armchair anthropologists, they treat myth as an autonomous text. But unlike Tylor or Frazer, they do not even speculate from their armchairs about why myth arose or worked.

Taken literally, myth for Bultmann is exactly what it is for Tylor: a primitive explanation of the world; an explanation incompatible with a scientific one; and an explanation therefore unacceptable to moderns, who by definition accept science. Read literally, myth for Bultmann should be rejected as uncompromisingly as Tylor rejects it. But unlike

Tylor, Bultmann reads myth symbolically. In his celebrated, if excruciatingly confusing, phrase, myth is to be "demythologized," which means not eliminated, or "demythicized," but instead rephrased in symbolic terms. To seek evidence of an actual worldwide flood, while dismissing the miraculous notion of an ark containing all species, would for Bultmann be to *demythicize* the myth of Noah. To interpret the flood as a symbolic statement about the precariousness of human life would be to *demythologize* the myth.

Demythologized, myth ceases to be about the world and is instead about the human *experience* of the world. Demythologized, myth ceases to be an explanation at all and instead becomes an expression, an expression of what it "feels" like to live in the world. Myth ceases to be merely primitive and becomes universal. It ceases to be false and becomes true. It depicts the "human condition." In Bultmann's words, "The real purpose of myth is not to present an objective picture of the world as it is, but to express man's understanding of himself in the world in which he lives. Myth should be interpreted not cosmologically, but anthropologically, or better still, existentially" (Bultmann 1953: 10).

Overall, the New Testament, when demythologized, presents the opposing ways in which the world is experienced: the alienation from the world felt by those who have not yet found God versus the at-homeness in the world felt by those who have found God. For those without God, the world is cold, callous, and scary. For those with God, the world is warm, inviting, and secure.

Taken literally, myth, as a personalistic explanation of the physical world, is incompatible with science and is therefore unacceptable to moderns: "Man's knowledge and mastery of the world have advanced to such an extent through science and technology that it is no longer possible for anyone seriously to hold the New Testament view of the world—in fact, there is no one who does.... We no longer believe in the three-storied universe which the creeds take for granted" (Bultmann 1953: 4). Once demythologized, however, myth is compatible with science because it now refers at once to the transcendent, nonphysical world and, even more, to humans' experience of the physical one.

Bultmann does not merely urge modern Christians to accept the New Testament but actually shows them how to do so—by translating the New Testament into existentialist terms. His justification for the translation is not, however, that otherwise moderns could not accept the Christian Bible but that its true meaning has always been existential.

Still, to say that myth is acceptable to scientifically minded moderns is not to say why it should be accepted. In providing an acceptable modern subject matter of myth, Bultmann provides no acceptable modern function. Perhaps for him the function is self-evident: describing the human condition. But why bother describing that condition, and why use myth to do so? Bultmann cannot contend that myth *discloses* the human condition, for he himself enlists philosophy to find that same meaning in myth.

Moreover, myth, even when demythologized, is acceptable to moderns only if they already believe in God. As desperate as Bultmann is to make myth acceptable to scientifically minded moderns, he is not prepared to interpret away—to demythicize—God altogether. To accept the mythology, one must continue to believe in God, however sophisticated the conception. Compatibility with science may be necessary for the espousal of myth today, but it is far from sufficient.

What would Bultmann make of the myth of Noah? To begin with, he would interpret away all aspects of the story that are incompatible with science or history. If there is no reliable modern evidence of a worldwide flood, then there presumably was no flood. If no human even now could manage to amass representatives of all species and to keep them alive for months, then no one could have done so back then. If no human even now could build a boat capable of withstanding forces that destroyed all of creation, then no one did so back then. Seeking a scientific or historical basis for this preposterous tale is misunderstanding myth.

For Bultmann, the myth of Noah, rightly understood, is not about a past event. It is not about a present event either. It is not about the physical world itself. It is about the opposing ways humans experience the physical world. Myth is not an explanation of those ways. It is the sheer presentation of them.

For those without God, whether the Jewish God or the Christian one, the world is indifferent. Not only floods and other natural catastrophes kill people. So does disease, and so does old age. The world is alien to humans. Events in it are caused but not motivated.

For those with God, the world is caring. People still suffer and still die, but God acts justly. Suffering and even death are deserved. Bultmann would concentrate not on any unique flood but on the covenant made afterwards between God and Noah. Demythologized, the story of Noah describes what it is like, any time and anywhere, to experience the world with a solicitous God on one's side.

Hans Jonas

Hans Jonas argues that ancient Gnosticism presents the same fundamental view of the human condition as that of modern existentialism. Both stress the radical alienation of human beings from the world: "the essence of existentialism is a certain dualism, an estrangement between man and the world .... There is only one situation ... where that condition has been realized and lived out with all the vehemence of a cataclysmic event. That is the gnostic movement" (Jonas 1963: 325).

Unlike Bultmann, who strives to bridge the gap between Christianity and modernity, Jonas acknowledges the divide between Gnosticism and modernity. He is not seeking to win converts to Gnosticism. Because ancient Gnosticism, unlike mainstream Christianity, sets immateriality against matter, humans remain alienated from the physical world even after they have found the true God. In fact, the true God can be found only by rejecting the physical world and its false god. Gnostics overcome alienation from this world only by transcending it. But then estrangement for Gnostics is only temporary, where for modern existentialists it is permanent. Yet for Jonas, Gnostic mythology can still speak to moderns—not to modern believers, as for Bultmann, but to modern skeptics. The mythology can do so because, rightly grasped, it addresses not the nature of the world but the nature of the experience of the world—that is, of this world. Like Bultmann, Jonas seeks to reconcile myth with science by recharacterizing the subject matter of myth.

To make ancient Gnosticism palatable to moderns, Jonas, like Bultmann, must bypass those aspects of the myths that overlap with science by presenting either the origin or the future of this world. The *fact* of human alienation from this world, not the source of it or the solution to it, is the demythologized subject of myth. Ignored therefore are Gnostic descriptions of the godhead, the emanations, the creator god, and the material world. Ignored above all is the Gnostic prospect of escape from this world. In actuality, then, the bulk of Gnostic mythology is reduced to mere mythology—to be discarded, or demythicized, like *all* of mythology for Tylor.

No more than Bultmann does Jonas offer any function of myth for moderns. Even if myth serves to express the human condition, why is it necessary to express that condition at all, let alone through myth, and again when philosophy does so? We are never told. Both Jonas and Bultmann limit themselves to the meaning, or subject matter, of myth.

The meaning of the myth of Noah for Jonas would be the same as the meaning of it for Bultmann.

Bultmann's and Jonas' approach to myth could scarcely be more opposed to Tylor's. Tylor takes for granted that to be taken seriously, myth must be taken literally. Bultmann and Jonas, as well as other theorists such as Campbell, argue the opposite: that to be taken seriously, myth must be taken symbolically. Where Tylor argues that myth is incredible to moderns precisely because they rightly take it literally, Bultmann and Jonas argue that myth is credible to moderns only insofar as they rightly take it symbolically. Yet Tylor truly objects not to those theorists who read myth symbolically for moderns but to those who also read it symbolically for "primitives." He would thus berate Bultmann and Jonas far more for what they say of early Christians and ancient Gnostics than for what they say of moderns.

Ironically, Tylor, Bultmann, and Jonas all write in defense of myth (see Cornford 1912 and 1952: chs. 1–11). The difference is that for Tylor the defense demands the abandonment of myth in the face of science, whereas for Bultmann and Jonas the defense requires the explication of the true meaning of myth in the face of science. That meaning is not a new one invented by moderns to save myth. It is the meaning that myth has always had but that, till pressed by the threat from science, has not been fully recognized. By forcing moderns to go back to the ancient texts to discover what they have really been saying all along, science has turned a necessity into a virtue.

Notes

Chapter 1

1. On euhemerism in more than the ancient world and in more than ancient times, see Roubekas 2017 and Pugh 2021.

2. In fact, Blumenberg singles out Ernst Cassirer as epitomizing the Enlightenment view. As Blumenberg rightly notes, Cassirer on the one hand maintains that myth is irreducible to science or any other symbolic form but on the other hand maintains that myth is incompatible with science, which succeeds it (see Blumenberg 1985: 168). See Cassirer 1955: 21 (on the one hand), 1955: xvii (on the other).

3. Oddly, Blumenberg cites *Totem and Taboo* rather than *The Future of an Illusion*, where Freud, in contrast to Blumenberg, does see myth—better, religion generally—as serving to facilitate escape from the world rather than coping with it (see Blumenberg 1985: 8).

4. The debate over whether myth creates (Enlightenment) or alleviates (Blumenberg) anxiety repeats the classical debate between Radcliffe-Brown and Malinowski over whether ritual creates (Radcliffe-Brown) or alleviates (Malinowski) anxiety: see Radcliffe-Brown 1939 and Malinowski 1954a: sections 4–6.

5. On the reduction of the unfamiliar to the familiar, see Blumenberg 1985: 5, 25.

6. On the difference between the work *of* myth and work *on* myth, see Blumenberg 1985: 118, 266; see also the translator's note, 112 note w.

7. On "reoccupation," see also Blumenberg 1983, especially 48–50 and part 1: ch. 6.

8. If in *Work on Myth* Blumenberg rails more fervently against the Enlightenment belief in progress than against the Romantic belief in continuity, in *The Legitimacy of the Modern Age* (part 1, especially chs. 3–4) he rails against Romanticism almost exclusively: he denies that the modern, Enlightened notion of progress is merely traditional religious eschatology in secular guise.

9. In his introduction to *Work on Myth* translator Robert Wallace defends Blumenberg's claim that he is skirting the issue of origin by restricting origin to "how" and categorizing "why" under function (Blumenberg 1985: xvii). But by that criterion many theorists of myth ignore the issue of origin—among them Eliade, Bultmann, Jonas, Radcliffe-Brown, and Malinowski. Only the last two of these theorists *profess* to be doing so.

Chapter 3

1. For a much earlier presentation of not only Frazer on Adonis but also Marcel Detienne and C. G. Jung on Adonis, see Segal 1991.

Chapter 4

1. On euhemerism as a theory of religion, see Roubekas 2017.
2. On Frazer's differing versions of myth ritualism, see Segal 1998b: 4–5.
3. See, among the more recent efforts to make Jesus mythical rather than historical, Murdoch 2011.
4. Ironically, Frazer's disciple Lord Raglan, while refraining from discussing the case of Jesus, pits history against myth in his analysis of dozens of heroes: see Raglan 1936.
5. On Frazer's euhemeristic interpretation of Osiris, see Cornford 1914b.

Chapter 5

1. On Frazer's literary influence, see Segal 1998b: 9–11 and part V.
2. On the differences between Frazer and Smith, see Segal 1998b: 3–5 and 17–34.

Chapter 6

1. On the differences between Campbell and Róheim, see Segal 1997: 48–50, 222–29.
2. For Jung's interpretation of heroism in both halves of life, see Jung 1968a: 151–81; 1967: 171–444; 1968d: 333–39; and 1976: 105–10.
3. On Rank's view of heroism, see also Campbell 1964: 73–74, 77.
4. On females as heroes, see Campbell 1964. See also chapter 12 in the present book. On female Jungian heroes, see Covington 1989.
5. On further differences between Campbell and Jung, see Segal 1997: ch. 12.

Chapter 7

1. To cite but one statement: "the situation of modern man, who believes himself—or wishes to be—without religion" (Eliade 1969a: 20–21).
2. On modern myths, which Eliade often mixes with rituals, see especially Eliade 1959a: 201–13; 1975: 181–93; 1967: ch. 1; 1959b: ch. 4; 1965: 127–36; 1963: 431–34; 1961: 16–21; 1969a: 155–59; 1969b: ch. 7; and 1976: chs. 1–4.

Chapter 8

1. On modern myths, which Eliade often mixes with rituals, see the references in this book in ch. 7, n. 2.

Chapter 9

1. On the difference see Segal 1992a and 2014.

Chapter 10

1. On the preservation of classical mythology, see Bush 1932 and 1937, Highet 1939, Seznec 1953 [1940]), and Bull 2005.
2. See Frazer, *The Golden Bough*, 2nd ed. (1900), 3rd ed. (1911–15), and abridged ed. (1922). Frazer does not develop myth ritualism until the second edition of the work.
3. See Murray, "Excursus on the Ritual Forms Preserved in Greek Tragedy" (1913a); *Euripides and His Age* (1913b: 60–68); *Aeschylus* (1940); and "Dis Geniti" (1951); Cornford, "The Origin of the Olympic Games" (1912); *The Origin of Attic Comedy* (1914a); "A Ritual Basis for Hesiod's *Theogony*" (1941); and *Principium Sapientiae* (1952: 191–256).
4. See Weston, *From Ritual to Romance* (1920); Butler, *The Myth of the Magus* (1948); Barber, *Shakespeare's Festive Comedy* (1959); Weisinger, *Tragedy and the Paradox of the Fortunate Fall* (1953); Fergusson, *The Idea of a Theater* (1949); Raglan, "Myth and Ritual" (1955); Frye, *Anatomy of Criticism* (1957: 131–239); and Hyman, "Myth, Ritual, and Nonsense" (1949).
5. See not only Fergusson's *The Idea of a Theater* but also his "'Myth' and the Literary Scruple" (1956).
6. See not only Frye's *Anatomy of Criticism* but also his "The Archetypes of Literature" (1951) and "Myth, Fiction, and Displacement" (1961), in Frye, *Fables of Identity* (1963: 7–20 and 21–38); "Literature and Myth" (1967), in Thorpe, *Relations of Literary Study* (1967: 27–55); "Symbolism of the Unconscious" (1959) and "Forming Fours" (1954), in Frye, *Northrop Frye on Culture and Literature* (1978: 84–94 and 117–29); and "Myth," *Antaeus* (1981).
7. See, as classical Jungians, Bodkin, *Archetypal Patterns in Poetry* (1934), and Knapp, *A Jungian Approach to Literature* (1984).
8. See, as archetypal psychologists, Hillman, *Re-Visioning Psychology* (1975), and Miller, *The New Polytheism* (1981).
9. See Girard, *Violence and the Sacred* (1977), "*To Double Business Bound*" (1978), *The Scapegoat* (1986), and *Things Hidden since the Foundation of the World* (1987).
10. I use "story" rather than "narrative," the term preferred today. On the distinction see Rimmon-Kenan, *Narrative Fiction* (2002: 3). On the yet further distinction among story, narrative, and plot—all of which I innocently use interchangeably—see Cobley, *Narrative* (2001: 4–7).

11. See Tylor, *Primitive Culture* (1958 [1913]), vol. 1, chs. 8–10.
12. See not only Burke's *The Rhetoric of Religion* but also his *A Grammar of Motives* (1945: 430–40) and "Myth, Poetry and Philosophy" (1960).
13. For someone who goes even further than Burke and reduces myth to literature, see the American literary critic Chase, "Notes on the Study of Myth" (1946); "Myth as Literature" (1948); and *Quest for Myth* (1969 [1949]: v–vii, 73–74, 80–81, 110–31).
14. See Blumenberg, *Work on Myth* (1985) and *The Legitimacy of the Modern Age* (1983).
15. In *Work on Myth* Blumenberg rails more fervently against the Enlightenment view of myth than against the Romantic view. In *The Legitimacy of the Modern Age* (1983: part 1, esp. chs. 3–4) he rails against Romanticism almost exclusively.
16. See von Hahn, *Sagwissenschaftliche Studien* (1876: 340).
17. See Propp, *Morphology of the Folktale* (1968 [1958]).
18. The citation to Campbell's *The Hero with a Thousand Faces* is to the second edition (1972).

Chapter 12

1. In an earlier essay Tylor (1863) amasses stories of children raised by beasts, but only in passing does he connect them to myths of future heroes. For a superb overview of the history of hero patterns, beginning with Tylor's, see Dundes 1977.
2. On Rank after his break with Freud, see Segal 2021: ch. 3.
3. See Dundes 1962.
4. On the differences between Campbell and Jung, see Segal 1987: ch. 11.
5. For Jung's interpretation of heroism in both halves of life, see his 1968b; 1967; 1968d: 333–39; and 1976: 105–10.
6. On the puer, see Jung 1967: 257–59, 340; and Jung 1968b: 106. See also Neumann 1970: 88–101 (Neumann himself using the term "son-lover" for puer); von Franz 1981; and Whitmont 1969: 182–83. On the puella, see von Franz 1981: 81–84, 150–51, 152–54; and Whitmont 1969: 178–80.
7. On Frank Miller, see Shamdasani 1990.
8. See Neumann 1970: 131–256; and 1972: 203–208.
9. See Campbell 1972: 318–34. On Rank's view of heroism, see also Campbell 1964: 73–74, 77; and 1988b: 124–25, where Campbell is more appreciative of heroism in the first half of life.
10. See Pearson and Pope 1981; Pearson 1989; and Pearson 1991. On female Jungian heroes, see Covington 1989.
11. See Frazer 3rd ed. (1911–15); abridged ed. (1922). Citations are to the abridgment.
12. See Raglan 1936: 89–136; 1945; and 1949, esp. chs. 9–10.
13. Strictly speaking, the chief god for Raglan is of the sky rather than, as for Frazer, of vegetation.
14. See Jezewski 1984.

Chapter 13

1. On Freud and Jung's rejection of the nineteenth-century view of Tylor and Frazer, see Segal 2003.
2. On the Gaia hypothesis, see Segal 2012.
3. On synchonicity, see Aziz 1990 and Main 1997, 2004, and 2007.

Chapter 14

1. On the history of creationism see Numbers 1992.
2. For a comparable attempt to "naturalize" myth from outside of the Bible, see Kramer 1961. The classic attempt not to replace but to reconcile a theological account of the plagues with a scientific account is that of Buber, for whom the believer, on the basis of faith, attributes to divine intervention what the believer acknowledges can be fully accounted for scientifically. See Buber 1958, esp. 60–68 and 74–79. Buber is the Jewish counterpart to Bultmann.
3. The classic work on finding science in myth is de Santillana and von Dechend, *Hamlet's Mill* (1969).
4. For the evidence of an actual universal flood, see Ryan and Pitman 1999. For a superb collection of the array of ways that flood stories worldwide have been approached, see Dundes 1988.
5. For a balanced corrective, see Brooke, *Science and Religion* (1991).
6. See Tylor 1871. Citations are to the 1958 reprint of the 5th (1913) edition.
7. *The Golden Bough* appeared in three editions (1890, 1900, and 1911–15) and then in an abridged ed. (1922).
8. For Blumenberg (1985), myth serves to alleviate anxiety about the world rather than to explain the world—an argument that rests partly on his narrow definition of explanation as ultimate origin.
9. See Malinowski, "Magic, Science and Religion" (1925) and "Myth in Primitive Psychology" (1926), in his *Magic, Science and Religion and Other Essays* (1954a and 1954b).
10. See also Akoun et al. 1972.
11. See Radin 1957 and 1973: ch. 3.
12. See Cornford 1912 and 1952: chs. 1–11.
13. See Bultmann 1953 and 1958; Jonas 1934 and 1954, and 1963.

Bibliography

Ackerman, Robert. 1987. *J. G. Frazer: His Life and Work*. Cambridge: Cambridge University Press.

Akoun, André, et al. 1972. "A Conversation with Claude Lévi-Strauss." *Psychology Today* 5 (May): 36–39, 74–82.

Apollodorus. 1921. *The Library*. Trans. J. G. Frazer. Loeb Classical Library. Cambridge, MA: Harvard University Press; London: Heinemann.

Aziz, Robert. 1990. *C. G. Jung's Psychology of Religion and Synchronicity*. Albany: State University of New York Press.

Barber, C. L. 1959. *Shakespeare's Festive Comedy*. Princeton, NJ: Princeton University Press.

Berger, Peter L. 1967. *The Sacred Canopy*. Garden City, NY: Doubleday.

Bidney, David. 1955. "Myth, Symbolism, and Truth." *Journal of American Folklore* 68 (270): 379–92. https://doi.org/10.2307/536765

Bidney, David. 1967. *Theoretical Anthropology*. 2nd ed. New York: Schocken [1st ed. 1953]. https://doi.org/10.7312/bidn94356

Blumenberg, Hans. 1983. *The Legitimacy of the Modern Age*, translated by Robert M. Wallace. Cambridge, MA: MIT Press.

Blumenberg, Hans. 1985. *Work on Myth*, translated by Robert M. Wallace. Cambridge, MA: MIT Press.

Bodkin, Maud. 1934. *Archetypal Patterns in Poetry*. London: Oxford University Press.

Brooke, John Hedley. 1991. *Science and Religion: Some Historical Perspectives*. Cambridge: Cambridge University Press.

Buber, Martin. 1958 [1946]. *Moses: The Revelation and the Covenant*. New York: Harper Torchbooks.

Bull, Malcolm. 2005. *The Mirror of the Gods: Classical Mythology in Renaissance Art*. London: Allen Lane.

Bultmann, Rudolf. 1953. "New Testament and Mythology" (1944). In *Kerygma and Myth*, edited by Hans-Werner Bartsch, translated by Reginald H. Fuller, vol. 1: 1–44. London: SPCK.

Bultmann, Rudolf. 1958. *Jesus Christ and Mythology*. New York: Scribner's.

Burke, Kenneth. 1945. *A Grammar of Motives*. New York: Prentice-Hall.

Burke, Kenneth. 1960. "Myth, Poetry and Philosophy." *Journal of American Folklore* 73 (290): 283–306. https://doi.org/10.2307/538489

Burke, Kenneth. 1961. *The Rhetoric of Religion*. Boston, MA: Beacon Press.

Bush, Douglas. 1932. *Mythology and the Renaissance Tradition in English Poetry*. Minneapolis: University of Minnesota Press.

Bush, Douglas. 1937. *Mythology and the Romantic Tradition in English Poetry*. Cambridge, MA: Harvard University Press.

Butler, E. M. 1948. *The Myth of the Magus*. Cambridge: Cambridge University Press; New York: Macmillan.

Campbell, Joseph. 1964. *The Masks of God: Occidental Mythology*. New York: Viking.

Campbell, Joseph. 1972. *The Hero with a Thousand Faces*. 2nd ed. Princeton, NJ: Princeton University Press. [1st ed. New York: Pantheon Books, 1949.]

Campbell, Joseph. 1973 [1972]. *Myths to Live By*. New York: Bantam Books.

Campbell, Joseph. 1988a. *An Open Life*, with Michael Toms, edited by John M. Maher and Dennie Briggs. Burdett, NY: Larsen Publications.

Campbell, Joseph. 1988b. *The Power of Myth*, with Bill Moyers, edited by Betty Sue Flowers. New York: Doubleday.

Carlyle, Thomas. 1966 [1847]. *On Heroes, Hero-Worship and the Heroic in History*, ed. Carl Niemeyer. Lincoln: University of Nebraska Press.

Cassirer, Ernst. 1955. *The Philosophy of Symbolic Forms*, vol. 2, translated by Ralph Manheim. New Haven, CT: Yale University Press.

Chase, Richard. 1946. "Notes on the Study of Myth." *Partisan Review* 13: 338–46.

Chase, Richard. 1948. "Myth as Literature." In *English Institute Essays 1947*: 3–22. New York: Columbia University Press.

Chase, Richard. 1969 [1949]. *Quest for Myth*. New York: Greenwood.

Cobley, Paul. 2001. *Narrative*. London and New York: Routledge. https://doi.org/10.4324/9780203823071

Collingwood, R. G. 1939. *An Autobiography*. London: Oxford University Press.

Cornford, F. M. 1912. "The Origin of the Olympic Games." In Jane Ellen Harrison, *Themis: A Study of the Social Origins of Greek Religion*, 1st ed., ch. 7. Cambridge: Cambridge University Press.

Cornford, F. M. 1914a. *The Origin of Attic Comedy*. London: Arnold.

Cornford, F. M. 1914b. Review of Frazer, *The Golden Bough*, 3rd ed., part 4 (*Adonis, Attis, Osiris*). *Cambridge Review* (May 20): 460–61.

Cornford, F. M. 1950. "A Ritual Basis for Hesiod's *Theogony*" (1941). In Cornford, *The Unwritten Philosophy and Other Essays*, edited by W. K. C. Guthrie, 95–116. Cambridge: Cambridge University Press.

Cornford, F. M. 1952. *Principium Sapientiae*, edited by W. K. C. Guthrie. Cambridge: Cambridge University Press.

Covington, Coline. 1989. "In Search of the Heroine." *Journal of Analytical Psychology* 34 (3): 243–54. https://doi.org/10.1111/j.1465-5922.1989.00243.x

De Santillana, Giorgio, and Hertha von Dechend. 1969. *Hamlet's Mill*. Boston, MA: Gambit.

Downie, R. Angus. 1940. *James George Frazer: The Portrait of a Scholar*. London: Watts.

Downie, R. Angus. 1970. *Frazer and The Golden Bough*. London: Victor Gollancz.

Dubuisson, Daniel. 2006. *Twentieth Century Mythologies: Dumézil, Lévi-Strauss, Eliade*, translated by Martha Cunningham. 2nd ed. London: Equinox [1st ed. 1993].

Dumézil, Georges. 1993 [1971]. *The Destiny of a King*, translated by Alf Hiltebeitel. Chicago: University of Chicago Press.

Dundes, Alan. 1962. "Earth-Diver: Creation of the Mythopoeic Male." *American Anthropologist* 64 (5): 1032–51. https://doi.org/10.1525/aa.1962.64.5.02a00110

Dundes, Alan. 1977. *The Hero Pattern and the Life of Jesus*. Berkeley: Center for Hermeneutical Studies in Hellenistic and Modern Culture. Reprinted in Dundes 1980: 223–61, and in Rank et al. 1990: 179–223.

Dundes, Alan. 1980. *Interpreting Folklore*. Bloomington: Indiana University Press.

Dundes, Alan, ed. 1988. *The Flood Myth*. Berkeley: University of California Press.

Durkheim, Emile. 1915 [1912]. *The Elementary Forms of the Religious Life*, translated by Joseph Ward Swain. London: Allen and Unwin. https://doi.org/10.1097/00000446-191609000-00024

Eliade, Mircea. 1959a [1957]. *The Sacred and the Profane*, translated by Willard R. Trask. New York: Harvest Books.

Eliade, Mircea. 1959b [1949]. *Cosmos and History [The Myth of the Eternal Return]*, translated by Willard R. Trask. New York: Harper Torchbooks.

Eliade, Mircea. 1961 [1952]. *Images and Symbols*, translated by Philip Mairet. London: Harvill Press.

Eliade, Mircea. 1963 [1949]. *Patterns in Comparative Religion*, translated by Rosemary Sheed. Cleveland, OH: Meridian Books.

Eliade, Mircea. 1965 [1958]. *Rites and Symbols of Initiation [Birth and Rebirth]*, translated by Willard R. Trask. New York: Harper Torchbooks.

Eliade, Mircea. 1967 [1957]. *Myths, Dreams, and Mysteries*, translated by Philip Mairet. New York: Harper Torchbooks.

Eliade, Mircea. 1969a [1962]. *The Two and the One [Mephistopheles and the Androgyne]*, translated by J. M. Cohen. New York: Harper Torchbooks.

Eliade, Mircea. 1969b. *The Quest*. Chicago: University of Chicago Press.

Eliade, Mircea. 1975 [1963]. *Myth and Reality*, translated by Willard R. Trask. New York: Harper Torchbooks.

Eliade, Mircea. 1976. *Occultism, Witchcraft, and Cultural Fashions*. Chicago: University of Chicago Press.

Evans-Pritchard, E. E. 1965. *Theories of Primitive Religion*. Oxford: Clarendon Press.

Fergusson, Francis. 1949. *The Idea of a Theater*. Princeton, NJ: Princeton University Press.

Fergusson, Francis. 1956. "'Myth' and the Literary Scruple." *Sewanee Review* 64 (2): 171–85.

Frankfort, Henri, H. A. Frankfort, John A. Wilson, Thorkild Jacobsen, and William A. Irwin. 1949. *The Intellectual Adventure of Ancient Man: An Essay on Speculative Thought in the Ancient Near East*. Chicago: University of Chicago Press, 1946. Reprint: *Before Philosophy: The Intellectual Adventure of Ancient Man*. Harmondsworth: Pelican Books, 1946.

Frazer, J. G. (James George). 1890. *The Golden Bough*. 1st ed. 2 vols. London: Macmillan.

Frazer, J. G. (James George). 1900. *The Golden Bough*. 2nd ed. 3 vols. London: Macmillan.

Frazer, J. G. (James George). 1909. *Psyche's Task*. London: Macmillan.

Frazer, J. G. (James George). 1911–15. *The Golden Bough*. 3rd ed. 12 vols. London: Macmillan.

Frazer, J. G. (James George). 1918. *Folk-Lore in the Old Testament: Studies in Comparative Religion, Legend and Law*. 3 vols. London: Macmillan.

Frazer, J. G. (James George). 1922. *The Golden Bough*. Abridged ed. 1 vol. London: Macmillan. https://doi.org/10.1007/978-1-349-00400-3

Freud, Sigmund. 1953. *The Interpretation of Dreams. The Standard Edition of the Complete Psychological Works of Sigmund Freud (SE)*, edited and translated by James Strachey et al., vols. 4 and 5: 339–627. London: Hogarth Press and Institute of Psychoanalysis.

Freud, Sigmund. 1958. "The Theme of the Three Caskets." *SE* 12: 289–301.

Freud, Sigmund. 1961 [1927]. *The Future of an Illusion. SE* 21: 3–56.

Frye, Northrop. 1957. *Anatomy of Criticism*. Princeton, NJ: Princeton University Press.

Frye, Northrop. 1963. "The Archetypes of Literature" (1951) and "Myth, Fiction, and Displacement" (1961). In Frye, *Fables of Identity: Studies in Poetic Mythology*, 7–20 and 21–38. New York: Harcourt, Brace.

Frye, Northrop. 1967. "Literature and Myth." In *Relations of Literary Study*, edited by James Thorpe, 27–55. New York: Modern Language Association.

Frye, Northrop. 1978. "Symbolism of the Unconscious" (1959) and "Forming Fours" (1954). In *Northrop Frye on Culture and Literature*, edited by Robert D. Denham, 84–94 and 117–29. Chicago: University of Chicago Press.

Frye, Northrop. 1981. "Myth." *Antaeus* 43: 64–84.

Girard, René. 1977. *Violence and the Sacred*, translated by Patrick Gregory. London: Athlone Press; Baltimore, MD: Johns Hopkins University Press.

Girard, René. 1978. *"To Double Business Bound."* London: Athlone Press; Baltimore, MD: Johns Hopkins University Press.

Girard, René. 1986. *The Scapegoat*, translated by Yvonne Freccero. London: Athlone Press; Baltimore, MD: Johns Hopkins University Press.

Girard, René. 1987. *Things Hidden since the Foundation of the World*, translated by Stephen Bann and Michael Metteer. London: Athlone Press; Baltimore, MD: Johns Hopkins University Press.

Gould, Stephen Jay. 2002 [1999]. *Rocks of Ages: Science and Religion in the Fullness of Life*. London: Vintage.

Guthrie, Stewart. 1993. *Faces in the Clouds*. New York and Oxford: Oxford University Press.

Harrison, Jane Ellen. 1913. *Ancient Art and Ritual*. New York: Holt; London: Williams and Norgate.

Hempel, Carl G. 1973. "Science Unlimited?" *Annals of the Japan Association for Philosophy of Science* 4 (3): 187–202. https://doi.org/10.4288/jafpos1956.4.187

Henderson, Joseph. 1967. *Thresholds of Initiation*. Middletown, CT: Wesleyan University Press.

Highet, Gilbert. 1939. *The Classical Tradition*. New York: Oxford University Press.

Hillman, James. 1975. *Re-Visioning Psychology*. New York: Harper & Row.

Horton, Robin. 1967. "African Traditional Thought and Western Science." *Africa* 37 (1): 50–71 (part 1), 155–87 (part 2). https://doi.org/10.2307/1157195

Hyman, Stanley Edgar. 1949. "Myth, Ritual, and Nonsense." *Kenyon Review* 11 (3): 455–75.

Jezewski, Mary Ann. 1984. "Traits of the Female Hero: The Application of Raglan's Concept of Hero Trait Patterning." *New York Folklore* 10 (1–2): 55–73.

Jonas, Hans. 1934. *Gnosis und spätantiker Geist*, vol. 1. Göttingen: Vandenhoeck & Ruprecht.

Jonas, Hans. 1954. *Gnosis und spätantiker Geist*, vol. 2, part 1. Göttingen: Vandenhoeck & Ruprecht.

Jonas, Hans. 1963. "Gnosticism, Existentialism, and Nihilism." In Jonas, *The Gnostic Religion*, 320–40. 2nd ed. Boston, MA: Beacon Press.

Jung, C. G. 1967 [1956]. *Symbols of Transformation, The Collected Works of C. G. Jung (CW)*, edited by Sir Herbert Read et al., translated by R. F. C. Hull et al., vol. 5, 2nd ed. Princeton, NJ: Princeton University Press; London: Routledge.

Jung, C. G. 1968a [1959]. *The Archetypes and the Collective Unconscious. CW* 9, part 1, 2nd ed. Princeton, NJ: Princeton University Press; London: Routledge.

Jung, C. G. 1968b [1959]. "Psychological Aspects of the Mother Archetype." *CW* 9, part 1, 2nd ed., 73–110. Princeton, NJ: Princeton University Press; London: Routledge.

Jung, C. G. 1968c [1959]. "The Psychology of the Child Archetype." *CW* 9, part 1, 2nd ed., 149–81. Princeton, NJ: Princeton University Press; London: Routledge.

Jung, C. G. 1968d [1953]. *Psychology and Alchemy. CW* 12, 2nd ed. Princeton, NJ: Princeton University Press; London: Routledge.

Jung, C. G. 1968e. *Alchemical Studies. CW* 13. Princeton, NJ: Princeton University Press; London: Routledge.

Jung, C. G. 1969. *The Structure and Dynamics of the Psyche. CW* 8, 2nd ed. Princeton, NJ: Princeton University Press; London: Routledge.

Jung, C. G. 1971. *Psychological Types. CW* 6. Princeton, NJ: Princeton University Press; London: Routledge.

Jung, C. G. 1973–76. *Letters*, edited by Gerhard Adler and Aniela Jaffé, translated by R. F. C. Hull. 2 vols. Princeton, NJ: Princeton University Press; London: Routledge.

Jung, C. G. 1976. *The Symbolic Life. CW* 18. Princeton, NJ: Princeton University Press; London: Routledge.

Knapp, Bettina L. 1984. *A Jungian Approach to Literature*. Carbondale: Southern Illinois University Press.

Kramer, Samuel Noah. 1961 [1944]. *Sumerian Mythology*. Rev. ed. New York: Harper Torchbooks.

Lang, Andrew. 1884. *Custom and Myth*. London: Longmans, Green.

Lang, Andrew. 1887. *Myth, Ritual and Religion*. 2 vols. 1st ed. London: Longmans, Green.

Lang, Andrew. 1897. *Modern Mythology*. 1st ed. London: Longmans, Green.

Lang, Andrew. 1898. *The Making of Religion*. 1st ed. London: Longmans, Green.

Lang, Andrew. 1901a. *Myth, Ritual and Religion*. 2 vols. 2nd ed. London: Longmans, Green.

Lang, Andrew. 1901b. *Magic and Religion*. London: Longmans, Green.

Lévi-Strauss, Claude. 1955. "The Structural Study of Myth." *Journal of American Folklore* 68 (270): 428–44. https://doi.org/10.2307/536768

Lévi-Strauss, Claude. 1966. *The Savage Mind*, translator unknown. Chicago: University of Chicago Press.

Lévi-Strauss, Claude. 1967 [1963]. *Structural Anthropology*, translated by Claire Jacobson and Brooke Grundfest Schoepf. Garden City, NY: Doubleday Anchor Books.

Lévi-Strauss, Claude. 1970 [1969]. *The Raw and the Cooked*, translated by John and Doreen Weightman. New York: Harper Torchbooks.

Lévi-Strauss, Claude. 1978. *Myth and Meaning*. Toronto: University of Toronto Press.

Lévy-Bruhl, Lucien. 1966 [1926]. *How Natives Think* [1910], translated by Lilian A. Clare. London: Allen and Unwin.

Lovelock, James. 1979. *Gaia: A New Look at Life on Earth*. Oxford: Oxford University Press.

Main, Roderick, ed. 1997. *Jung on Synchronicity and the Paranormal*. Princeton, NJ: Princeton University Press; London: Routledge.

Main, Roderick. 2004. *The Rupture of Time*. London and New York: Brunner-Routledge. https://doi.org/10.4324/9780203501467

Main, Roderick. 2007. "Recaptured Time and the Re-enchantment of Modernity." In *Who Owns Jung?*, edited by Ann Casement, 19–38. London: Karnac Books. https://doi.org/10.4324/9780429484988-3

Malinowski, Bronislaw. 1954a [1948]. "Magic, Science and Religion" (1925). In his *Magic, Science and Religion and Other Essays*, edited by Robert Redfield, 17–92. Garden City, NY: Doubleday Anchor Books.

Malinowski, Bronislaw. 1954b [1948]. "Myth in Primitive Psychology" (1926). In his *Magic, Science and Religion and Other Essays*, edited by Robert Redfield, 93–148. Garden City, NY: Doubleday Anchor Books.

Malinowski, Bronislaw. 1960 [1944]. *A Scientific Theory of Culture and Other Essays*. New York: Oxford Galaxy Books.

May, Herbert G., and Bruce M. Metzger, eds. 1977. *The New Oxford Annotated Bible with the Apocrypha*. New York: Oxford University Press.

Miller, David L. 1981. *The New Polytheism*. Dallas, TX: Spring Publications.

Müller, Friedrich Max. 1860. "Semitic Monotheism." In his *Chips from a German Workshop*, vol. 1: 337–74. New York: Scribner, 1869. Reprinted in Stone 2002: 25–42.

Müller, Friedrich Max. 1867. "Comparative Mythology" (1856). In his *Chips from a German Workshop*, vol. 2: 1–141. London: Longmans, Green.

Müller, Friedrich Max. 1869. *Chips from a German Workshop*, vol. 1. New York: Scribner.

Müller, Friedrich Max. 1878. *Lectures on the Origin and Growth of Religion*. 1st ed. London: Longmans, Green.

Müller, Friedrich Max. 2002 [1898]. "Science of Religion: A Retrospect." In Stone 2002: 353–56. New York and Houndsmill: Palgrave Macmillan. https://doi.org/10.1007/978-1-137-08450-7_20

Murdoch, D. M. 2011. *Christ in Egypt*. Seattle: Stellar Publishing.

Murray, Gilbert. 1913a. "Excursis on the Ritual Forms Preserved in Greek Tragedy." In Jane Ellen Harrison, *Themis: A Study of the Social Origins of Greek Religion*, 1st ed., 341–63. Cambridge: Cambridge University Press.

Murray, Gilbert. 1913b. *Euripides and His Age*. 1st ed. New York: Holt; London: Williams and Norgate.

Murray, Gilbert. 1913–14. "Hamlet and Orestes: A Study in Traditional Types." *Proceedings of the British Academy* 6: 389–412.

Murray, Gilbert. 1940. *Aeschylus*. Oxford: Clarendon Press.

Murray, Gilbert. 1951. "Dis Geniti." *Journal of Hellenic Studies* 71: 120–28. https://doi.org/10.2307/628192

Neumann, Erich. 1970 [1954]. *The Origins and History of Consciousness*, translated by R. F. C. Hull. Princeton, NJ: Princeton University Press.

Neumann, Erich. 1972 [1955]. *The Great Mother*, translated by Ralph Manheim. 2nd ed. Princeton, NJ: Princeton University Press.

Numbers, Ronald L. 2006. *The Creationists*. Expanded ed. [1st ed. 1992]. Cambridge, MA: Harvard University Press.

Pearson, Carol. 1989 [1986]. *The Hero Within*. Expanded ed. San Francisco: HarperSanFrancisco.

Pearson, Carol. 1991. *Awakening the Heroes Within*. San Francisco: HarperSanFrancisco.

Pearson, Carol, and Katherine Pope. 1981. *The Female Hero in American and British Literature*. New York: Bowker.

Pettazzoni, Raffaele. 1954. *Essays on the History of Religions*, translated by H. J. Rose. Leiden: Brill.

Popper, Karl R. 1962. *Conjectures and Refutations: The Growth of Scientific Knowledge*. 1st ed. London: Routledge and Kegan Paul; New York: Basic Books.

Propp, Vladimir. 1968 [1958]. *Morphology of the Folktale*, translated by Laurence Scott, 2nd ed., rev. and ed. Louis A. Wagner. Publications of the American Folklore Society Bibliographical and Special Series, vol. IX. Indiana University Research Center in Anthropology, Folklore, and Linguistics Publication 10. Austin: University of Texas Press.

Pugh, Syrithe, ed. 2021. *Euhemerism and Its Uses: The Mortal Gods*. Abingdon and New York: Routledge.

Radcliffe-Brown, A. R. 1939. *Taboo*. Frazer Lecture. Cambridge: Cambridge University Press.

Radin, Paul. 1957. *Primitive Man as Philosopher*. 2nd ed. New York: Dover [1st ed. 1927].

Radin, Paul. 1971. *The World of Primitive Man*. New York: Dutton.

Raglan, Lord. 1936. *The Hero*. London: Methuen. Part 2, on myth, reprinted in Rank et al. 1990: 89–175. Citations are to this reprint. Chs. 16–17 of *The Hero* were originally published, with minor differences, as "The Hero of Tradition," *Folklore* 45 (3) (1934): 212–31. https://doi.org/10.1080/0015587X.1934.9718559

Raglan, Lord. 1945. *Death and Rebirth*. London: Watts.

Raglan, Lord. 1949. *The Origins of Religion*. London: Watts.

Raglan, Lord. 1955. "Myth and Ritual." *Journal of American Folklore* 68 (270): 454–61. https://doi.org/10.2307/536770

Rank, Otto. 1914 [1909]. *The Myth of the Birth of the Hero*, 1st ed., translated by F. Robbins and Smith Ely Jelliffe. New York: Journal of Nervous and Mental Disease Publishing. Citations are to the reprint in Rank et al. 1990: 3–86.

Rank, Otto. 1929 [1924]. *The Trauma of Birth*. London: Kegan Paul; New York: Harcourt, Brace.

Rank, Otto. 1992 [1912]. *The Incest Theme in Literature and Legend*, translated by Gregory C. Richter. Baltimore, MD: Johns Hopkins University Press.

Rank, Otto. 2004. *The Myth of the Birth of the Hero*, 2nd ed., translated by Gregory C. Richter and E. James Lieberman. Introduction by Robert A. Segal. Baltimore, MD: Johns Hopkins University Press.

Rank, Otto, Lord Raglan, and Alan Dundes. 1990. *In Quest of the Hero*. Introduction by Robert A. Segal. Princeton, NJ: Princeton University Press. https://doi.org/10.1515/9780691234229

Rimmon-Kenan, Shlomith. 2002 [1983]. *Narrative Fiction*. 2nd ed. London and New York: Routledge. https://doi.org/10.4324/9780203426111

Róheim, Géza. 1943. *The Origin and Function of Culture*. Nervous and Mental Disease Monograph Series, 69. New York: Journal of Nervous and Mental Disease Publishing.

Roubekas, Nickolas. 2017. *An Ancient Theory of Religion: Euhemerism from Antiquity to the Present*. London: Routledge. https://doi.org/10.4324/9781315725871

Ryan, William, and Walter Pitman. 1999. *Noah's Flood*. London: Simon and Schuster.

Schleiermacher, Friedrich. 1996 [1799]. *On Religion*, translated by Richard Crouter. Cambridge: Cambridge University Press.

Segal, Robert A. 1987. *Joseph Campbell: An Introduction*. New York: Garland Publishing, 1987. Revised paperback edition: New York: Penguin/NAL, 1990. Reprinted trade paperback edition: New York: Penguin/Meridian, 1997.

Segal, Robert A. 1989. "In Defense of Reductionism" (1983). In Segal, *Religion and the Social Sciences*, ch. 1. Atlanta, GA: Scholars Press.

Segal, Robert A. 1991. "Adonis: A Greek Eternal Child." In *Myth and the Polis*, edited by Dora C. Pozzi and John M. Wickersham, 64–85. Ithaca, NY: Cornell University Press.

Segal, Robert A. 1992a. *Explaining and Interpreting Religion: Essays on the Issue*. New York: Peter Lang.

Segal, Robert A., ed. 1992b. *The Gnostic Jung*. Princeton, NJ: Princeton University Press; London: Routledge.

Segal, Robert A., ed. 1998a. *Jung on Mythology*. Princeton, NJ: Princeton University Press; London: Routledge.

Segal, Robert A., ed. 1998b. *The Myth and Ritual Theory: An Anthology*. Malden, MA, and Oxford: Blackwell.

Segal, Robert A. 1999. *Theorizing about Myth*. Amherst: University of Massachusetts Press.

Segal, Robert A. 2003. "Jung's Very Twentieth-Century View of Myth." *Journal of Analytical Psychology* 48 (5): 593–617. Reprinted in Segal 2021: ch. 4. https://doi.org/10.1111/1465-5922.00422

Segal, Robert A. 2012. "Does the Gaia Hypothesis Bring Myth Back to the World?" In *Science and the World's Religions*, edited by Patrick McNamara and Wesley J. Wildman, vol. 1: 117–49. Santa Barbara, CA: Praeger/ABC-CLIO. Reprinted in Segal 2021: ch. 12.

Segal, Robert A. 2014. "Explanation and Interpretation." In *Jung and the Question of Science*, edited by Raya A. Jones, 82–97. London and New York: Routledge.

Segal, Robert A. 2015. *Myth: A Very Short Introduction*. Rev. ed. Oxford: Oxford University Press [1st ed. 2004].

Segal, Robert A. 2021. *Myth Analyzed*. London and New York: Routledge. https://doi.org/10.4324/9780429273537

Seznec, Jean. 1953 [1940]. *The Survival of the Pagan Gods: The Mythological Tradition in Renaissance Humanism and Art*, translated by Barbara F. Sessions. New York: Pantheon Books.

Shamdasani, Sonu. 1990. "A Woman Called Frank." *Spring* 50: 26–56.

Smith, William Robertson. 1894. *Lectures on the Religion of the Semites*. 2nd ed. [1st ed. 1889]. Edinburgh: Black.

Spencer, Herbert. 1874. *The Study of Sociology*. New York: Appleton [1873].

Stone, Jon R., ed. 2002. *The Essential Max Müller*. New York and Houndsmill: Palgrave Macmillan.

Tylor, E. B. (Edward Burnett). 1863. "Wild Men and Beast-Children." *Anthropological Review* 1 (1): 21–32. https://doi.org/10.2307/3024982

Tylor, E. B. (Edward Burnett). 1871. *Primitive Culture*. 2 vols. 1st ed. London: Murray. Citations are to the reprint of the 5th ed. (1913) edition (New York: Harper Torchbooks, 1958).

Van den Bosch, Lourens P. 2002. *Friedrich Max Müller*. Leiden: Brill. https://doi.org/10.1163/9789004379176

Van der Leeuw, Gerardus. 1938 [1933]. *Religion in Essence and Manifestation*, translated by J. E. Turner. London: Allen & Unwin.

Von Franz, Marie-Louise. 1981. *Puer Aeternus*. 2nd ed. Santa Monica, CA: Sigo [1st ed. 1970].

Von Hahn, Johann Georg. 1876. *Sagwissenschaftliche Studien*. Jena: Mauke.

Wach, Joachim. 1962 [1944]. *Sociology of Religion*. Chicago: University of Chicago Press.

Weber, Max. 1963 [1922]. *The Sociology of Religion*, translated by Ephraim Fischoff. Boston, MA: Beacon Press.

Weisinger, Herbert. 1953. *Tragedy and the Paradox of the Fortunate Fall*. London: Routledge and Kegan Paul; East Lansing: Michigan State College Press.

Weston, Jessie L. 1920. *From Ritual to Romance*. Cambridge: Cambridge University Press. Reprint with foreword by Robert A. Segal: Princeton, NJ: Princeton University Press, 1993. https://doi.org/10.1515/9780691217741

Whitmont, Edward. 1969. *The Symbolic Quest*. New York: Putnam.

Winnicott, D. W. 1982 [1971]. "Transitional Objects and Transitional Phenomena." In his *Playing and Reality* (London and New York: Routledge), ch. 1. Original version (1951) in Winnicott, *Through Paediatrics to Psychoanalysis* (London: Karnac Books, 1992 [1958]): ch. 18.

Winnicott, D. W. 1987 [1964]. *The Child, the Family, and the Outside World*. Reading, MA: Addison-Wesley.

Index

Ackerman, Robert 64, 65–66, 69
Adonis 4–5, 45–54, 55, 57, 58–59, 61, 64,
    105, 135, 154–55
Aeneas 28, 77
animism 15, 151–52
Apollodorus 49, 51, 107
Aristotle 31
Arlow, Jacob 2
Attis 2, 4, 46–47, 49, 52, 53, 55, 57, 59, 61,
    64, 135
Augustine 30–31

Barber, C. L. 63, 104
Berger, Peter 25
Bidney, David 2, 12
Blumenberg, Hans 2, 4, 7, 1–32, 111–17,
    155–56
Bodkin, Maud 108
Buber, Martin 165, 166
Bultmann, Rudolf 2, 4, 6, 9, 12, 28, 85,
    87, 90, 91, 98, 139, 140–41, 143, 147,
    166–68, 169–70
Burke, Kenneth 2, 12, 110–11, 121, 163
Burkert, Walter 12
Butler, E. M. 63, 104

Campbell, Joseph 2, 4, 3, 5, 6, 7–8, 12, 16,
    26, 27, 28, 63–69, 70–77, 85, 114–15,
    116, 126, 130–35
Camus, Albert 2, 4, 6, 9, 71–72, 87, 90, 91,
    139, 140–41
Carlyle, Thomas 95
Cassirer, Ernst 9, 12, 163–64, 166
Collingwood, R. G. 27, 87
Cornford, F. M. 2, 12, 17, 63, 104, 107, 166

Creationism 11, 49, 148–49

Darwin, Charles 148
Dawkins, Richard 14, 153
Deism 3
De Santillana, Georgio 2, 12
Detienne, Marcel 5, 54 n. 1
Dionysus 4, 16, 46, 47, 52–53, 55, 57, 59,
    61, 64, 135
Downie, R. Angus 65
Dubuisson, Daniel 7, 97–102
Dumézil, Georges 2, 7, 97–102
Durkheim, Émile 28, 34, 35, 64, 101, 118

Electra 103
Eliade, Mircea 2, 3, 6–7, 16, 29, 30, 35,
    78–85, 86–96, 97–102, 118, 139–40, 147,
    158–59
Eliot, T. S. 63, 103, 105
Emerson, Ralph Waldo 68
euhemerism 5, 16–17, 55, 57, 59–60,
    109–10
Evans-Pritchard, E. E. 34

Fergusson, Francis 2, 63, 105, 106, 107
Frankfort, Henri, and H. A. 9, 19, 164–66
Frazer, J. G. 3, 4, 5, 6, 7, 9, 12, 17, 28, 40,
    41, 45–54, 55–62, 63–69, 85, 87, 88,
    89–90, 95, 96, 98, 101, 104, 105, 106,
    107, 108–109, 113, 115–16, 135–37, 138,
    140, 154–57, 165
Freud, Sigmund 2, 6, 8, 12, 24, 25, 27, 28,
    29, 70–77, 82, 83, 91, 98, 103, 113–14,
    123–24, 126–30, 139, 141–42
Frye, Northrop 2, 7, 63, 105, 106–107

Gaia 143
Girard, René 108
Gould, Stephen Jay 14, 152–53
Guthrie, Stewart 44

Harrison, Jane Ellen 2, 7, 12, 63, 104, 106,
    108
Heidegger, Martin 140
Henderson, Joseph 77
Hesiod 20, 25, 30, 31, 38, 112
Hillman, James 108
Homer 14, 20, 86, 112, 148, 152
Hooke, S. H. 2, 12
Horton, Robin 2, 12
Hyman, Stanley Edgar 7, 63, 105

Jesus 5, 14, 60–62, 135
Jezewski, Mary Ann 137
Jonas, Hans 2, 4, 9, 12, 87, 90, 91, 139,
    141, 143, 166, 169–70
Joyce, James 3, 63, 103
Jung, C. G. 2, 4, 5, 6, 8, 12, 16, 26, 27, 28,
    40, 55–62, 70–77, 82, 85, 87, 91, 98,
    103, 106, 107, 114–15, 123–24, 130–35,
    137–40, 141–45, 161

Kant, Immanuel 3
Kramer, Samuel Noah 2, 29
Kuhn, Adalbert 2, 12

Lang, Andrew 2, 4, 5, 42–44, , 70–77, 113
Lawrence, D. H. 63
Lévi-Strauss, Claude 2, 7, 9, 12, 20, 29,
    97–102, 110, 111, 146, 159–61
Lévy-Bruhl, Lucien 2, 9, 19, 29, 156–57,
    162–66
Lovelock, James 143

Main, Roderick 144–45
Malinowski, Bronislaw 2, 6, 9, 28, 29, 65,
    86, 87, 89–90, 91–92, 96, 98, 99, 139–40,
    147, 158–59
Mann, Thomas 31
Marlowe, Christopher 122–23
Miller, David 108
Milton, John 103, 117, 120–23
Mother Goddess 135
Moyers, Bill 67, 69

Müller, Friedrich Max 2, 4, 12, 17, 35–44,
    106
Murray, Gilbert 2, 7, 12, 63, 104, 106, 107

Neumann, Erich 132
Nietzsche, Friedrich 12
Noah 9, 146–70
Norman, Dorothy 134–35

Odysseus 28, 75
Oedipus, Oedipal 74, 103, 106, 113, 114,
    127, 128, 129–30, 137
Osiris 4, 40, 46, 47, 50, 52, 53, 55–62, 135
Ovid 49, 51

Pauli, Wolfgang 9, 124
Pearson, Carol 134–35
Persephone 49, 50, 51, 135
Pettazzoni, Raffaele 34
Plato 30, 86, 112, 147, 148, 152
Plotinus 30, 112
Pope, Katherine 134
Popper, Karl 9, 161–62
postmodernism 11, 16, 21
Prometheus 27, 32
Propp, Vladimir 7, 112–13, 116

Radcliffe-Brown, A. R. 2, 12, 28, 65
Radin, Paul 9, 162–63
Raglan, Lord 8–9, 63, 105, 106, 113,
    115–16, 126, 135–37
Rank, Otto 2, 7, 8, 9, 34, 71–75, 113–16,
    126–30
Róheim, Géza 2, 25, 63, 71, 74, 75
Rubinstein, William 147

Schleiermacher, Friedrich 76
Smith, William Robertson 8, 34, 65, 66,
    104, 118–20, 165
Spencer, Herbert 95
survival 11
synchronicity 9, 82, 138–45, 161

Thales 30, 31, 112
Thoreau, Henry David 65
Tylor, E. B. 2, 4, 6, 7, 9, 10–32, 34, 35, 38,
    39–44, 63, 66, 85, 87, 88–90, 95, 96, 98,
    108–10, 111–12, 126, 138, 140, 151–54,

155–57, 159–60, 161, 162, 163, 165,
166–67, 170

Van der Leeuw, Gerardus 25, 34
Von Dechend, Hertha 12
Von Hahn, Johann Georg 2, 3, 112

Wach, Joachim 34
Weber, Max 34

Weisinger, Herbert 63, 105
Weston, Jessie 2, 7, 63, 104, 105, 106
White, Andrew Dixon 151
Winnicott, D. W. 8, 124–25
Wordsworth, William 39

Yeats, William Butler 63

Zeus 41, 87

www.ingramcontent.com/pod-product-compliance
Lightning Source LLC
Chambersburg PA
CBHW051433270326
41935CB00018B/1813